Pictorial Metaphor in Advertising

Over the past few decades, research on metaphor has focused almost exclusively on its verbal and cognitive dimensions. In *Pictorial Metaphor in Advertising*, Charles Forceville argues that metaphor can also occur in pictures. By using insights taken from a range of linguistic, artistic, and cognitive perspectives, for example, interaction and relevance theory, Forceville shows not only how metaphor can occur in pictures, but also provides a framework within which these 'pictorial' metaphors can be analysed.

The theoretical insights are applied to thirty advertisements and billboards of British, French, German, and Dutch origin. Apart from substantiating the claim that it makes sense to talk about 'pictorial metaphors', the detailed analyses of the advertisements suggest how metaphor theory can be employed as a tool in media studies. The final chapter of this book looks at ways in which the insights gained can be used for further research.

This book will be of interest to advanced undergraduate and graduate students of Communication Studies, Language, and Linguistics.

Charles Forceville is Lecturer in the Department of English, also affiliated to the Department of Comparative and Empirical Literature at the Free University in Amsterdam.

Pictorial Metaphor in Advertising

Charles Forceville

London and New York

First published 1996
by Routledge
11 New Fetter Lane, London EC4P 4EE

Simultaneously published in the USA and Canada
by Routledge
29 West 35th Street, New York, NY 10001

First published in paperback 1998

Typeset in Times by RefineCatch Limited, Bungay, Suffolk
Printed and bound in Great Britain by T.J. International Ltd, Padstow, Cornwall

British Library Cataloguing in Publication Data
A catalogue record for this book is available from the British Library

Library of Congress Cataloguing in Publication Data
A catalogue record for this book has been requested

ISBN 0–415–12868–4 (hbk)
ISBN 0–415–18676–5 (pbk)

Contents

List of illustrations

Every attempt has been made to obtain permission to reproduce copyright material, and publisher and author would like to thank the copyright holders who granted permission to reprint their advertisements and billboards in this book. If any proper acknowledgement has not been made, we would invite copyright holders to inform Routledge of the oversight.

Acknowledgements

A metaphor is the result of the interaction between two different domains; completing a book on metaphor is the result of the interaction with numerous people. First of all I want to thank Elrud Ibsch and Lachlan Mackenzie (both Vrije Universiteit Amsterdam), who monitored and commented upon the progress of this book from its earliest beginnings. I have benefited much both from their expertise and their enthusiasm. Apart from closely watching over the book's overall structure, Elrud managed to convince me that the book would gain by the incorporation of an empirical component. To Lachlan I want to express my gratitude for giving me the first taste of metaphor. His inspiring seminar on the subject in the early 1980s was for me the beginning of what may well prove a life-long addiction. Furthermore, the text owes much to his thoughtful comments and meticulous editing.

Among my colleagues in the Department of English and the Department of Comparative and Empirical Literature at the Vrije Universiteit Amsterdam I would like to thank specifically Johan Hoorn, Dick Schram, and Gerard Steen. The formal and informal discussions in this group helped foster the kind of research climate without which no scholar can thrive.

While the academic community tends to agree readily that interdisciplinary research deserves priority in funding decisions, the extent to which this conviction is practised is often disappointing. I am therefore much indebted to NWO (Netherlands Organization for Scientific Research) for subsidizing the somewhat unconventional project of which this book is the fruit, and for the grants that allowed me to present my research abroad.

Various chapters or parts of chapters in this book have been, or will be, published in scholarly journals and collections of essays.[1] In writing and rewriting for the journals I learnt much from critical reports on submitted articles.

Among the many academics whose suggestions and encouragement came at moments when this was particularly welcome I would like to single out Guy Cook, Leo Hoek, John Dixon Hunt, Mark Johnson, John Kennedy, and Jaap H. Spoor.

Many people have commented over the years on ads and billboards in seminars, lectures, and during conferences. The fact that often I do not even know their names does not detract from the fact that many of their observations have found their way into my analyses.

For years Marieke Nieuwland of the Nederlandse Vereniging van Erkende Reclame Adviesbureaus (VEA) and Marie-Lou Florisson of the Art Directors Club Nederland (ADCN) generously allowed me to consult their archives, and helped me find the information I needed. I much enjoyed the brief glimpses into the world of advertising, so vastly different from the academic one, which my visits to the VEA and the ADCN afforded me.

To both Marcel Kampers, friend, and Etienne Forceville, brother, I owe a great debt. In an important sense Marcel was there when all this began, and for me our discussions were an inexhaustible source of new perspectives on old problems. Over the years Etienne increasingly became an appreciated sounding-board and sparring partner in discussions about the project. With our many shared ideas as a starting point, he constantly forced me to ponder and formulate my ideas in more precise terms. Vincent Forceville, brother and flatmate, I thank for his good humour and laconic advice, as well as for doing more than his share of the household chores when the going got rough.

Finally, I want to thank Gesien van Altena, my partner, friend, and personal manager, for her patience, common-sense counsel, and insistence that there is more to life than work: she helped me keep sane.

Charles Forceville
February 1995
Vrije Universiteit Amsterdam

1   Introduction

The past few decades have witnessed an avalanche of publications on metaphor. Three bibliographies on metaphor (Shibles 1971, van Noppen *et al.* 1985, van Noppen *et al.* 1990) together list some 10,000 books, articles and conference papers originating in a wide range of academic disciplines. Although there is an increasing interest from cognitive scientists in metaphor, the vast majority of the publications focus on verbal metaphors, or at least on verbal manifestations of metaphor. However, as Lakoff and Johnson claim in their influential book *Metaphors We Live By*, 'metaphor is primarily a matter of thought and action, and only derivatively a matter of language' (1980: 153). This perspective paves the way for an investigation of the question whether other media than language can manifest metaphor as well. In this book I argue that metaphor can occur in pictures, more specifically in printed advertisements and billboards, and I propose a theoretical framework within which these pictorial metaphors can be analysed. The most important aim of this study is to make a contribution to a theory of pictorial metaphor. After the theoretical framework has been outlined, a substantial number of advertisements and billboards will be analysed in the light of this theory, the analyses themselves naturally leading to further subdivisions of the concept 'pictorial metaphor'. Accordingly, the second aim of the book is to show how the theory can be applied in the analysis of specific advertisements. Finally, it is hoped that validation of the concept 'pictorial metaphor' in turn will help to advance the more encompassing theory of metaphor as a cognitive phenomenon.

Whereas the order of the chapters in this book is motivated by the overall goal of developing a model for the analysis of pictorial metaphor, an attempt has been made to ensure that chapters that may be of interest to those whose primary concern is with other topics than pictorial metaphor proper – such as 'verbal metaphor', 'word and image relations', 'Relevance Theory', or 'advertising' – can, with minimal difficulty, be read independently. The structure of the book is as follows.

Chapter 2 contains a detailed discussion of Max Black's (1962, 1979a) interaction theory of verbal metaphor. This theory, enriched by the insights of later scholars of metaphor, will in slightly adapted form serve as the starting point for the analysis of pictorial metaphors in Chapters 6 and 7. Some elliptical passages in Black's two articles are clarified and expanded on, and the objections of Kittay (1987) to the interaction theory are examined at length. This chapter is intended to be of intrinsic interest to students of verbal and cognitive metaphor.

Chapter 3 evaluates a number of earlier studies which pertain to the concept 'pictorial metaphor'. A critical survey of these studies, some of which focus on artistic texts while others also include non-artistic texts in their corpora, highlights some of the theoretical problems attending an attempt to present a theory of pictorial metaphor. On the basis of the strengths and weaknesses of these previous approaches I explain my choice of static advertisements as corpus material.

Chapter 4 discusses in what ways context plays a role in the interpretation of advertisements generally, and pictorial metaphors occurring in them specifically. Within a communicative framework adapted from the well-known model by Jakobson (1960), a distinction is made between text-internal and text-external elements of context. The former can be further subdivided into pictorial and verbal context, drawing on Roland Barthes' (1964/1986) concept of 'anchoring'. It is argued that an examination of text-internal context does not suffice, however; in addition, text-external factors such as cultural conventions, expectations, and genre-attributions need to be considered as well.

Although Chapter 4 outlines various aspects outside the advertisement text proper that affect interpretation, two major factors are there left out of consideration: the role played by the communicator of the advertisement message, and its addressee, respectively. Chapter 5 delineates how the identities and interests of the originator of the advertising message and its envisaged reader/viewer crucially co-determine its possible interpretations. In an application of the theory of Sperber and Wilson (1986), who claim that the principle of relevance is the key concept governing human communication, it is shown what consequences their approach has for the analysis, first of metaphors, and then of advertisements. Of particular importance are their claim that relevance is always relevance to an individual and the distinction they propose between strongly and weakly communicated aspects of a message. Apart from constituting a vital step in the elaboration of a model of pictorial metaphor, this chapter can also be read independently as an application of Sperber and Wilson's relevance theory beyond the realm of language, namely to messages that are (partly) non-verbal, and mass-medial.

Chapter 6, a key chapter of the book, combines Black's interaction theory with the insights of Sperber and Wilson to analyse pictorial phenomena in some thirty advertisements and billboards in terms of pictorial metaphor. On the basis of the various text-internal (verbal and pictorial) contextual levels that can be distinguished, a subdivision is proposed into pictorial metaphors with one pictorially present term (MP1s), pictorial metaphors with two pictorially present terms (MP2s), verbo-pictorial metaphors (VPMs), and pictorial similes. While the discussions of the advertisements and billboards are first and foremost intended to substantiate the validity of the concept pictorial metaphor in itself, the analyses hopefully are of independent interest to students of advertising, and of word and image relations more generally.

Since the advertisements and billboards discussed in Chapter 6 are all interpreted by myself, the analyses – in line with Sperber and Wilson's claim that relevance is always relevance to an individual – necessarily suffer from a degree of subjective bias. By way of a modest counterbalance, Chapter 7 reports the results of an exploratory experiment testing the responses of some forty people to three billboards all purportedly containing a verbo-pictorial metaphor. Apart from assessing whether the participants are capable of identifying the metaphors as such, the experiment gives some idea of the degree of freedom in interpretation a pictorial metaphor allows. In addition, the results provide evidence that some viewers, when given a chance to do so, are happy to volunteer interpretations that run counter to those in all likelihood intended by the advertiser. This latter finding suggests that there may be a discrepancy between how viewers realize they are *supposed* to respond to the billboards and how they *actually* react. In view of the exploratory character of the experiment, the chapter reflects amply on methodological matters.

Chapter 8, finally, briefly hints at ways in which the insights of this book may give rise to further research into issues concerning pictorial metaphor, word and image relations, advertising, and other pictorial tropes.

2 Max Black's interaction theory of metaphor

INTRODUCTION

The theory of metaphor upon which I will ground my account of pictorial metaphor is Max Black's (1962, 1979a) interaction theory. Despite minor shortcomings this theory can be regarded as the most satisfactory theory of metaphor hitherto developed. Many writers on metaphor are explicitly or implicity committed to it: they accept its central tenets wholly or with small variations, or at least take its premises as a foundation on which to expand or vary (see for instance Ricoeur 1977, Verbrugge 1980, MacCormac 1985, Kjärgaard 1986, Kittay 1987, Hausman 1989, Indurkhya 1991, 1992). Apart from its widespread acceptance, Black's theory has another great merit: it has been formulated in such a manner that theoretical explicitness goes hand in hand with transparent principles of operation – that is, Black gives a very lucid account of how metaphor works. In this latter respect it is superior to the account of Richards (1965/1936), the other theorist commonly associated with the interaction theory.[1] As Ricoeur points out, 'Richards made the breakthrough; after him, Max Black and others occupy and organize the terrain' (1977: 84). Thirdly, Black shows an awareness of the importance of metaphor's pragmatics that is still insufficiently shared by many contemporary commentators: metaphorical meaning cannot be adequately discussed without resorting to metaphorical use.

Since Black's two articles constitute the basis for my account of pictorial metaphor, I will in this chapter discuss his interaction theory in some detail. It is to be realized that Black's account pertains to the realm of verbal metaphor, with no more than brief digressions on metaphorical thinking and no references at all to pictorial metaphor. At this stage I will follow Black in largely limiting myself to verbal and cognitive metaphor. After all, since I will heavily rely on Black in later chapters, my first task is to show that the theory is sound on its own terms before making a use of it that Black himself did not, at least not explicitly, envisage. Moreover, a careful examination of Black's theory enables me to evaluate some obscure or controversial passages in his articles with reference to improvements and elaborations suggested by other commentators. In the latter part of this chapter, I will briefly discuss, still with Black's views as a starting point, some well-known problems besetting the theory of metaphor. Here I will refer to Lakoff and Johnson, since these authors extensively develop an idea that Black only briefly touches upon, namely the idea that metaphor is a matter of cognition rather than language (see also Indurkhya 1992). As will become clear, this notion, captured in their insight that 'the essence of metaphor is *understanding* and *experiencing* one kind of thing in terms of another' (Lakoff and Johnson 1980: 5, my emphasis), is crucial for my own undertaking.

With respect to the issues discussed in the latter part of this chapter (starting with the section 'Other views held by Black'), it is to be emphasized that no exhaustive treatment has been attempted. The main point of these sections is to make clear to which positions concerning these questions I am committed when in later chapters I turn to pictorial metaphor, although students of verbal metaphor may find certain sections useful in their own right. I will end the chapter with a summary of my enriched, and slightly modified version of Black's theory – a version that I think is true to all of the spirit and most of the text of Black's two brilliantly brief, clear, and profound articles on metaphor.

MAX BLACK'S INTERACTION THEORY OF METAPHOR: A FIRST OUTLINE

Black (1979a) opens with the statement that 'this paper is intended to supplement the earlier study in which I introduced and defended an "interaction view of metaphor"'. The sensible approach, therefore, is to take the later article as the more representative of Black's views, and return to the earlier piece (referred to as *Metaphor* by Black himself) only when this sheds light on issues about which the later piece is silent or unclear. The essence of the interaction view is summarized by Black himself in a page and a half, worth quoting in its entirety:

1 A metaphorical statement has two distinct subjects, to be identified as the 'primary' subject and the 'secondary' one.

In *Metaphor*, I spoke instead of the 'principal' and 'subsidiary' subjects. The duality of reference is marked by the contrast between the metaphorical statement's *focus* (the word or words used non-literally) and the surrounding literal *frame*.

2 The secondary subject is to be regarded as a system rather than an individual thing.

Thus, I think of Wallace Stevens's remark that, 'Society is a sea' as being not so much about the sea (considered as a thing) as about a system of relationships (the 'implicative complex' discussed below) signaled by the presence of the word 'sea' in the sentence in question. (In *Metaphor*, I proposed that the primary subject, also, be taken as a system. But it seems in retrospect needlessly paradoxical, though not plainly mistaken, to say that Stevens was viewing society, too, as a system of social relationships.) In retrospect, the intended emphasis on 'systems', rather than upon 'things' or 'ideas' (as in Richards), looks like one of the chief novelties in the earlier study.

3   The metaphorical utterance works by 'projecting upon' the primary subject a set of 'associated implications', comprised in the implicative complex, that are predicable of the secondary subject.

The label 'implicative complex' is new. 'Projection' is, of course, a metaphor, [sic] that will need further discussion. In the earlier study, I spoke of a 'system of associated commonplaces' (which later provoked some pointed criticisms by Paul Ricoeur). My notion was that the secondary subject, in a way partly depending upon the context of metaphorical use, determines a set of what Aristotle called *endoxa*, current opinions shared by members of a certain speech-community. But I also emphasized, as I should certainly wish to do now, that a metaphor producer may introduce a novel and nonplatitudinous 'implication-complex'.

4   The maker of a metaphorical statement selects, emphasizes, suppresses, and organizes features of the primary subject by applying to it statements isomorphic with the members of the secondary subject's implicative complex.

The mechanism of such 'projection' (a still serviceable metaphor) are discussed and illustrated in the next section.

5   In the context of a particular metaphorical statement, the two subjects 'interact' in the following ways: (a) the presence of the primary subject incites the hearer to select some of the secondary subject's properties; and (b) invites him to construct a parallel implication-complex that can fit the primary subject; and (c) reciprocally induces parallel changes in the secondary subject.

This may be considered a crux for the interaction view (an attempted explication of Richards's striking image of the 'interanimation of words'). Although I speak figuratively here of the *subjects* interacting, such an outcome is of course produced in the minds of the speaker and hearer: it is they who are led to engage in selecting, organizing, and projecting. I think of a metaphorical statement (even a weak one) as a verbal action essentially demanding *uptake*, a creative response from a competent reader. In *Metaphor*, I said – scandalizing some of my subsequent critics – that the imputed interaction involves 'shifts in meaning of words belonging to the same family or system as the metaphorical expression' (p. 45). I meant, of course, a shift in the *speaker's* meaning – and the corresponding *hearers* [sic] meaning – what both of them understand by words, as used on the particular occasion.

(Black 1979a: 28–9)

This dense passage is best discussed point by point.

A metaphorical statement has two distinct subjects, to be identified as the 'primary' subject and the 'secondary' one. To facilitate the discussion, it will be convenient to refer to an example. In tribute to Black I will align myself with the army of metaphorists that have echoed Black's example (itself probably derived from Hobbes' famous *homo homini lupus*):

1   Man is a wolf.

In Black's terminology, 'man' is the primary subject of the metaphor and 'wolf' the secondary subject. Black's emphasis on the metaphorical *statement* is crucial. A metaphor does not obtain at the level of the *word* but at the level of *discourse*. As Black himself formulated it, 'a "statement", in my intended sense, will be identified by quoting a whole sentence, or a set of sentences, together with as much of the relevant verbal context, or the nonverbal setting, as may be needed for an adequate grasp of the actual or imputed speaker's meaning' (1979a: 24). Moreover, Black here points to the potential relevance of the nonverbal context – a notion that I will have occasion to come back to time and again and that will be elaborated in later chapters. The terms 'frame' and 'focus' refer to, respectively, the literal and the metaphorical elements in the metaphorical statement. Black defines the 'focus' as 'the salient word or expression, whose occurrence in the literal frame invests the utterance with metaphorical force' (1979a: 26). Our truncated example 1) is not very illuminating when it comes to explaining these terms, since the frame here more or less coincides with the primary subject, and the focus with the secondary subject. But if we expand 1) into 1a),

1a   Yesterday Harmen and Marcel were discussing the nature of man. Harmen stated as his belief that man is fundamentally good, but Marcel firmly rejected that notion. 'He is a wolf', Marcel maintained,

the difference is clearer. Here the frame of the metaphorical statement comprises everything in (1a) except the word 'wolf' – which is its focus.

The necessity of studying metaphor primarily at a level higher than the word, i.e., at the level of the sentence and beyond, is also maintained by Ricoeur: 'Metaphor, and above all newly invented metaphor, is a phenomenon of discourse . . .' (1977: 180). The move from word to sentence(s), and thereby to discourse, is an important one, for 'in the phenomenon of the sentence, language passes outside itself; reference is the mark of the self-transcendence of language' (ibid.: 74). Because of its predicative character, metaphor contains observations about the (or rather 'a') world.

The secondary subject is to be regarded as a system rather than an individual thing. While Black considers his earlier view that this claim holds with equal force for the primary subject 'not plainly mistaken', he apparently does no longer want to endorse it without qualification. This is an unfortunate lapse from the older, and highly correct, notion. It is not clear where this hesitation stems from[2] – but it certainly is mistaken, for it is essential that the primary subject is regarded as a system of things. But Black himself in his formulations elsewhere in the 1979 article suggests that in fact he *is* committed to the view that the primary subject is a 'system of things'. Thus, in the section 'how metaphorical statements work' Black refers to 'the relations between the meanings of the corresponding key words of the two implication *complexes*' and 'the connection between the two implication-*complexes*' (1979a: 30), and in the section 'metaphors and similes' he remarks about the metaphor 'poverty is a crime' that '"crime" and "poverty" are nodes of isomorphic *networks*' (ibid.: 31, my emphases). Since these phrases suggest 'systems of things' rather than mere 'things', I would argue that in spite of the partial disclaimer in the summary quoted above, a sympathetic reading of Black's entire article yields the conclusion that he holds the view that both primary and secondary subject are systems of things rather than mere individual things. Black is certainly right about seeing the emphasis on 'systems' as a vital contribution to the theory of metaphor. Indeed, it is not exaggerated to claim that this insight is one of the premises underlying for instance Lakoff and Johnson's (1980) influential study.

The metaphorical utterance works by 'projecting upon' the primary subject a set of 'associated implications', comprised in the implicative complex, that are predicable of the secondary subject.

The implicative complex of the secondary subject must be envisaged as the theoretical totality of properties, features, notions, beliefs, metonymic extensions that in one way or another adhere to the secondary subject. In our example, properties that could be projected from the secondary subject 'wolf' to the primary subject 'man' would probably be, say, 'cruel', 'scavenging', 'carnivorous'. In his 1979 article, Black does not much elaborate the notion of the implicative complex, but in the earlier study – discussing the concept under the label of 'associated commonplaces' – he makes a number of valuable comments on this issue. To start with, he points out that a metaphor cannot be understood by someone who is ignorant about the nature of its secondary subject. In 1), that is, the addressee of the metaphor must know about wolves and not only, or even in the first place, be aware of the dictionary meaning of 'wolf', but be familiar with a number of properties or beliefs associated with it. These need not even be factual properties: 'From the expert's standpoint, the system of commonplaces may include half-truths or downright mistakes (as when a whale is classified as a fish); but the important thing for the metaphor's effectiveness is not that the commonplaces shall be true, but that they should be readily and freely evoked' (1962: 40). Black goes on to make the observation that because what matters in the implicative complex of a concept is not merely a number of factual properties, but also comprises beliefs, superstitions and so on, a metaphor is also dependent on a cultural context. As he points out, 'men who take wolves to be reincarnations of dead humans will give the statement "Man is a wolf" an interpretation different from the one I have been assuming' (ibid.: 40).

Finally, Black in this section reiterates the observation already made in *Metaphor* that the author of a metaphor can, in the text leading up to it, in one way or another manipulate the implication complex of the secondary subject in such a way that it may be enriched by certain ad hoc properties and features. The result of this is that the properties conventionally associated with it are replaced, or supplemented, by the property (or properties) developed ad hoc – and such a 'modified' secondary subject in turn affects any primary subject with which it is coupled metaphorically in a different way than if it had been used in its conventional sense: 'Metaphors can be supported by specially constructed systems of implications, as well as by accepted commonplaces; they can be made to measure and need not be reach-me-downs' (1962: 43). Black himself specifically mentions 'a poem, or a piece of sustained prose' (1962: 43) as examples of texts where this is possible.

The maker of a metaphorical statement selects, emphasizes, suppresses, and organizes features of the primary subject by applying to it statements isomorphic with the members of the secondary subject's implicative complex. . . . In the context of a particular metaphorical statement, the two subjects 'interact' in the following ways: a) the presence of the primary subject incites the hearer to select some of the secondary subject's properties; and b) invites him to construct a parallel implication-complex that can fit the primary subject; and c) reciprocally induces parallel changes in the secondary subject.

Points 4 and 5 can hardly be separated and are thus best discussed together. Black stresses that the projection of properties from the secondary subject upon the primary subject leads to a reorganization of the primary subject, at least for as long as the metaphor is entertained. Black somewhat confusingly talks here of 'statements' that are isomorphic with the members of the secondary subject's implicative complex, while elsewhere he refers to features or properties, but this is of course merely a manner of talking. One can either say that certain features (for instance the feature 'cruel' and/or 'carnivorous') of 'wolf' are projected upon 'man' or alternatively that the statement '[a wolf] is cruel' is made to fit, through the metaphorical connection, the concept 'man' so that the metaphorized man is said to be cruel. An alternative way of putting it would be to say that it is the predicate 'is cruel' that is projected from 'wolf' upon 'man'. This latter formulation emphasizes the predicative, dynamic character of a metaphor, and avoids the possibly misleading idea suggested by the use of the term 'feature' or 'property' that what is projected is somehow objectively given (see also Ortony 1979: 190). For convenience's sake I will, however, continue to use the nouns 'feature' and 'property' along with the notion of 'predication'.

The appropriateness of the processes of 'selecting', 'emphasizing', 'suppressing', and 'organizing' features can be demonstrated as follows. If we postulate, for argument's sake, that the one feature transferred from 'wolf' to 'man' is 'cruelty', then we would have to say that in the particular metaphor 'man is a wolf' the feature selected from that infinitely complex concept 'man' is 'cruelty'. Put differently, the feature 'cruelty' is emphasized, whereas numerous other features of 'man' are, by default, 'suppressed'.[3] Thus, man's (alleged or potential) stupidity is suppressed, though in a rather passive way: stupidity simply is one of the numerous features that do not – barring exceptional ad hoc contexts – figure in the implicative complex of 'wolf'. (We need not, of course, leave the zoo to find an animal that *does* have the characteristic of prototypical stupidity very prominently in its implicative complex: with the metaphor 'man is an ass' we have precisely what we want.) It is worth pointing out, however, that among the numerous features of man that are suppressed by (1), that of cruelty's antonym – say, compassion – is not merely suppressed by default, but is suppressed very strongly. That is, the transferred predicate '. . . is cruel' entails no information about many other predicates about man that are compatible with it (for instance '. . . is stupid', '. . . is beautiful', '. . . is cowardly', '. . . is humorous'), but it is incompatible with the predicate '. . . is compassionate'. Thus, the metaphor reorganizes the one aspect of man's alleged cruelty. Various other characteristics of 'man' remain unaffected, since the metaphor does not modify them.

Black not only emphatically asserts that certain features in the *primary* subject are selected; he claims, in 5a), that the same holds for the *secondary* subject. Whereas some features obviously qualify for projection upon the primary subject (in our example: 'cruelty'), and the projection of some others is debatable (e.g., 'dark-loving'), there are also features that (as always: barring some specifically constructed context) will *not* be transferred. As a matter of fact these will constitute the vast majority. One can here think of such obvious predicates as '. . . having four legs', 'being furred', 'possessing a tail', and numerous others. Thus, only a selection of all characteristics of the secondary subject that could be thought of is actually transferred to the primary subject. It is precisely the partiality of projectable (or 'transferrable', or 'mappable') features which constitutes the 'tension' between primary subject and secondary subject that is associated with the interaction theory of metaphor (see Black 1979a: 22). After all, if all features were mappable, the result would be complete identity; and if none of the features were mappable, the result would be nonsense. Ricoeur argues that the tensive character that inheres in metaphor resides in the copula 'to be'. As he explains, 'in order to elucidate [the] tension deep within the logical force of the verb *to be*, we must expose an "is not", itself implied in the impossibility of the literal interpretation, yet present as a filigree in the metaphorical "is". Thus, the tension would prevail between an "is" and an "is not"' (1977: 248). Hence it is the combination of similarity and dissimilarity obtaining between primary and secondary subject that gives metaphor its tensive character.

Finally, besides the mappable and the non-mappable features there usually are features that the primary subject and the secondary subject already shared before they were conjoined in the metaphor. The feature 'being a living creature' is an example of such a pre-existing feature. The following scheme shows some of the pre-existent, mappable, and non-mappable features of 'Man is a wolf', symbolized by an open line, an arrow and a blocked line respectively. Three dots indicate that none of the categories is exhaustive. Depending on the context in which the metaphor is used they can be extended or reduced.

Table 2.1 The selection of mappable features in a verbal metaphor

Primary subject		*Secondary subject*
MAN	IS	WOLF
Living creature		—— Living creature
		—— …
		←—— Being aggressive, cruel, bloodthirsty
		←—— …
		×—— Having four legs, a tail
		×—— …

Returning to Black's theory we can state, then, that for a metaphor to be understood as a matching process between primary and secondary subject, a kind of mutual adjustment or matching between properties of both subjects must be realized. Black shows how he sees this process operating by discussing another, less worn metaphor, namely 'marriage is a zero-sum game'. He formulates the salient properties (in the form of predicates) in the implicative complex of 'zero-sum game' as follows:

(G1)   A 'game' is a *contest*;
(G2)   between two opponents;
(G3)   in which one player can win only at the expense of the other.

The corresponding system of imputed claims about marriage depends crucially upon the interpretations given to 'contest', 'opponents', and especially to 'winning'. One might try:

(M1)   A marriage is a sustained struggle;
(M2)   between two contestants;
(M3)   in which the rewards (power? money? satisfaction?) of one contestant are gained only at the other's expense.

   Here, the 'projected' propositions can be taken literally – or almost so, no matter what one thinks of their plausibility (the metaphor's aptness not being here in question).

(Black 1979a: 29–30)

In the next section this passage will be examined in more detail.

In my reading of points 4 and 5, Black endorses the idea that the two subjects of a metaphor cannot be reversed without changing the metaphor altogether. To elucidate what this important matter is about, let me rephrase it as a question. Can one simply reverse the order of primary subject and secondary subject in a metaphor? The answer is an unequivocal 'no'. As Miller, discussing similarity in metaphors and other analogies, points out, 'as soon as we consider how authors use analogies ... we find that the context imposes a direction, that it is no longer possible to rearrange freely the order of the terms' (1979: 215). The remark can be illustrated by comparing the following metaphors:

2)   Surgeons are butchers.
3)   Butchers are surgeons.

In 2), something is predicated about surgeons. Surgeons are here understood in terms of butchers, and one or more features from the secondary subject 'butchers' is/are transferred to 'surgeons'. We could describe the transferred features as 'ruthlessness', 'cold-bloodedness', 'indifference to the body they are working on'. Presumably, a negative value is moreover co-transferred from 'butchers' to 'surgeons': the remark is thus more likely to carry an insulting than a complimentary force. In 3), on the other hand, something is predicated about butchers in terms of surgeons. Here the transferred features are presumably something like 'precision', 'care', 'reliability'. Here, we may surmise, the observation is a complimentary one. Comparing 2) and 3), then, shows that reversing the terms of the metaphor results in an entirely different metaphor. As stated, I believe that Black can be shown to hold this correct view, albeit implicitly. Both Lakoff and Turner (1989) and Hausman (1989), however, think that Black unproblematically allows a reversal of the two terms of a metaphor. For Hausman, who builds his theory of 'metaphor and art' on Black's interaction theory, this misconception has serious consequences. Since the matter is best discussed in the context of Hausman's ideas, I will postpone a more detailed discussion of this topic, including Lakoff and Turner's criticisms, to Chapter 3.

AN EVALUATION OF KITTAY'S (1987) CRITICISMS OF BLACK'S THEORY

A theorist of metaphor who devotes a fairly long discussion to Black's interaction theory is Kittay (1987). As she herself acknowledges, Kittay owes much to Black's interaction theory. She considers her own account sufficiently different from Black's, however, to warrant the use of a different name: hers is labelled a *perspectival* account of metaphor. I propose, in turn, to discuss at some length Kittay's criticisms of Black. This discussion has a twofold purpose. In the first place it allows me to analyse some passages in Black's articles that are potentially controversial or simply obscure; and secondly it gives me an opportunity to examine critically whether Kittay's suggested improvements to Black's model are indeed improvements.

Apart from some terminological quibbles (see Kittay 1987: 25), Kittay begins by objecting that 'first, the systems are not "associated common-places" but *semantic fields*; secondly, both the vehicle [= Black's secondary subject] and the topic [= Black's primary subject] belong to systems, not only the vehicle . . .' (ibid.: 31). As for the second criticism, I have argued in the preceding section that Black, despite one half-hearted disclaimer, is really committed to the idea that both primary and secondary subject are 'systems', so Kittay need not worry on this score. More importantly, however, she wants to replace the 'associated commonplaces' by 'semantic fields'. She argues that Black is too restrictive about the features or properties of the secondary subject that are projected upon the primary subject if he understands these only in terms of Aristotle's *endoxa*. It is only necessary, Kittay maintains, to rely exclusively on these endoxa 'when using metaphors which are dislodged from their originating discourse. . . . When-ever we have a sufficiently rich context, we construct a system of implica-tions guided in part by *endoxa* and in part by the specificity of the contextual constraints and leads' (ibid.: 32). Kittay is right, of course, but I cannot see that this in any way refutes Black's ideas. To repeat, Black stated, 'my notion was that the secondary subject, *in a way partly depending upon the context of metaphorical use*, determines a set of what Aristotle called *endoxa*, current opinions shared by members of a certain speech-community' (Black 1979a: 28–9; first emphasis mine). Black here explicitly refers to the context in which the metaphor occurs. And the very possibility of 'novel and nonplatitudinous implication-complexes', mentioned in Black's next sentence, only exists because an author in a particular text steers a reader/listener to unconventional, ad hoc properties *not* embodied in the *endoxa*. Nor is this the only passage proving Black's awareness that the context importantly contributes to answering the question which fea-tures qualify for transfer from the secondary to the primary subject. After affirming that whenever he uses the word 'metaphor' he actually means 'metaphorical statement', Black continues, as we saw above, 'a "statement", in my intended sense, will be identified by quoting a whole sentence, *or a set of sentences together with as much of the relevant verbal context, or the nonverbal setting*, as may be needed for an adequate grasp of the actual or imputed speaker's meaning' (1979a: 24, my emphasis). Kittay, therefore, is fighting straw men here.

Expanding on the idea that both the primary subject (topic) and the secondary subject (vehicle) of a metaphor are systems rather than things, Kittay argues that both ought to be seen as part of 'semantic fields'. She defines and elaborates:

When a set of words, a *lexical set*, is applied to a domain unified by some content, a *content domain*, we have a *semantic field*. The semantic fields are comprised of terms which cover some specifiable conceptual ground and which bear certain relations of affinity and contrast to one another. . . . Both vehicle and topic are elements of semantic fields – or more precisely the vehicle is an element of a semantic field while the topic is part of some content domain that may not be articulated by a set of lexical items. . . . It should be possible to draw a specification of the systems operative in metaphor within a general account of meaning, where the general theory identifies the meaning of a term as systematically involving relations to the meaning of other terms in a language. Semantic field theory will provide for us just such a ground on which to build a theory of metaphorical meaning.

(Kittay 1987: 33–5)

Some examples of semantic fields Kittay gives are those of colours (comprising such terms as 'red', 'blue', 'green', 'yellow'); fishing (containing for instance 'fishing', 'fish', 'trout', 'fisherman'). A semantic field can also include relations such as synonymy ('big', 'large'); graded antonymy ('hot', 'warm', 'cool', 'cold'); hyponymy ('bird', 'robin'); cyclical series ('summer', 'winter', 'autumn', 'spring'); noncyclical series ('birth', 'childhood', 'adolescence'); ranks ('general', 'colonel', 'sergeant', 'private') (ibid.: 34).

Following her commitment to semantic field theory, Kittay reprimands Black for discussing projections from the secondary to the primary subject in terms of predicates. Instead, she argues, 'we are more likely to regard metaphorical transfers of meaning as transfers of *relations* across different domains' (ibid.: 36, my emphasis). A little later she continues:

Metaphorical transfers of meaning are transfers from the field of the vehicle to the field of the topic of the relations of affinity and opposition that the vehicle term(s) bears to other terms in its field. More precisely, in metaphor what is transferred are the relations which pertain within one semantic field to a second, distinct content domain. That, in short, is how I characterize metaphor.

(ibid.: 36)

First, it is unclear why transferring relations is incompatible with the notion of transferring predicates. Surely the observation that properties transferred from the secondary subject to the primary subject may cohere does not, as I already argued, preclude a (re)formulation of these properties in terms of predicates. This is exactly what Black does in the elaboration of the marriage-as-zero-sum-game metaphor discussed above. This having been said, I think that introducing the concept of 'semantic fields' usefully highlights the idea that both primary subject and secondary subject are *systems* of things, and that in a metaphorical transfer coherent configurations of properties/predicates may be transferred. However, I see several problems with Kittay's insistence on the pertinence of semantic fields for metaphor theory. The most serious problem, indeed one of the major weaknesses of Kittay's entire study, is that her commitment to semantic fields puts too much weight on the *linguistic* character of verbal metaphor. Admittedly, Kittay herself realizes the importance of a pragmatic component as well: 'Metaphors, I argue, have meaning and they therefore require a semantic account. But I also hold that a semantic account does not give us a full comprehension of the ways in which we understand metaphor and must be supplemented by pragmatic considerations' (ibid.: 10). Her 'pragmatic considerations', however, are restricted to situations where it is the context – verbal or non-verbal – that must be invoked to decide whether such sentences as 'Smith is a plumber' (ibid.: 69) or 'the seal dragged himself out of the office' (ibid.: 69 *et passim*) are metaphorical or not. Certain other pragmatic considerations, while no less important, are entirely ignored by Kittay. Black, on the contrary, is highly aware of them.

Black had realized early on that a metaphor is never merely linguistic: 'There is ... a sense of "metaphor" that belongs to "pragmatics" rather than to "semantics" – and this sense may be the one most deserving of attention' (1962: 30). In a passage quoted earlier, Black draws attention not only to the verbal, but also to the nonverbal context of a metaphor, and in his two articles he repeatedly emphasizes that beliefs, attitudes, and emotions are often, as it were, co-transferred with the properties from the secondary subject to the primary subject. Thus, since

> a wolf is (conventionally) a hateful and alarming object ... to call a man a wolf is to imply that he too is hateful and alarming (and thus to support and reinforce dyslogistic attitudes). Again, the vocabulary of chess has its primary uses in a highly artificial setting, where all expression of feeling is formally excluded: to describe a battle as if it were a game of chess is accordingly to exclude, by the choice of language, all the more emotionally disturbing aspects of warfare.
>
> (ibid.: 42)

Similarly, it seems likely that when former president George Bush metaphorically compared Saddam Hussein to Hitler in the early stages of the Gulf conflict, he indeed intended to activate above all the emotionally charged features of the secondary subject 'Hitler'.[4]

It is precisely an awareness of these important aspects of the secondary subject that is missing from Kittay's account. Put differently, there are a number of value-laden, emotionally prominent characteristics, beliefs, and intertextual echoes adhering to a secondary subject that – by definition – do not occur in its semantic field but may nonetheless prove elementary in the metaphorical transfer. Apart from Black's emphasis on the wolf's characteristic 'fear-inspiring' nature or its being (in a different culture) a reincarnation of a dead person, we can also be (made) aware that the wolf ate the grandmother of Little Red Riding Hood, or that, in another fairy-tale, the wolf was after the seven little goats. Needless to repeat that it depends on the context, verbal and non-verbal, which predicates are eligible for transfer from the secondary subject to the primary subject. What matters is that the set of projectable features of terms in a metaphor often far exceeds what would be found in a semantic field.

Apart from limiting the transfer of features to those occurring in a semantic field, Kittay's insistence on the pertinence of a semantic field theory has yet another unfortunate aspect. Her emphasis on the way any secondary subject is embedded in a semantic field leads her to postulate, as we saw, that it is not properties that are transferred from secondary to primary subject, but relations. This is indeed what tends to happen in the more interesting metaphors, i.e., those involving secondary subjects that are part of a whole network of concepts, attitudes, emotions, etc., a great deal of which is mappable on to the primary subject.[5] Shakespeare's 'the world's a stage' comes to mind as an example. But this is by no means always what happens. In some metaphors it is no more than an isolated feature that is transferred. Imagine the following utterances:

(4a)   'Roy managed to carry the refrigerator upstairs all on his own. Truly, the man is an elephant.'

(4b)   'Even thirty years later, Roy still remembered the names of all those present at the occasion. Truly, the man is an elephant.'

(4c)   'Roy had hardly sat down when the chair collapsed. Truly, the man is an elephant.'

(4d)   'Roy immediately after the funeral started urging remarriage on the widow. Truly, the man is an elephant.'

My claim is that in each of these utterances a different salient feature from the implicative complex of 'elephant' is transferred to the primary subject – a man called Roy. In 4a) it is the feature 'possessing great physical strength'; in 4b) that of 'having an excellent memory'; in 4c) that of 'being extraordinarily heavy'; and in 4d) that of 'being very tactless'. Notice that in 4d), the salient feature does not depend on our *knowledge* that elephants are, in fact, 'tactless'; it probably derives from our notion of an (in itself: metaphorical) 'thick skin'. In each of the utterances the salient features of the other three are irrelevant. Each utterance picks out *one isolated* salient feature and leaves the others alone. Nothing like an entire semantic field, or even part of it, is activated here. Notice, incidentally, that the one-line metaphorical sentence 'Truly, the man is an elephant' gives us no clue which feature is to be transferred in the metaphor; it is the surrounding verbal context – or the non-verbal, situational context – which steers the interpreter to the selection of the correct feature. Put differently, the metaphor's 'frame' must be expanded beyond the sentence for the metaphor to be understood.

In Chapter 5 of her book, 'Alternative approaches: a critique', Kittay resumes her criticisms of Black's interaction theory, in particular with respect to its support of the 'predicate transfer thesis'. Before she launches her attack, she quotes Black at length. For a good understanding of what is

going on here I find it necessary to quote Kittay quoting Black (1962: 41) –
adding, however, in square brackets what Kittay leaves out:

> The effect, then, of (metaphorically) calling a man [a] 'wolf' is to evoke
> the wolf-system of related commonplaces. If the man is a wolf, he preys
> upon other animals, is fierce . . . [The ellipsis reads: 'hungry, engaged in
> constant struggle, a scavenger, and so on.'] Each of these implied
> assertions has now to be made to fit the principal subject (the man)
> either in normal or in abnormal senses. . . . [The ellipsis reads: 'If the
> metaphor is at all appropriate, this can be done – up to a point at least.']
> A suitable hearer will be led by the wolf-system of implication ['-s to
> construct a corresponding system of implications'] about the principal
> subject. But these implications will *not* be those comprised in the common-
> places *normally* implied by literal uses of 'man'. The new implications
> must be determined by the pattern of implication[s] associated with
> literal uses of the word 'wolf'. Any human traits that can without undue
> strain be talked about in 'wolf-language' will be rendered prominent,
> and any that cannot will be pushed into the background. The wolf-
> metaphor suppresses some details, emphasizes others – in short, *organizes*
> our view of man.
>
> (Kittay 1987: 181)

The omission of the indefinite article and the plural -*s*s is the kind of
editorial oversight that pesters any book, and is forgivable. The disappearance of an entire phrase ('to construct a corresponding system of implications') is worse, for as it stands Black's line is incomprehensible. The two
deliberate ellipses, however, are more than unfortunate, as will become
clearer if we turn to Kittay's comments immediately following the
quotation:

> This sounds helpful, but it cannot be quite right. To begin, the implica-
> tions of 'the wolf-system of related commonplaces' must be indefinite
> and perhaps infinite. Therefore it is absurd to think that *each* of these
> implied assertions (and why must they be assertions?) gets applied to the
> principal subject. . . . We can note that, even if we confine ourselves to
> commonplace beliefs concerning the subsidiary subject (the vehicle),
> there are many predicates which can be formed, such as 'are not ironing-
> boards', believed to be true of wolves, which have no import whatsoever
> in the interpretation of the metaphor.
>
> (ibid.: 181–2)

Kittay is quite correct to emphasize that there are numerous trivial, irrelevant implied assertions adhering to wolf that are *not* applied to 'man' –
but (as before) she is wrong to suggest that Black would think otherwise.
Kittay's first ellipsis in Black's quotation is misleading here. Black's noun
phrase 'these implied assertions' does not, as Kittay suggests, invoke all
thinkable attributes that could be predicated of 'wolf', but quite precisely

refers back to 'preying upon other animals', 'being fierce', 'being hungry', 'being engaged in constant struggle', 'being a scavenger'. Maybe Black was a bit careless to add 'and so on' without further commentary, but it takes a malicious reading to imply that 'not being an ironing-board' would be among the attributes included in 'and so on'.

A different primary subject in a metaphor, Kittay goes on to point out, would lead to a projection of different attributes: in the sentence 'In the deserted land, the wind, a lone wolf, howled in the night', the features projected from 'wolf' upon 'wind' will not be 'scavenging' and 'carnivorous' but other ones. Again, this observation is completely correct – but this was already argued by Black himself, as Kittay grudgingly admits (ibid.: 182) (see point 5a quoted earlier in this chapter).

But there is still more in Black's theory Kittay is unhappy about. 'We recall that in speaking of the man as wolf metaphor, Black suggested that those human traits which became prominent could "without undue strain be talked of in wolf-language"; the rest would be "pushed in the background"' (Kittay 1987: 182). Kittay objects that 'there are predicates applicable to wolves which offer no strain whatsoever when applied to man. These are the predicates or implications which apply [to] (or concern) *both* the topic and the vehicle of the metaphor'. As examples she mentions that men, like wolves, are living, animate beings; mammals; and carnivorous, but that all this 'would be of no interest or help in interpreting "man is a wolf"' (ibid.: 183). Secondly she has problems with Black's 'undue strain', claiming that 'most interesting metaphors involve a great deal of strain on language and thought' (ibid.: 183).

As before, Kittay stubbornly persists in reading against the spirit and the text of Black's articles. As to the first point, in the very passage quoted earlier by Kittay herself Black emphasizes that 'a suitable hearer will be led by the wolf-system of implications to construct a corresponding system of implications about the principal subject. *But these implications will not be those comprised in the commonplaces normally implied by literal uses of "man"*' (my emphasis).[6] As to the second point, Black's formulation may here be a bit unfortunate, but it is implausible to assume that the formulator of the creativity thesis of metaphor (see the next section) himself should be unaware of the imaginative leaps that can or must sometimes be made in mappings from the secondary on to the primary subject.

Kittay's parting shot at Black pertains to the question 'how we are to understand statements that result from the projection of predicates from the secondary subject on to the primary subject' (ibid.: 184). She takes a closer look at Black's example 'marriage is a zero-sum game'. Kittay complains that she does not believe that M1–M3 can be understood as literal assertions. Her first grievance is that 'marriage, understood as an institution or contractual agreement, is not the sort of thing that can be properly described as a "struggle"' – the latter describing an 'activity' – although she admits that 'living the married life may perhaps be literally so described' (ibid.: 184). This objection can be simply dismissed as quibbling about words: Black opted for the word 'marriage' but no doubt would have cheerfully accepted 'married life' instead. Kittay's further comments prove that she entirely misses the mark. 'Still, literally to predicate of marriage that it is a struggle need imply nothing about contestants. We mean to say only that it is difficult to achieve the happiness, harmony, etc. desired of the married life. Both partners can struggle together, rather than against each other' (ibid.: 184–5). True, 'to predicate of marriage that it is a struggle need imply nothing about contestants' – but to predicate of marriage that it is a zero-sum game certainly does! That is, Kittay could have been right – if the metaphor under discussion had simply been 'marriage is a struggle' instead of the more complicated 'marriage is a zero-sum game'. What Black does is project (some of) the salient features, properties, attributes, predicates (or whatever label is chosen), of the secondary subject 'zero-sum game' upon the primary subject 'marriage', and while a zero-sum game can be described as a struggle, it happens to be more specifically a type of struggle in which the winner necessarily wins at the expense of the loser. This last feature is precisely one of the elements that distinguishes the metaphor 'marriage is a zero-sum game' from the metaphor 'marriage is a struggle'. It is true that Black's metaphor yields a rather cynical view of marriage, but that is entirely irrelevant. As Kittay herself has – correctly – reminded us by baptizing her approach a perspectival theory of metaphor, 'to call our theory perspectival is to name it for the function metaphor serves: to provide a perspective from which to gain an understanding of that which is metaphorically portrayed' (13–14). Kittay obviously does not like this view of marriage – and who would? (Perhaps the marriage metaphors Quinn [1987] examines provide one that is more to her taste.) Her heavy-handed criticism, however, ignores both Black's parenthetical remark that the metaphor's aptness is not in question and his ironical observation that a marriage considered in terms of a zero-sum game is obviously 'not the kind made in heaven' (1979a: 30). Indeed, here surfaces a virtue of Black's account of metaphor that, as indicated before, is so painfully missing from Kittay's own: the awareness that besides elements from the semantic field of 'zero-sum game', also 'the suggestions and valuations that necessarily attach themselves to a game-theory view of marriage' (ibid.) play a role in the metaphor.

Kittay winds up by objecting that the marriage partners are '"contestants" only if marriage is already metaphorically conceived of as a game or struggle invoking contestants – they are not literally "contestants" at all' (1987: 185). A similar objection is raised against what Black asserts under M3.

Kittay is right that the use of the word 'contestants' implies a view of marriage-as-zero-sum-game, i.e., it is a concept that already is 'transformed' by the metaphor. What Black gives under M1–M3 is the transformed implicative complex. Since Black could be accused of skipping one stage in the process he traces (that of the 'untransformed' implicative complex of 'marriage'), I will take the opportunity to sketch here, step by step, what I see as the application of point 5 of his theory. Let us recall this point:

> In the context of a particular metaphorical statement, the two subjects 'interact' in the following ways: a) the presence of the primary subject incites the hearer to select some of the secondary subject's properties; and b) invites him to construct a parallel implication-complex that can fit the primary subject; and c) reciprocally induces parallel changes in the secondary subject.
>
> (Black 1979a: 29)

Ad a). The primary subject being 'marriage', the hearer has to pick out predicates from the secondary subject 'zero-sum game' that can sensibly be projected upon 'marriage'. These, or at least some of these, are given by Black under G1–G3. Not all of the salient attributes are selected: for instance, arguably 'zero-sum game' also has as one of its properties 'playfulness'. This attribute is irrelevant, therefore downplayed, and hence not co-projected upon 'marriage'.

Ad b). G1–G3 now lead to the construction of a parallel implication-complex in the primary subject, such that the possibility of correspondences between the two complexes is created. Black does not himself elaborate on this phase in the present example. I supplement:

Sup 1   A marriage involves a relation
Sup 2   between a man and a woman
Sup 3   that yields certain benefits.

Ad c). At this stage, a situation has been developed in which we have two 'isomorphic' (as Black calls them) implication complexes. The correspondences have been established. These correspondences, I propose, can be seen as a kind of bridges.[7] The bridges have been built, then, and now the salient properties from the implication complex of 'zero-sum-game' can cross (be transferred) to fuse with the corresponding salient properties of the implication complex of 'marriage', thus reorganizing the view of marriage (at least for as long as the metaphor is entertained). In this 'journey across the bridge' the zero-sum game's 'contest' turns the marriage's 'relation' into a 'struggle'; the two opponents become two adversaries or contestants, one a husband, the other a wife; and the rewards of the zero-sum game turn the marriage's 'benefits' into the kind that the two participants can obtain only at each other's expense. The result of the metaphor, then, is a new implicative complex, an implicative complex that, properly speaking, is not a (new) implicative complex of marriage, but of 'marriage-as-zero-sum-game'. The expression of this new complex is formulated by Black as M1–M3. Black's *practice* is quite clear, but his formulation of it under (c) is confusing. The changes induced in the complex of the secondary subject would be, presumably, those from 'salient-properties-of-zero-sum-game' to 'salient-properties-of-zero-sum-game-as-applicable-to-marriage'. Moreover, the process need not stop here: the 'oscillation' between the subjects may go on and lead to further elaborations of the metaphor.

In view of the above, it is worthwhile repeating that something 'happens' to the salient features of the secondary subject at the moment when they cross the bridge to the primary subject: they are, to a larger or lesser degree, transformed. This point was made already by Richards. He discusses the metaphor 'the (poet's) mind is a river' (from a poem by Denham), and comments:

> Take *deep*. Its main implications as regards a river are, 'not easily crossed, dangerous, navigable, and suitable for swimming, perhaps.' As applied to a mind it suggests 'mysterious, a lot going on, rich in knowledge and power, not easily accounted for, acting from serious and important reasons'.
>
> (Richards 1965/1936: 122)

Ortony (1979), cited by Kittay (1987: 189), draws attention to the same phenomenon in discussing 'blood vessels are like aqueducts'. It is thus best to say that predicates, when transferred from the secondary subject, always require some degree of 'adaptation' or 'transformation'[8] before they are applicable to the primary subject.

Summarizing Kittay's criticisms of Black, I find that most of the improvements she suggests are in fact anything but improvements, and that there is thus no reason to substitute Kittay's perspectival account for Black's interaction theory. These invalid objections apart, however, Kittay makes at least two useful suggestions for expanding on Black's theory. First, Kittay elaborates on the serviceable notion that in many cases the properties/predicates that can be transferred from secondary to primary subject are somehow systematically related, leading to the view that it is not merely isolated properties, but rather relations of properties that are transferred, as long as it is borne in mind that 1) the concept of a 'semantic field' is too restrictive to account for this, and 2) in some metaphors it is not relations but isolated features that are transferred. Second, Kittay provides more insight into the role of context in metaphor by introducing the notion of 'default value', a notion she borrows from Hofstadter (1985). Particularly when one-line metaphors are cited, as is quite customary in metaphor studies, it might seem that there is somehow no further context. As a matter of fact, there always is a silently presupposed context: a context consisting of numerous assumptions shared by 'all or some of the members of a language community' (Kittay 1987: 55). The sum total of these contextual assumptions is indicated by the term 'default values'. Kittay defines default values as follows:

> By default assumptions I mean those assumptions upon which speakers rely, in both verbal and non-verbal behaviour, in the absence of any

contextual evidence cancelling or questioning such assumptions. Because speakers are scarcely conscious of employing such assumptions, they presume, again with little consciousness of making such presumptions, that their audience has the same assumptions. They are *default* assumptions because they are what we assume in the absence of any contradictory evidence.

(ibid.:55)

It is important to realize that default values, of course, are never objectively given but, as Kittay indicates, relative to a certain community. This community can vary in size: at its largest it probably comprises the entire human race – for instance when such universal human activities as eating, sleeping, copulating and motor functions (see Johnson 1987) are concerned – whereas at its smallest it consists of two people who have in certain areas developed their own default values. But default values can also be text-bound. As Black pointed out, an author can build up an ad hoc implicative complex for a term in a certain text. Any metaphor involving such a term must then be measured not against the general default values but against those that have been developed in that text. Such a text can also generate discourse-specific default values because of its genre. Thus Kittay convincingly argues that 'the seal dragged himself out of the office' is a metaphor in the context of general default values, but not in the context of a Disney-like fairy-tale populated by personified animals, since here the genre has changed the default values.

OTHER VIEWS HELD BY BLACK

Creating similarity

One of the crucial claims of the interaction theory is the creative character of many metaphors: 'It would be more illuminating in some . . . cases to say that the metaphor creates the similarity than to say that it formulates some similarity antecedently existing' (Black 1962: 37). It is this aspect of metaphor that turns it into an instrument that can play such an exciting role in both poetry and science. The notion of 'creating similarity' constitutes such a momentous insight that it is worth dwelling on at greater length. For a systematic treatment of the role of poetic metaphor, we had best have a brief look at Lakoff and Turner (1989). In this book Lakoff and Turner apply and expand insights generated by Lakoff and Johnson (1980) to the realm of poetry. A key pre-supposition is that human language reveals how we structure certain concepts in terms of other concepts. Thus, Lakoff and Johnson argue, utterances like 'your claims are *indefensible*; he *attacked every weak point* in my argument; 'his criticisms were *right on target*; I *demolished* his argument' (1980: 4) are systematically related by the existence in our minds of the conceptual metaphor ARGUMENT IS WAR.[9] Similarly,

Lakoff and Turner point out, it is thanks to the existence of such conceptual metaphors that we are able to understand and interpret many passages in poetry. Thus, Robert Frost's lines (from 'The Road Not Taken'):

Two roads diverged in a wood, and I –
I took the one less traveled by,
And that has made all the difference

presuppose the conceptual metaphor LIFE IS A JOURNEY. Once this metaphor is accessed, all kinds of elaboration become possible. Since the concept 'journey' is a fairly structured one – journeys have beginnings, middles, ends; they involve a means of transport, a trajectory, fellow-passengers, delays, intermediate stops, costs, unexpected barriers, dangers, etc. – the concept provides an enormous number of elements potentially mappable upon the implicative complex, or domain,[10] of LIFE. Thus, the target domain LIFE as transformed by the metaphorical coupling with the source domain JOURNEY would yield something like the following: birth, growing up, and death correspond to the beginning, middle and end of the journey; the means of transport could be anything, dependent on circumstances, from an inheritance, an ambition, an obsession – anything that could be conceived of as that which propels one in life. Fellow-passengers would be family, friends, colleagues; delays could be illnesses, divorces, setbacks in a career; intermediate stops could be memorable events such as a marriage, the birth of a child, an accident, a retirement . . .

On the one hand, poets rely on their readers to access metaphors of the LIFE IS A JOURNEY type – that is, metaphors of a conventional nature; on the other hand poets can creatively expand on these conventional metaphors. But metaphors in poetry are by no means always expansions of conventional metaphors. Indeed, it is precisely many of the most interesting, truly creative metaphors that have *no* grounding in conventional mappings. Black (1979a: 21) referred to Wallace Stevens's 'a poem is a pheasant', where ad hoc context and readerly imagination must make sense of the metaphor. Here the similarity can be said to be created rather than to be pre-existent (unless we prefer to conceive of the similarity as 'pre-existent-but-waiting-to-be-discovered').

In essence, the creative character of metaphor works the same in science as in art. In an account illustrated by examples taken from science, Indurkhya (1991) usefully helps focus Black's creativity thesis by formalizing it. Indurkhya points out that – in Black's terminology – both primary and secondary subject are part of a context (which Indurkhya calls 'environment'). On the basis of the nature of the interaction between the two subjects and their respective environments, he distinguishes three kinds of metaphor: syntactic, suggestive, and projective. Basically in what Indurkhya calls syntactic metaphor the two subjects of the metaphor are already largely 'isomorphic': the salient properties of the secondary subject can be easily made to fit salient properties in the primary subject. That is, the internal structures of the two subjects as well as the ways in which they relate to their environments are already largely familiar and there is little difficulty in making the correspondences between the two domains. As an example of syntactic metaphor, Indurkhya cites the well-known 'electrical circuits are hydraulic systems'. There is little 'oscillation' between the two domains, the mutual adaptations between the (domains of the) two subjects necessary for the metaphor to work posing little difficulty. Consequently, no spectacularly new insights are generated – although this type of metaphor has its uses (Indurkhya 1991: 11–16). In suggestive metaphor, by contrast, the primary subject has little structure by itself – and it is this very structure that is imposed upon it by the secondary subject. Suggestive metaphors are typically used to gain more insight into unknown areas of knowledge. By metaphorically coupling a structured source domain with a target domain possessing little structure, the latter domain can be enriched. Indurkhya gives as an example a metaphor used by Gick and Holyoak (1980) in an experiment testing how a richly structured, and appropriate, source domain (an army faced with the problem of how to capture a fortress surrounded by mines) could help laymen solve the medical problem of how to treat a tumour without destroying the surrounding healthy tissue (the target domain). This kind of metaphor is also useful in triggering scientific discoveries. There is bound to be a lot of oscillation between the two subjects, a lot of matching (Indurkhya uses the term 'fine tuning'), since it is a matter of trial and error to assess which elements and which structural relations in the source domain can be made to correspond with elements and structural relations in the target domain.

Indurkhya's third type is projective metaphor. While a suggestive metaphor respects whatever little structure is known to exist in the primary subject, and merely augments this structure by importing the internal relationships of a richly structured secondary subject, in projective metaphor both the structures of primary and secondary subjects are largely familiar. What is new is their unexpected coupling. This metaphor presents the primary subject in an unexpected way and thus highlights properties of it that remained hidden under the conventional mode of perceiving the primary subject (and, conversely, downplays properties that were formerly highlighted). Obviously, in a scientific environment with highly complex primary and secondary subjects, a change of secondary subject can trigger a complete change of paradigm, an entire reconceptualization of a primary subject. Indurkhya gives as an example of projective metaphor the case of the paintbrush-as-pump reported in Schön (1979), where an important technical breakthrough resulted from the insight that a certain kind of brush should not be understood as 'smearing' paint on a surface, but rather as 'pumping' it. Other examples are provided by Vroon and Draaisma (1985), who discuss various ways in which mankind has in the course of time conceived of the brain – such as a clock, a telephone switchboard, a radio, a radar, a computer – and some of the consequences of each change of metaphor.

Metaphor and truth

In view of his emphasis on the potential creativity of metaphor, it is not at all surprising that Black warns against imposing true/false tests on metaphors. A creation, after all, is never subject to that test: inasmuch as a metaphor is creative, it can be true or false just as little as a painting or a poem can be. As Black points out, 'it is a violation of philosophical grammar to assign either truth or falsity to strong [i.e., innovative, thought-provoking] metaphors' (1979a: 41). He goes on to claim that 'what lies behind the desire to stretch "true" to fit some cases . . . is a recognition that an emphatic, indispensable metaphor does not belong to the realm of fiction, and is not merely being used, as some writers allege, for some mysterious aesthetic effect, but really does say something' (ibid.; see also Ricoeur 1977: 232).

Lakoff and Johnson (1980) at first sight seem less averse to applying a true/false dichotomy to metaphor than Black, but end up holding a position that is not incompatible with Black's. The apparent differences stem from the fact that while Black focuses on novel, creative metaphors, Lakoff and Johnson are primarily interested in metaphors that are already embedded in a culture. Recall that one of the key themes of *Metaphors We Live By* is the extent to which we *systematically* conceptualize certain domains of experience in terms of other domains of experience, and how this metaphorical thinking manifests itself in language. Lakoff and Johnson's interest in the systematicity of these conceptualizations explains their emphasis on *conventional* metaphors, i.e., 'metaphors that structure the ordinary conceptual system of our culture, which is reflected in our everyday language' (1980: 139). Two of the numerous examples discussed in their book are the ARGUMENT IS WAR and LIFE IS A JOURNEY metaphors alluded to above. The account of truth Lakoff and Johnson give, therefore, is coloured by their concern with, and the examples they give of, conventional metaphors. Let us have a closer look at their notion of truth with reference to metaphor.

In the first place Lakoff and Johnson argue that the 'truth' of many metaphors can only be judged in the context of the reality defined by those very metaphors. 'If you see reality as defined by the metaphor . . . then you can answer the [true/false] question relative to whether the metaphorical entailments fit reality' (ibid.: 158). Giving the example of a president's announcement that his administration has won a major energy battle, Lakoff and Johnson claim that if you see the energy crisis as a war, then you can judge the truth or falsity of an utterance based on this metaphor. Thus, if the oil-producing nations had been forced to cut the price of oil by fifty per cent, then indeed the metaphorical statement could be said to be true. If, however, only a temporary freeze had been negotiated, one could call it false.

When we are dealing with conventional metaphors, therefore, the matter of their truth or falsity is hardly more problematic than in the case of 'literal language'.[11] The reason for this is that conventional metaphors are so embedded in a language that their metaphoricity is often no longer recognized as such. Intuitively, we would have no more difficulty in pronouncing on the truth or falsity of 'Theo *attacked* my proposal' or 'Arnold's claims were *indefensible*' – both verbal manifestations of the conventional metaphor ARGUMENT IS WAR – in a given situation than on that of 'Theo is a philosopher' or 'Arnold has three children'.[12] But what happens if we shift from conventional metaphors to unconventional ones?

It is telling that when Lakoff and Johnson extend their claim that truth and falsity can be predicated of metaphors from conventional to new or nonconventional ones, they take as an example the Shakespearean 'Life . . . is a tale, told by an idiot . . .' expanding, as they themselves point out, on the metaphor LIFE IS A STORY – which is a conventional metaphor. Once we turn to metaphors that are highly *unconventional*, however, such as those Black is particularly interested in, the claim that it makes sense to discuss them in terms of truth and falsity becomes more difficult to uphold. Again, Wallace Stevens's 'a poem is a pheasant' is a case in point. Indeed, Lakoff and Johnson themselves seem to realize that they are on thin ice in declaring the truth/falsity distinction applicable to nonconventional metaphor, for immediately after their Shakespearean example they state,

> although we have seen that such new, nonconventional metaphors will fit our general account of truth, we should stress again that issues of truth are among the least relevant and interesting issues that arise in the study of metaphor. The real significance of the metaphor LIFE'S A TALE TOLD BY AN IDIOT is that, in getting us to try to understand how it could be true, it makes possible a new understanding of our lives.
>
> (ibid.: 175)

Inasmuch as there is a difference between Lakoff and Johnson's acceptance of the true/false distinction with reference to metaphor, and Black's rejection of it, this reflects their respective emphasis on conventional metaphor – metaphor that is usually experienced as literal language – and on creative, daring, innovative metaphor – metaphor that by definition is not (yet) part and parcel of our conceptual frameworks. Whereas the claims concerning metaphor's truth or falsity made by Black on the one hand and by Lakoff and Johnson on the other strike me as compatible, the view that creative, non-conventional metaphors can be true or false seems to me to be misleading.[13]

Literal versus figurative; conventional versus unexpected

The question whether metaphors are subject to true/false judgments is related to another much-discussed dichotomy, i.e., that between the literal and the figurative. Black's very subdivision between frame and focus presupposes the necessity of distinguishing between what is traditionally labelled the literal and the figurative in a metaphor. In each metaphor there is a tension between frame and focus, and more specifically between primary and secondary subject, which urges the addressee to reject a literal reading in favour of (or complement a literal reading by) a figurative one – whether because the literal reading yields a plain falsity, nonsense, or a trivial truth. Indeed, without this tension there can simply be no metaphor.

However, the labels 'literal' and 'figurative' are not unproblematic. Let us briefly return to Lakoff and Johnson's notion of conventional metaphor, which I discussed in the preceding sections. Lakoff and Johnson argue that a sentence like 'The *foundations* of your theory are not very solid', which *is* a verbal manifestation of the conceptual metaphor THEORIES ARE BUILDINGS, is 'part of our ordinary literal language about theories' (1980: 52). In Lakoff and Johnson's terms, then, while we have a metaphor here, the distinction could not be between a literal and a figurative part, since the expression as a whole belongs to literal use. The reason that the expression belongs to literal use is that the element 'foundation' of the concept BUILDING belongs to the conventionally 'used' part of the metaphor THEORIES ARE BUILDINGS. Another commonly 'used' part of that metaphor, according to Lakoff and Johnson, is the 'shell' element of the concept BUILDINGS – that is, the outer, visible part of a building. This use of the 'shell' element of the metaphor is reflected in such sentences as 'we need to *buttress* the theory' and 'we need some more facts or the argument will *fall apart*'. On the other hand, 'the roof, internal rooms, staircases, and hallways are parts of a building not used as part of the concept THEORY' (ibid.). These conventionally 'unused' parts of the THEORIES ARE BUILDINGS metaphor could, however, be activated in such utterances as 'his theory has *thousands of little rooms and long, winding corridors*' and 'he prefers massive *Gothic* theories *covered with gargoyles*' (ibid.: 53). These utterances, unlike those exemplifying used parts of the conceptual metaphor, 'fall outside the domain of normal literal language and are part of what is usually called "figurative" or "imaginative" language' (ibid.).

The distinction between the used part and the unused part of a conceptual metaphor is a valuable one. We intuitively feel that the former is indeed part and parcel of our ordinary, literal language, whereas the latter reflects a more innovative, imaginative use, while we nonetheless recognize that the same conceptual metaphor underlies both types. All this suggests that the 'literal/figurative' pair is not a very fortunate choice.

Lakoff discusses the problem in more detail. He argues that the concept 'literal' in fact comprises at least four senses, which he describes as follows:

Literal 1, or *conventional literality*: ordinary conventional language – contrasting with poetic language, exaggeration, approximation, embellishment, excessive politeness, indirectness, and so on.
Literal 2, or *subject matter literality*: language ordinarily used to talk about some domain of subject matter.
Literal 3, or *nonmetaphorical literality*: directly meaningful language – not language that is understood, even partly, in terms of something else.
Literal 4, or *truth-conditional literality*: language capable of 'fitting the world' (i.e., of referring to objectively existing objects or of being objectively true or false).

(Lakoff 1986: 292)

Lakoff claims that only if these senses were always to converge would it be possible to maintain such traditional distinctions as literal versus figurative. As it is, however, a sentence may for instance be literal in the sense that it is made up of ordinary conventional language (sense 1), but non-literal in the sense that one type of thing is understood in terms of another kind of thing (sense 3) – which as we have seen is Lakoff and Johnson's hallmark of metaphoricity. Similarly, a sentence need not be literal in sense 3 while still being literal in sense 4. Thus, Lakoff shows that the sentence 'He's passed away' – said of someone who has died – is metaphorical in the sense that it is a manifestation of the conventional metaphor DEATH IS GOING TO A LOCATION AWAY FROM HERE, where dying is conceived of in terms of leaving (i.e., non-Literal 3) but literal in the sense that it is a common, conventional way of talking about dying (i.e., Literal 1) and in the sense that the sentence can be judged true or false (i.e., Literal 4). In a second example Lakoff, with reference to Gentner and Gentner (1982), considers the two common ways of understanding and reasoning about electricity: as fluid flow and as crowd movement. Since both are conventional modes of talking and thinking about the domain of electricity, they are both Literal 1 and Literal 2. But as each of them presents one kind of thing (electricity) in terms of another (fluid flow, crowd movement), both are non-Literal 3. And because we have no way of assessing what electricity 'really' is, Lakoff argues, we would have to answer the question whether they are Literal 4 in the negative: since the two modes have different, but equally conventional ontologies, they cannot both be 'objectively' true or false.

Because Lakoff does not elaborate on the differences between 'Literal 1' and 'Literal 2', the most important insight arising from this article (but anticipated already in Lakoff and Johnson 1980) is that a sentence may be simultaneously Literal 1 and 2, but non-Literal 3, while the application of Literal 4 is variable. That is, an expression may be simultaneously conventional and metaphorical. To avoid confusion, Lakoff proposes to avoid the term 'literal' as much as possible and if it is nonetheless used to reserve it for his Literal 3, the only one of the four Literals to contrast with 'metaphorical'. It should be borne in mind, however, that, as with truth/

false judgments, the literal/metaphorical distinction is mainly problematic when *conventional* metaphors – or, more precisely, the conventionalized, 'used', parts of these metaphors – are at stake. Black, on the contrary, is primarily interested in new, creative, *unconventional* metaphors – and from this perspective at least senses 2, 3, and 4 of 'literal' (and their implied contrasts) are likely to converge.

Since the pictorial metaphors I will be discussing are closer to Black's unconventional metaphors than to Lakoff and Johnson's conventional ones, it might seem acceptable to stick to the old literal/figurative or literal/metaphorical labels. If these labels are nonetheless not ideal this is because they are so strongly associated with *verbal* metaphor. If we were to retain them, we would have to talk about the literal and the figurative part of a picture. This would, at the very least, be awkward. It is counterintuitive to talk about the 'literal' part of a picture, while the word 'figurative' has a very different meaning in the discussion of pictures, being usually contrasted with 'abstract'. Therefore, whenever it is necessary to distinguish between the literal and figurative part of a picture, I will use the medium-neutral terms Black introduced: 'frame' and 'focus'.

Noun-metaphor and other kinds of metaphor

Although Black mentions metaphors other than those having the form 'Noun A is noun B' – such as 'the chairman plowed through the discussion' (1962: 26) – his theory and analyses are based on examples of the 'Noun A is noun B' variety. This naturally suggests the question whether metaphors with a different grammatical structure (see for instance Brooke-Rose 1958) are amenable to Black's model. I do think they are, although involving different grammatical categories can pose special problems. I will briefly consider two specimens: Miller's (1979) 'rusty joints' and Levin's (1979) 'the brook smiled'.

Miller's 'rusty joints' can be 'taken as a figurative description of an old man' or alternatively 'conjures up a rusty machine' (1979: 213). In the absence of context – and Miller does not provide any – it is not immediately obvious which is the frame and which is the focus of the metaphor. If we take 'joints' as the frame, then 'rusty' is the focus and the underlying conceptual metaphor must be construed as something like A MAN IS A MACHINE, i.e., in this metaphor a man is understood in terms of a machine. Alternatively, if we take 'rusty' as the frame and 'joint' as the focus, the underlying conceptual metaphor must be construed as A MACHINE IS A MAN. Usually, of course, the context, here so conspicuously absent, provides us with a sufficient clue to decide which construal is appropriate.

Levin's example poses similar problems. He argues that

[5] 'the brook smiled'] may be construed either with the concept of brook being modified or with the concept of smiling modified. In the

former case [5a] we get an interpretation in which the brook, provided with certain characteristics, smiled; in the latter case [5b] we get an interpretation in which the brook glistened or sparkled. In terms of comparison, we might say that in [5a] the brook is compared to the concept of smiling in the respect that smiling is an activity normally engaged in by humans. In [5b] we might say that the activity of smiling is compared to the concept of a brook in respect of the latter's being a liquid object. In [5a] the result is a personification of the brook; in [5b] the result is a dispersonification of smiling.

(Levin 1979: 129)

I agree with Levin's main point that, as in the case of the rusty joints, the interpretation of the metaphor differs according to whether 'the brook' or 'smiled' is construed as the frame of the metaphor. The rest of his analysis strikes me, however, as somewhat unfortunate. In the first place this analysis only holds in the unnatural situation where we have no further context, so that we can only fall back on Kittay's 'default values'. Secondly, while it may not be plainly wrong to say that the resulting interpretation is either 'a personification of the brook' or 'a dispersonification of smiling', it seems at the very least a rather truncated way of presenting the metaphor. Let me elaborate on this second problem.

If 'brook' is, or belongs to, the frame of the metaphor, then 'smiled' is the focus and thus calls for metaphorical construal. Put differently, a certain activity that can be literally, or conventionally, predicated of brooks is conceived of in terms of 'smiling', say 'flowing'. In this construal, then, the underlying conceptual metaphor is, say, FLOWING IS SMILING. The properties of SMILING that are mapped on to FLOWING, we may speculate (and in the absence of context speculate is all we can do), are 'radiating pleasantness', 'suggesting intimacy', 'constituting a temptation' – or something else that belongs in the domain of SMILING (Levin understands the result of the mapping in terms of the brook's 'sparkling' or 'glistening'). In addition to all this, I would argue, the brook does not remain altogether unaffected, in that it is, to some degree, personified. This is pointed out by Levin as well, but contrary to him, I see this personification *as a result of the metaphorization of 'flowing-as-smiling', not of 'brook'*. A situation in which this reading of the metaphor is appropriate might run something like this:

Mary and Peter had been wandering through the forest for hours. It was a very hot day, and they were dying for a swim, but they had not yet come across the brook that was rumoured to run through the wood. At last Mary caught a glimpse through the trees. 'Look', she exclaimed, and indeed – there, less than a hundred yards away, the brook smiled at them.

But what, then, happens when 'the brook' is the focus of the metaphor, and 'smiled' (part of) the frame? In this case, there is an X that is understood metaphorically in terms of 'the brook'. What or who is this X? We cannot know, because there is no context to provide us with clues. But since X belongs to the frame just like 'smiled' does, we can at least say that this X must be capable of smiling and is hence bound to be human. The underlying metaphor thus would run THE (HUMAN) X IS A BROOK.[14] Let us invent an appropriate context.

> Hans each summer suffers from terrible bouts of hay fever. On these occasions, the tears stream down his face. Although I feel truly sorry for him, I can't help seeing the irony of the situation – for there is no more merry guy than Hans. So when I told him he produced more water than an average brook he took it well: the brook smiled.

In this context the property of BROOK that is transferred to HANS (X) is something like 'causing a lot of water to flow'.

My point in discussing 'rusty joints' and 'the brook smiled' is to suggest that even though they are not noun metaphors they work no differently from the paradigmatic 'Noun A is Noun B' type. The crucial characteristic of metaphor, to recall Lakoff and Johnson's formulation, is 'understanding and experiencing one kind of thing in terms of another'. That means that what is at the heart of metaphor is the metaphorical IS that, as Ricoeur pointed out, is simultaneously an IS NOT. This metaphorical IS/IS NOT, however, occurs on the conceptual level, and does not necessarily manifest itself as a form of the verb 'to be' on the linguistic level – a point amply illustrated in Lakoff and Johnson (1980), where a wealth of metaphorical sentences, displaying a wide variety of grammatical structures, are always traced back to a conceptual metaphor of the form A IS B. My analyses of 'rusty joints' and 'the brook smiled', then, are to suggest that all types of metaphor can ultimately be traced back to a conceptual A IS B.

But apart from that they point up something that is too often ignored in paradigmatic noun metaphors: many metaphors need construal. As we have seen, both the decision which is the focus and which the frame of the metaphor, and hence which is its primary and which its secondary subject, and the assessment which features are mapped from the secondary subject on to the primary subject may depend on the context – a context that is notably absent in both Miller's and Levin's examples. As will transpire in Chapter 4, it is precisely this kind of construal that is required in the analysis of pictorial metaphors.

Metaphor and simile

Perhaps the least satisfactory part of Black's articles is his discussion of metaphor versus simile. Although granting that both metaphor and simile are 'grounded in similarity and analogy' (1979a: 31), and even that in certain contexts there is no fundamental difference between a metaphor and

its corresponding simile ('poverty is a crime' vs. 'poverty is like a crime'),
Black fears that failing to make a distinction between the two ignores
metaphor's creative power.

> To suppose that the metaphorical statement is an abstract or précis of a
> literal point-by-point comparison, in which the primary and secondary
> subjects are juxtaposed for the sake of noting dissimilarities as well as
> similarities, is to misconstrue the function of a metaphor. In discursively
> comparing one subject *with* another, we sacrifice the distinctive power
> and effectiveness of a good metaphor. The literal comparison [= simile]
> lacks the ambience and suggestiveness, and the imposed "view" of the
> primary subject, upon which a metaphor's power to illuminate depends.
>
> (Black 1979a: 32)

Black furthermore argues that a simile (unlike most metaphors) is often
followed by a point-by-point elaboration of the similarities and dissimilari-
ties between primary and secondary subject, and observes that the notion
'is like' has many uses.

Despite these differences there is something counterintuitive about placing
metaphors and similes in separate categories, and several theorists have
rejected a rigid dichotomy. Thus, Ricoeur believes that simile does not
differ fundamentally from metaphor: it is only a weakened version of it. He
argues that '"to be like/as" must be treated as a metaphorical modality of
the copula itself; the "like/as" is not just the comparative term among all
the terms, but is included in the verb *to be*, whose force it alters' (1977:
248). Miller also downplays the differences between the two. 'Similes are
less interesting than metaphors only in that the terms of the similitude are
explicit and require less work from a reader. As far as interpretation is
concerned, it is important to recognize that similes can pose all the appercep-
tive problems that metaphors can' (1979: 222). Lakoff and Turner, too,
argue that simile and metaphor are basically versions of the same phenomenon. They attribute the tendency to put them in different categories to
overemphasizing the linguistic character at the expense of the conceptual
nature of metaphor. 'Statements of both forms can employ conceptual
metaphor. The kind called a simile simply makes a weaker claim. . . . In
both cases, one concept . . . is being understood in terms of another . . . On
the whole, the syntactic form of an utterance has little, if anything, to do
with whether metaphor is involved in comprehending it' (1989: 133).

I subscribe to the view, therefore, that there is no essential difference
between metaphor and simile. This leaves uninvalidated, however, that
there is a surface difference between the two in that a simile, unlike a
metaphor, is explicitly signalled by the occurrence of 'like', '(such) as' or
one of their equivalents. In Chapter 6 it will be argued that this surface
difference applies in the pictorial no less than in the verbal realm.

Metaphor, thought, and action

The matter of differentiating between metaphor and simile discussed in the preceding section points to an issue that has already been fleetingly touched upon in this chapter, but deserves separate discussion, i.e., metaphor's roots in thinking. Richards already pointed out that 'fundamentally [metaphor] is a borrowing between and intercourse of *thoughts*, a transaction between contexts. *Thought* is metaphoric, and proceeds by comparison, and the metaphors of language derive therefrom' (1965/1936: 94). Black calls meta-phorical thought a 'neglected topic of major importance' and proposes to get a better grasp of it by pondering what it is to 'to *think* of A as B' (Black 1979a: 32, my emphasis), and the fact that Black's article itself appeared in a book called *Metaphor and Thought* (Ortony 1979) may testify to the growing interest in the relationships between metaphor and cognition. It is Lakoff and Johnson, however, who for the first time devoted an extended study to the relationship between the linguistic and the conceptual aspects of metaphor. One of their central claims is that 'metaphor is primarily a matter of thought and action and only derivatively a matter of language' (1980: 153) or, formulated even more succinctly, metaphor is 'not a figure of speech, but a mode of thought' (Lakoff 1993: 210).

As to the 'thought' part of the claim, the passages from Lakoff and Johnson cited in earlier sections sufficiently illustrate their point. Until recently, metaphor was automatically associated with *verbal* metaphor. Lakoff and Johnson, however, argue that verbal metaphors are better seen as linguistic manifestations of metaphorical *thought* processes. On the one hand, this shift in focus from metaphorical language *per se* to metaphorical language as a reflection of metaphorical thought, as we have seen above, leads to a downplaying of differences that arise from a metaphor's linguistic form – such as the traditional distinction between metaphor and simile, and between noun metaphor and metaphors featuring other grammatical struc-tures. On the other hand, the claim that metaphor is primarily relevant on a cognitive level means that, in principle, it can manifest itself in other media than language alone. Since this book is devoted to developing a model of *pictorial* metaphor, Lakoff and Johnson's emphasis on the essentially cogni-tive character of metaphor is one of the presuppositions upon which my account depends.

The 'action' part of Lakoff and Johnson's programmatic statement, I take it, refers to their thesis that since metaphors always embody a way of understanding one kind of thing in terms of another, they are never merely neutrally descriptive. On the contrary, they reflect certain values, often moral ones. It is this which turns certain conceptual metaphors, those that are so deeply rooted in our conceptual systems we are hardly aware of them as metaphors, into 'metaphors we live by'. It should never be forgotten that the (conscious or unconscious) acceptance of a particular metaphor makes possible certain actions and consequences that are consonant with it and downplays others. Each metaphor, after all, gives only a partial, and hence partisan structure to the concept embodied in a primary subject. The metaphor MARRIAGE IS A JOURNEY stresses other aspects of MARRIAGE than does MARRIAGE IS A PARTNERSHIP; MARRIAGE IS AN INVESTMENT; or MARRIAGE IS BUILDING A DURABLE PRODUCT (see Quinn 1982, 1987). It is of crucial importance to realize this, since the internal 'logic' of conceptual metaphors such as the above might tempt one to forget that what is here presented is a certain perception of an (aspect of) reality, and not a factual observation about it (see also Forceville 1987). The significance of this realization becomes especially prominent when a metaphor is championed by a person or institution that simultaneously has some sort of interest to promote and wields some sort of power, for as Lakoff and Johnson (quoting Charlotte Linde, in conversation) point out, 'whether in national politics or in everyday interaction, people in power get to impose their metaphors' (1980: 157) and this means that they can initiate or enforce actions consonant with the metaphors they uphold. To put it in a sweeping albeit grossly simplifying way: if a politician is committed to the metaphor 'man is a wolf' he will advocate the building of more prisons; if he believes that 'man is an ass' he will pump money into education; and if he is convinced that 'man is a pig' he may well consider subsidizing launderettes.

Briefly to anticipate the corpus that will be discussed in the present book, advertisements are of course no less value-laden than political statements, and it will come as no surprise therefore that in an age where images are increasingly supplementing or even superseding the word as a vehicle of information the advertising business makes grateful use of the strategies of what I hope to demonstrate are 'pictorial metaphors'.

SUMMARY

My version of Black's interaction theory can be summarized as follows: a metaphor is, explicitly or implicitly, always a metaphorical statement, that is, inasmuch as metaphor is a phenomenon of language it pertains to units larger than the word, sometimes even than the sentence. However, in Lakoff and Johnson's formulation, metaphor is 'primarily a matter of thought and action and only derivatively a matter of language' (1980: 153). Any verbal metaphor, therefore, is a manifestation of a conceptual metaphor, which it resembles to a greater or lesser extent. While a verbal metaphor can occur in a variety of grammatical forms, the conceptual metaphor(s) underlying it invariably take the form 'A IS B' – reflecting Lakoff and Johnson's insight that 'the essence of metaphor is understanding and experiencing one kind of thing in terms of another' (ibid.: 5). This metaphorical IS, as Ricoeur points out, is best seen as incorporating simultaneously an IS and an IS NOT. It is the combination of identity and non-identity that gives metaphor its characteristic tension. The emphasis on the conceptual over and above the linguistic level of metaphor also entails that there is no fundamental difference between metaphor and simile.

Metaphor has a predicative character and is capable of referring to an extra-linguistic reality – although this reality is not necessarily an already existing one. The processing of a metaphor involves more than making sense of the semantic elements of which it consists. The production and interpretation of metaphor include reference to many contextual elements that are at best only partly linguistic in character. Since situational context plays such a dominant role in metaphor, a semantic view of metaphor must always be complemented by a pragmatic one.

In a verbal metaphor, part of the statement draws on the literal, conventional use of language. This part of the metaphor is called its 'frame'. The part of the metaphorical statement used non-conventionally is called the 'focus'. A metaphor contains, in principle, two subjects. The literal, conventional subject, which by definition always belongs to the frame, is labelled its 'primary subject'; the metaphorical subject, which by definition is or belongs to the focus, is called its 'secondary subject'. Each of the subjects is a 'system of things'. This is taken to mean that it labels a complex network of properties or features. These properties or features can be reformulated in terms of predicates of the form '. . . is Y'. The properties, moreover, are of a widely different nature: they may designate characteristics deemed to be inherent in them; they may only constitute acknowledged half-truths; they may reflect popular beliefs, superstitions, emotions, attitudes conventionally associated with them (more or less Black's Aristotelian *endoxa*). But these properties are not always those embodied in generally accepted *endoxa*. Due to a specially created context, verbal or non-verbal, they may acquire *ad hoc* aspects that exceed, or even supplant, their conventional meanings.

Apart from being 'systems of things' themselves, the two subjects of a metaphor also belong to systems of things, that is, they are elements in a larger domain. This domain is partly explicable in terms of a semantic field, and partly contains encyclopaedic and folklore information about the term in question. In order to cover both semantic and pragmatic aspects of this field, the term 'domain' will be employed. Following the usage of Lakoff and Johnson (1980) the domain to which the secondary subject belongs will be called the 'source domain' and the domain of the primary subject the 'target domain'.

In a metaphor, one or more features (properties, predicates) are projected from the secondary subject upon the primary subject.[15] This transfer of features often necessitates an adjustment in the primary subject before they can be incorporated; it is this process of 'adjusting' that Black refers to under 5b above. In turn, this adjustment can result in new adjustments in the secondary subject (see Black's point 5c). Basically what is described here is the process of fitting or matching the two subjects. There is, thus, an 'oscillation' between primary subject and secondary subject. Black limits the stages in this process to three (5a, b and c) but there is no reason, particularly in highly interesting, resonant metaphors, why this process should stop here. As Indurkhya's (1991, 1992) accounts of suggestive and projective metaphor suggest, a resonant scientific metaphor can be explored in considerable depth, meaning that each 'revised' or 'adjusted' view of one of the subjects can in turn trigger off new projections of features. This process of mutual adjustment should not be taken to mean, however, that primary subject and secondary subject are reversible. A IS B is a totally different metaphor from B IS A, and in a given context there is, in principle, no confusion about what is the primary and what the secondary subject of the metaphor.[16]

While conventional metaphors (or at least their 'used' parts) such as those discussed in Lakoff and Johnson (1980) have become lexicalized in our culture to such an extent that they can be subjected to questions pertaining to their truth or falsity, this does not hold for the novel, creative metaphors that Black focuses on. Creative metaphors are to be seen as providing a certain perspective on the primary subject. Thus, innovative metaphors are intriguing, illuminating, dull, or obfuscating, but not true or false. Inasmuch as a perspective may be compelling, persuasive, or guided by hidden interests, novel metaphors are never value-free. The perspective provided by a metaphor may point to a whole way of thinking, as Black's phrase 'every metaphor is the tip of a submerged model' (1979a: 31) suggests. Conversely, the conscious or subconscious acceptance of a metaphor may have practical consequences for actions in daily life.

A question that has here been dealt with as if it yields no special problems is the question which are the features or predicates that are projected from the source domain of the metaphor upon its target domain. As a matter of fact, this issue, which concerns the crucial issue of the interpretation of metaphor, is by no means a simple one. The complexity of the problem thus forbids a brief summary. Since this question applies to pictorial metaphors no less than to verbal ones, however, I will have ample occasion to come back to it in subsequent chapters.

3 Towards a theory of pictorial metaphor
Relevant studies

INTRODUCTION

In this chapter several studies addressing the subject of metaphor in pictures will be examined in some detail. I will discuss what from my point of view are their strengths and weaknesses, and will thus pave the way for my own account of pictorial metaphor, based on Black's interaction theory.

WOLLHEIM (1987)

In Lecture 6 of his *Painting As an Art*, entitled 'Painting, metaphor, and the body: Titian, Bellini, De Kooning, etc.', the art historian Richard Wollheim discusses how 'a painting gains *metaphorical meaning*' (1987: 305) and repeatedly uses the label 'pictorial metaphor' (ibid.: 305, *et passim*). It is illuminating to consider Wollheim's theoretical presuppositions – or rather the lack of them – in some detail, since his failure to address several crucial problems helps suggest directions which a more fruitful account of pictorial metaphor may take.

Wollheim adopts the views on metaphor developed by Donald Davidson as the basis for his own exposition of pictorial metaphor, as he acknowledges in a note. This note deserves to be quoted in full:

> The account of metaphor upon which I draw derives from Donald Davidson, 'What Metaphors Mean,' *Critical Inquiry*, Vol. 5, no. 1, Autumn 1978, reprinted in *On Metaphor*, ed. Sheldon Sacks (Chicago, 1979), pp. 29–45, and in his *Inquiries into Truth and Interpretation* (Oxford, 1984). A brief way of characterizing Davidson's account is to say that it removes metaphor from the domain of semantics to that of pragmatics. I do not believe that this point can be applied to painting with any greater exactness than I attempt in the main body of the text, if only for the reason that the distinction between semantics and pragmatics does not hold for pictorial meaning. Other contributions to the Sacks anthology are relevant to the present discussion.
>
> (1987: 374)

This justification begs several questions. First, one wonders why Wollheim chooses Davidson's rather than any other theorist's account of metaphor as the basis for his own analyses. Possibly the reason for this decision is that, according to Wollheim's own 'brief characterization', Davidson holds that metaphor is a matter of pragmatics, and not of semantics, and this allows Wollheim to de-emphasize the linguistic character of metaphor. But immediately after identifying Davidson's approach in these terms, Wollheim seems to imply that this approach is not really pertinent anyway, since 'the distinction between semantics and pragmatics does not hold for pictorial meaning'. So apart from failing to justify his choice of theory, the fundamental distinction made in the chosen theory apparently does not matter in the first place. Finally, Wollheim's unqualified recommendation of other articles in the Sacks volume is curious – to say the least – since this book contains an article by Max Black in which Davidson's views are repudiated (Black 1979b), as well as scattered objections to Davidson by several other contributors (Harries 1979, Goodman 1979). Wollheim, unlike Davidson himself,[1] is apparently unaware of the latter's controversial position among theorists of metaphor.

Let us now leave Wollheim's disputable note, and return to his main text where, following Davidson, he discusses 'the three major features of linguistic metaphor, [which] . . . are also exhibited by what I have called pictorial metaphor'. Briefly:

> In the first place, linguistic metaphor does not require that the words that effect the metaphor lose their normal sense . . . Secondly, linguistic metaphor does not require that there is a special or pre-existent link between what the words carrying the metaphor pick out and the thing metaphorized . . . Finally, the aim both of linguistic and of pictorial metaphor is to set what is metaphorized in a new light.
>
> (Wollheim 1987: 307)

Although this is by no means a complete account of (verbal) metaphor, I can accept these points. Matters become more problematic in the next section, however, when Wollheim explains the 'big difference between linguistic and pictorial metaphor':

> Linguistic metaphor illuminates what it metaphorizes by pairing it with something else . . . This is the essential metaphoric strategy, which pictorial metaphor follows to the extent of pairing the object metaphorized with something other than that object. But – and this is the crucial point – in the case of painting this something is the picture itself. It is not – as linguistic metaphor might suggest – something that the picture picks out: even though the picture, at any rate normally, has to pick out something, indeed has to represent something, in order to fit itself to be a metaphor. When the way of metaphor works, what is paired with the object metaphorized is the picture as a whole.
>
> (ibid.)

From a theoretical point of view this introductory discussion of pictorial metaphor raises several problems. First of all, Wollheim nowhere explicitly addresses the question when a phenomenon under scrutiny should be considered as a metaphor rather than as literal usage. That is, he insufficiently convinces the reader/spectator that a 'literal reading' of the paintings he examines is inadequate, and that they ought to be 'read' metaphorically. As far as I can see there is in the paintings he adduces as examples no deviance of any kind that requires, or suggests, a metaphorical resolution in order for them to make (better) sense. Secondly, Wollheim's insistence on metaphorically equating the object not with another object but with the painting as a whole remains highly puzzling, since the author nowhere satisfactorily justifies or explains what he means by this, let alone how this type of metaphor is supposed to operate. Thirdly, the author seems to be confused about the order of the two terms of what he calls metaphor. In the second paragraph of his Lecture, Wollheim argues that

> when the way of metaphor works, and the painting acquires metaphorical meaning, there is something for which the painting becomes a metaphor or, as I shall barbarously put it, something which the painting 'metaphorizes'. And 'something' here means 'some *thing*'. It is always an object that the painting metaphorizes. In point of fact I further believe that the fundamental cases of pictorial metaphor are those where a corporeal thing is metaphorized: the painting becomes a metaphor for the body.

> (ibid.: 305)

Leaving aside the matter why it should be the *body* rather than something else that, in 'the fundamental cases of pictorial metaphor', is metaphorized, one thing at least seems clear from this passage: the metaphor invites us to understand the concept BODY in terms of the concept PAINTING, and not the other way round. This is corroborated by a passage, partly quoted already, two pages later on. Referring back to two examples of verbal metaphor he has used earlier ('Juliet is the sun' and 'Religion is the opium of the people'), Wollheim tells us: 'The aim of both linguistic and of pictorial metaphor is to set what is metaphorized in a new light. Juliet, religion, the body – we see whatever it is afresh' (ibid.: 307). 'The thing metaphorized' is obviously *the body*, and it is apperceived in terms of 'something other than that object, [and] in the case of painting this something is the picture itself'. In terms derived from Black, the primary subject of the metaphor is BODY, and its secondary subject PAINTING, yielding the metaphor BODY IS PAINTING.

A few lines later, however, Wollheim remarks that 'it is the picture as a whole that is the first term to the metaphoric relation. . . . When, in what is for me the fundamental case, the picture metaphorizes the body, I shall say that the experience that grounds this relation attributes to the picture the global property of *corporeality*' (ibid.: 307–8). Here Wollheim apparently is talking about the picture, or painting, as the *first* term of the metaphor, that is, the term to be metaphorized: Black's primary subject. This 'first term' seems to refer to the *painting* or *picture* as the object metaphorized, as were 'Juliet' and 'religion' in the examples quoted earlier. The suspicion that this use of the expression 'first term' is not a mere slip of the pen gains plausibility in the context of Wollheim's remark, in the second part of the just-quoted passage from page 305, that the property attributed from 'body' to 'picture' is 'corporeality'. Here it is suddenly the painting which is metaphorized by the body, the latter transferring the property of 'corporeality' to the former. The two terms of the metaphor have been reversed, resulting in PAINTING IS BODY instead of the earlier BODY IS PAINTING.

Thus, at the very outset of his Lecture, Wollheim appears to be confused about the order of the two terms of the metaphor. Are we to understand PAINTING in terms of BODY or BODY in terms of PAINTING? Now because Wollheim does not clearly define what he means by the two complex concepts BODY and PAINTING, we might perhaps be insufficiently aware of the importance of this question. However, one cannot simply reverse the two terms of a metaphor without completely changing it (see p. 12; Forceville 1995b). Taking Wollheim's own example of Marx's famous statement, it is immediately clear that claiming that RELIGION IS OPIUM is entirely different from proposing that OPIUM IS RELIGION, if only because the first metaphor is predicating something about religion and the second about opium. Thus, Wollheim here ignores the crucial fact that for anything to be called a metaphor, it must be assessed which of the terms is the primary subject and which is the secondary subject of the metaphor – this distribution in itself determining the direction of the metaphor's feature-transfer.

In the analyses of the paintings he discusses, Wollheim keeps insisting that they 'metaphorize the body'. Due to the absence of both a clear definition of the concepts used and a consistent application thereof in the analyses, the references to metaphor become virtually vacuous. The recurring theme seems to be that the paintings under discussion somehow exemplify, or 'achieve', a strong sense of 'corporeality' – its specific variant differing per artist – and that this corporeality informs, or dominates, the entire painting.[2] While this may be a perfectly valid conclusion, it makes no sense to connect such observations to the theory of metaphor. One strongly gets the impression that Wollheim wished to say certain things about certain paintings and that the label 'metaphor', and what he knew about that subject, sounded vaguely appealing and useful to him. Whatever Wollheim's merits in analysing paintings, his inadequate application of the label 'pictorial metaphor' dangerously jeopardizes attempts to give that concept any meaning.[3]

HAUSMAN (1989)

Another author who has invoked the theory of metaphor because of the contributions it might yield to a better understanding of art is Carl Hausman. *Metaphor and Art* (1989) is of particular relevance for present purposes because Hausman bases himself on Black's interaction theory of metaphor. For this reason Hausman's study will be investigated at some length. This investigation does not purport to be a review of the entire book. Rather I will concentrate on those parts where Hausman examines Black's theory and considers how it can be applied to painting. More particularly my criticisms will focus on Hausman's ideas that the two terms of a metaphor can be unproblematically reversed (a point already touched upon in the discussion of Wollheim) and that a metaphor often has more than two terms.

Hausman's views on 'creativity'

Hausman's interest in Black's account of metaphor stems from the fact that its central theses appear to apply equally to the way art works. Most importantly, a metaphor, at least a novel one, *creates* similarity rather than draws on pre-existent similarity or, in Hausman's words, on 'antecedently fixed meanings and references' (1989: 65). Inasmuch as metaphors are radically innovative, they by definition cannot reflect something that already exists in the world. Hence, creative metaphors call their referents into being.[4] An important consequence of the fact that the referent is created by the very act of producing the metaphor is that no truth/falsehood test can be applied. But the fact that a creative metaphor is not amenable to a truth/falsehood judgment does not entail that it has no cognitive import. Since it is possible to pronounce on a creative metaphor's appropriateness or aptness, a creative metaphor can contribute something to our understanding and perceptions of the world.

The mystery of how something new in the world can spring from a combination of familiar elements and yet cannot be explained in terms of the sum of those elements – in short, the mystery of creativity – is pertinent not only to metaphor, but also to art, Hausman argues. Art, just like metaphor, cannot be adequately explained in terms of anterior meanings; it is not subject to truth/falsehood tests; and it has nonetheless something to contribute to our perception of the world. On the basis of these striking parallels Hausman claims that metaphor does not only occur in language, but has also non-verbal manifestations. Focusing on art he contends that non-verbal arts such as painting and music feature 'metaphorical structure', too. As Hausman himself puts it, 'it seems to me that the ways that words and larger linguistic verbal units function within metaphors and, in turn, within the contexts of metaphors, are comparable to the functions of the components of works of the visual arts and music' (ibid.: ix).

Hausman's discussion of Black's interaction theory

Hausman's discussion of Black's theory is presented in his Chapter 2, 'A reconsideration of interactionism'. As the three key features of metaphors he mentions '(1) tension, (2) the presence of two "subjects" or "anchoring" meaning units and (3) the interrelation of meaning units in an integration or family resemblance that functions like a community' (1989: 59). What Hausman discusses under 'tension' is the familiar notion that in a metaphor there is an incompatibility between the domains of the primary and the secondary subject. It is this incompatibility which bars a literal reading and invites a metaphorical reading in the first place. Hausman's views on this matter are by and large consonant with Black's. The circumlocution in (3) I take to refer to the integrating process in metaphor that is the necessary counterpart of its tensional aspect. Neither of these points, although they are rather laboriously argued, poses serious problems. My criticisms will focus on (2), as it is with regard to this point that Hausman's treatment of Black is controversial. Hausman states that 'the main point to be emphasized at the moment is that metaphorical expressions include *at least* two anchoring terms or key meaning units that interact, each affecting the other' [my emphasis] (ibid.: 67). The argument leading up to this statement runs as follows:

> Either of the key subjects may, though not necessarily, function as the lens or filter, or as the vehicle [i.e., secondary subject] of a metaphor. . . . I shall . . . point out here that if, for example, the world (antecedently known) is regarded through a qualifier, a filter, 'unweeded garden' in the metaphor 'The world is an unweeded garden', then so an unweeded garden will be regarded through 'the world'. What it is to be an unweeded garden is not the same once it has interacted with what it is to be the world. Indeed, the point of interactionism, as I see it, is that it is not the antecedent world that is regarded through the screen or filter of the implicatures of unweeded garden. It is, rather, a world that is an unweeded garden and that was not antecedently there to be referred to through a filter. The world referred to is not the world of prior literal reference.
>
> (Hausman 1989: 67)

First a matter of terminology needs to be settled. In the latter part of this passage the issue is whether the 'world' in the metaphor is the world of prior literal reference or not. It seems misleading to claim that 'it is not the antecedent world that is regarded through the screen or filter of the implicatures of unweeded garden'. True, the 'world' is reorganized through the metaphorical mapping of features from 'unweeded garden' on to itself, but it is only *after* this transfer that the 'world' is no longer the 'antecedent world'. Up till that moment it is. The antecedently known 'world' interacts with the antecedently known 'unweeded garden', and *as a result of this metaphorical interaction* the 'world' has changed – at least for as long as we entertain the metaphor. But this seems to be a mere slip of the pen. When Hausman states a little later that 'it can be seen that the influence of [the terms] on one another in a metaphor effects an integration that is not controlled by the meaning units viewed in their standard function [so that] a new meaning as a whole is generated' (ibid.: 68), I read this as confirming my point.

More troublesome is Hausman's view of the relation between the two terms of the metaphor as implied in his claim that 'either of the key subjects may, though not necessarily, function as the lens or filter, or as the vehicle of a metaphor', as this seems to imply that the two terms are interchangeable. That notion recurs in other passages in the text. Earlier, Hausman discusses the situation of 'someone sitting by a river bank, looking at a stream of bubbling, gleaming, and flowing water', who says, 'It is life'. The extralinguistic context, as Hausman correctly claims, suggests that 'it' refers to 'the river'. But then he proceeds as follows: 'Assuming the relevance of the river, the speaker's statement could be translated as the metaphor "The river (or the flow of the river) is life" or "Life is a river" ' (ibid.: 51–2).

Hausman gives a third example of the reversibility of the terms in a metaphor, when discussing the opening quatrain of Shakespeare's sonnet 73 (not 72, as he states in footnote 17). This quatrain runs:

That time of year thou mayst in me behold
When yellow leaves, or none, or few, do hang
Upon those boughs which shake against the cold
Bare ruin'd choirs, where late the sweet birds sang.

Hausman comments:

'Bare ruin'd choirs' relates to an explicit term, 'those boughs which shake against the cold', as well as other terms in the verse. The verse is a complex metaphor, containing metaphors within metaphors. The bare ruined choirs are boughs shaking in the cold; they are also places where birds sang; and they are qualifications of a time of year and of the 'poetic speaker'. The metaphor focused in the 'ruin'd choirs' is presented within an explicit context of connected words. But there is a host of implicit meanings associated within each of the meaning units.

(Hausman 1989: 64)

Although Hausman is not explicit on the issue, he seems to suggest that the 'other terms in the verse' are actually terms in the metaphor, and that there are more than two terms. In line with what he himself believes about the unproblematic reversibility of primary subject and secondary subject, Hausman makes no attempt to identify them as such. Now whereas with reference to the two earlier examples Hausman discussed ('The world is an unweeded garden' and '[the river] is life') I argued that the terms cannot be simply reversed without radically altering the metaphor, matters in these

Shakespearean lines are more complicated. Two things are at issue. In the first place there is the by now familiar question of the (ir)reversibility of the terms of a metaphor; in the second place, there are the additional questions which are the terms of the metaphor and whether there are actually more than two terms.

In order to sort out the metaphors in this complex quatrain, let us briefly return to Lakoff and Turner, who happen to discuss the same lines. As was discussed in Chapter 2, they argue that we are able to understand many poetic metaphors because they draw on conventional conceptual metaphors. One of these conventional metaphors is PEOPLE ARE PLANTS.

> In this metaphor, people are viewed as plants with respect to the life cycle – more precisely, they are viewed as that part of the plant that burgeons and then withers or declines, such as leaves, flowers, and fruit, though sometimes the whole plant is viewed as burgeoning and then declining, as with grass or wheat.
>
> (Lakoff and Turner 1989: 6)

Another conventional metaphor is A LIFETIME IS A YEAR: 'In this conception of the life cycle, springtime is youth, summer is maturity, autumn is old age, and winter is death' (ibid.: 18). Both these metaphors, Lakoff and Turner argue, play a role in the first quatrain of Shakespeare's sonnet 73:

> The first four lines evoke the PEOPLE ARE PLANTS metaphor, in which the stages of life correspond to stages of the plant life cycle. The yellow leaves signal the approach of the end of the cycle, which is old age in the metaphor. . . .
>
> The first four lines evoke a superimposition of images. First, 'yellow leaves' and 'boughs' call up the concept of a tree. The phrase 'in me' calls up the concept of a man. One way we connect these is through the conventional PEOPLE ARE PLANTS metaphor, in which people are metaphorically plants with respect to the life cycle. Another way we can connect these is through the superimposition of the image of a tree upon the figure of a man, with limbs corresponding to limbs and trunk to trunk. . . .
>
> Second, the expression 'bare ruined choirs' describing 'boughs' suggests the superimposition of the image of a church choir on the image of a tree, with the ranks of the choir corresponding to the boughs of the tree and the singers to the birds. A major purpose served by this superimposition of the choir loft on the tree, and hence on the man, is to see the man through the choir: as the once intact and song-filled choirs are now ruined and empty, so the once vigorous and vibrant man is now decrepit and diminished.
>
> (ibid.: 27–8)

Apart from the conventional metaphors PEOPLE ARE PLANTS and A LIFETIME IS A YEAR, then, the passage draws on the novel metaphor that can be abbreviated to 'boughs ... are bare ruined choirs'. Abstracting the latter metaphor to PLANTS ARE CHURCH CHOIRS, a clear pattern emerges, in which all the 'terms' Hausman identifies ('bare ruined choirs', 'boughs that shake in the cold', 'places where birds sang', 'qualifications of a time of year', and 'qualifications of the poetic speaker') can be incorporated. A paraphrase would run something like this: the poetic speaker presents himself in terms of an autumnal wood, whose bare trees in turn are metaphorically coupled with empty church choirs. The source domain of the empty church choirs, with all its relevant connotations, is mapped on to the target domain of the autumnal wood, and the autumnal wood – metaphorically 'enriched' by the metaphorical coupling with the church choir – in turn becomes the source domain to be mapped on to the target domain of the poetic speaker, namely by virtue of the PEOPLE ARE PLANTS metaphor.

Now this analysis of the metaphors in Shakespeare's quatrain, based on Lakoff and Turner's discussions, sheds light on the question at issue: are the terms in a metaphor reversible, and can there be more than two terms in a metaphor? The answer to the first question is, once more, an unequivocal no. The poetic speaker is conceived of in terms of an autumnal wood (PEOPLE ARE PLANTS) and not the other way round (PLANTS ARE PEOPLE). Similarly, trees, or boughs, are conceived of in terms of church choirs, and not church choirs in terms of trees. The second question has partly a simple, partly a difficult answer. The simple answer is that the discussion in terms of Lakoff and Turner's analyses confirms that there are not five terms, as Hausman implies, but no more than three.[5] The difficult answer is that while we can say that there are two metaphors here, PEOPLE ARE PLANTS and TREES ARE CHURCH CHOIRS, we could also say, equalling PLANTS and TREES on the conceptual level, that there is one metaphor with three terms: PEOPLE ARE PLANTS ARE CHURCH CHOIRS. I would contend, however, that the apparent difference between these two formulations is mainly a question of terminology and that it does not matter fundamentally whether one perceives two interacting separate metaphors or a single complex one. The only thing one can quarrel about is whether there can be a *direct* mapping of elements from 'empty church choir' on to the poetic speaker, or whether this mapping necessarily is filtered through an intermediate mapping upon the boughs. What is beyond discussion, however, is that the order of the terms is not arbitrary. Even if we accept the reading of one metaphor with three terms, the order can only be PEOPLE ARE PLANTS ARE CHURCH CHOIRS. The PLANTS ARE CHURCH CHOIRS is embedded in the PEOPLE ARE PLANTS metaphor.[6]

Hausman on Black's view of the (ir)reversibility of terms

Hausman's idea that the two terms in a metaphor can be unproblematically reversed may now be considered refuted. What remains to be investigated is Hausman's conviction that the reversibility of terms is supported by Black.

And since, as we will see, Hausman is not alone in considering this to be the case, it is worthwhile pursuing the matter a little further. In the following passage, Hausman explicitly discusses the point with reference to Black:

> Black speaks of the principal subject as viewed through a filter. One subject, it might be said, is presented *as* the second subject, or the ascribing or framing, metaphorically functioning meaning. Notice that Black uses the example 'Man is a wolf', and he says that the metaphor is not a comparison of a man's face with a wolf mask (as some have proposed) but is, rather, 'seeing the human face *as* vulpine.' However, this interpretation can be misleading. The term *as* too easily suggests either a fiction or a comparison, the very relationship that Black argues against. To see the human face as vulpine suggests seeing the human face *as if* it were vulpine, seeing it as *like* what is vulpine, or seeing it in terms of what can be readily translated as a simile. ... Furthermore, the seeing-as thesis overlooks the multidirectionality of interaction in metaphors. If man is seen as vulpine, wolves may also be seen as human. Black himself suggests this. Whatever filter we start with in order to see a subject metaphorically, the filter itself changes and must screen differently; it is unlike the established lens it was at the outset.
>
> (Hausman 1989: 70)

This passage calls for comment. Before offering this comment it will be helpful to quote the passage by Black that Hausman refers to. This passage occurs in Black (1962) – and not in Black (1979a), as Hausman states – footnote 16 on p. 37, here given in full:

> Much more would need to be said in a thorough examination of the comparison view [of metaphor]. It would be revealing, for instance, to consider the contrasting types of case in which a formal comparison is preferred to a metaphor. A comparison is often a prelude to an explicit statement of the grounds of resemblance whereas we do not expect a metaphor to explain itself. (Cf. the difference between *comparing* a man's face with a wolf mask by looking for points of resemblance – and seeing the human face *as* vulpine.) But no doubt the line between *some* metaphors and *some* similes is not a sharp one.
>
> (Black 1962: 37)

Forgoing a discussion of Hausman's dubious claim that the formulation 'seeing as' promotes a comparison-view of metaphor,[7] I will focus on the question whether Black can be read as endorsing the 'multidirectionality' of metaphor, i.e., the reversibility of its terms. Hausman states, 'If man is seen as vulpine, wolves may also be seen as human. Black himself suggests this'. That is, Hausman claims that primary subject and secondary subject in a metaphor are interchangeable and moreover that Black subscribes to this view. Surprisingly, Lakoff and Turner claim the very same thing. Pointing out that one of the mistakes often found in traditional theories of metaphor is 'the claim that metaphors do not have a source and a target domain, but are merely bidirectional linkages across domains' (Lakoff and Turner 1989: 110–1), they appear to associate this error with Richards's (1965/1936) and Black's (1962, 1979a) interaction theory:

> Unfortunately ... the target domain is described as 'suffusing' the source domain, and it is claimed that the metaphor is bidirectional – from target to source as well as from source to target. Indeed, according to this theory, there is no source or target. There is only a connection across domains, with one concept seen through the filter of the other.
>
> (Lakoff and Turner 1989: 131)

I completely agree with Lakoff and Turner's rejection of the principle of bidirectionality, but I think they misread Black if they think he accepts it. The confusion probably is caused by a few rather obscure or even sloppy passages in Black's articles. Let me try to clarify these.

To begin with, in Black (1962), where the labels 'principal' and 'subsidiary subject' are used for what in Black (1979a) are rebaptized as 'primary' and 'secondary subject', the following passage occurs: 'We can say that the principal subject is "seen through" the metaphorical expression – or, if we prefer, that the principal subject is "projected upon" the field of the subsidiary subject' (1962: 41). Taken at face value, this statement indeed suggests that the transfer of features runs from A to B as well as from B to A. It seems more likely, however, that this is merely a slip of the pen. Surely, what Black *meant* to say here is '... or, if we prefer, that the *subsidiary* subject is "projected upon" the field of the *principal* subject' [my emphases]. The interjection 'if we prefer' strongly suggests that Black intends to say the same thing twice using different descriptions (or indeed 'metaphors'):[8] *seeing* A *through* B is the same as *projecting* B *upon* A. Moreover, Black, when summing up the matter of feature-projection, in both versions of his theory explicitly limits the transfer of features to that of B to A: 'The metaphor works by applying to the principal subject a system of "associated implications" characteristic of the subsidiary subject' (ibid.: 44) and 'The metaphorical utterance works by "projecting upon" the primary subject a set of "associated implications", comprised in the implicative complex, that are predicable of the secondary subject' (1979a: 28). These characterizations, therefore, provide circumstantial evidence that the passage quoted above is probably no more than a momentary lapse, and should not be seen as proof that Black argues in favour of the bidirectionality of metaphor.

Another source of puzzlement may be Black's pronouncements on the matching process that takes place between the two subjects of a metaphor. More specifically, Black's claim that the primary subject of a metaphor induces certain changes in the secondary subject (see Chapter 2, discussion of Black's point 5) may have been misread as suggesting that the two terms of a metaphor are reversible. Let me recall Black's point and expand somewhat on it. In a given metaphor, the primary subject activates certain properties in the source domain that are subsequently projected upon the target domain. This projecting of properties from source to target domain sometimes entails a degree of adaptation or translation. In the metaphor SCHOOLS ARE PRISONS, for instance, the prisoners and guards from the source domain PRISONS presumably correspond to the SCHOOL's pupils and teachers respectively.[9] In this projection or transfer, then, the features 'harbours prisoners' and 'employs guards' in the source domain correspond to 'harbours pupils' and 'employs teachers' in the target domain. The metaphor transforms the pupils into prisoners and the teachers into guards. Whatever we thought about pupils and teachers *before* being confronted with the metaphor SCHOOLS ARE PRISONS is affected for as long as we entertain that metaphor. Our adaptation of pupils and teachers into pupils-as-prisoners and teachers-as-guards is an example of what, in my view, Black means by 'construct[ing] a parallel implication-complex that can fit the primary subject' (ibid.: 29). Now let us assume that the above adaptations were those that induced the use of the metaphor in the first place. The metaphor, however, lends itself to elaboration; it reconceptualizes, for instance, the relations between teachers and pupils. Whereas teachers commonly are expected to help pupils acquire knowledge about and insight into a wide variety of subjects, they are now primarily seen as enforcing their authority on the pupils and as exercising a controlling function. Furthermore, the metaphor emphasizes the pupils' limited freedom: the intervals between teaching hours in the school-day's routine can be viewed as 'airings' at fixed times; homework can be matched with the compulsory activities to which prisoners are subjected.[10] These 'matches' or 'correspondences' between the two domains (and no doubt many more can be found) in effect boil down to building up the domains of both primary and secondary subjects. For in the metaphor it is not only the target domain that is momentarily transformed, but also the source domain. Every feature of PRISONS that can *not* be matched by one in SCHOOLS is eliminated or downplayed. Thus, for instance the fact that prison cells usually contain only one person, or a few, while the average school class contains considerably more, makes 'number of people involved' a difficult feature to match; hence this feature of PRISON is downplayed in the metaphor. Similarly, prison cells are locked, whereas classrooms, while in use, normally are not. In short, the domain of the secondary subject that is built up for the purposes of a particular metaphor is a selection from, and adaptation of, a far richer complex of facts, beliefs and associations that adheres to the concept PRISON. It is in this spirit, I take it, that Black formulated his observation that 'changes in the secondary subject' are effected (ibid.: 29).

There is a third passage in Black that may have misled his critics. Returning for a moment to Hausman's claim that 'Black himself suggests' the reversibility of terms in a metaphor, we might guess – in the absence of a specific reference in Hausman (1989) – that Hausman concludes this on the basis of Black's somewhat enigmatic line that 'if to call a man a wolf is to put him in a special light, we must not forget that the metaphor makes the wolf seem more human than he otherwise would' (1962: 44).[11] Unfortunately, that is all Black says about this issue in his 1962 article, and he does not take up the theme in Black (1979a). However, a line a bit before the one quoted is illuminating: 'The nature of the intended application helps to determine the character of the system to be applied' (ibid.: 43–4). What Black means here, I propose, is that since only features from the domain of WOLF are selected that can be matched with features from the domain of MAN, this necessarily focuses on qualities that allow adaptation to the human domain, and ignores qualities of WOLF that are not adaptable. It is in *this* sense that the wolf seems 'more human than he otherwise would'.

In short, Hausman has tenuously little to go on in Black's articles to buttress his idea that the metaphorical transfer between the terms of the metaphor is 'multidirectional', i.e., that it goes in equal measure from primary to secondary subject and from secondary to primary subject. In my view, Black cannot be read as supporting the interchangeability or reversibility of primary subject and secondary subject in a metaphor. I understand Black as subscribing to the view that, whatever happens in the process of mutual adjustment of primary and secondary subject, in the last resort the latter always remains subservient to the former. Therefore, Hausman's interpretation of Black's theory is seriously deficient. In the next section I will take a closer look at Hausman's applications of Black's theory.

Hausman's application of Black's interaction theory to painting

In his Chapter 4, 'Metaphorical interaction and the arts', Hausman opens the section 'The presence of two subjects' by stating:

> In most if not all the arts, one can distinguish multiple subjects. Each representational component can be regarded as a subject or term interacting with others, as 'world' and 'unweeded garden' interact in 'The world is an unweeded garden'. Art historians often analyze works of art in terms of various symbols that can be identified within the works. And components such as these may be regarded as subjects. However, in nonverbal expressions, as in verbal metaphors, there are certain meaning units that have prominence. There are two ways in which prominent meaning units function as two subjects. The first way is obvious. One unit helps control the way the other is seen or heard. In Cézanne's *Mt St Victoire*, a mountain image is seen architecturally in part because of the solidlike carved space of a sky as well as the buildup of overlapping color patches.
>
> (Hausman 1989: 137–8)

The first lines of this passage corroborate Hausman's commitment to the view that there are several elements within a painting that can function as subjects, and that the most prominent of these can (or do?) interact metaphorically. When discussing the first of the 'two ways in which prominent meaning units function as two subjects', he means, I take it, that in the case of the Cézanne painting there is a metaphor that could be verbalized as, say, MT ST VICTOIRE IS A BUILDING or MT ST VICTOIRE IS A CATHEDRAL. With the restriction that such a metaphor is one that the spectator can, but is not forced to, perceive in the painting, this strikes me as an acceptable metaphoric reading, and I would agree that this could be termed a (pictorial) metaphor. Indeed, this example of Hausman comes close to what I term 'pictorial metaphors', as discussed in my Chapter 6.

Hausman goes on to claim that there is a second, less obvious way in which two subjects can interact metaphorically in the arts. Here, a context may have to be constructed for the subjects to be recognized as such. Hausman argues that the real mountain Mt. St. Victoire in Southern France can function as one such subject:

> The significance of the extra-aesthetic mountain is relevant to one distinct component of the painting, the painted mountain. Otherwise, Cézanne's transformation of its form could not be recognized. Even if one has never seen the actual mountain, the apprehension of the representational form of the mountain in the painting signals the possibility of a model, a landscape in space and time that is independent of the painting.
>
> (Hausman 1989: 138)

He concludes that

> there is a second subject or key term for Cézanne's painting – in this case, the extra-aesthetic image of the actual mountain, an image that is assumed to be available to normal vision and that is subject to pragmatic tests of confirmation. . . . Once the painting is regarded as a presentation of a prominent image (among others) that functions aesthetically and as a transformation, for aesthetic purposes, of a counterpart preaesthetic image, then we have an interaction parallel to a verbal metaphor. Considering once more 'Man is a wolf', it can be said that man functions initially in the same way that a preaesthetic image of a nonverbal metaphorical expression does. In the case of this verbal metaphor, the metaphorical image, man, is a conceptualizable image referring to man but, at the same time, having this reference changed as it interacts with wolf.
>
> (ibid.: 138–9)

Here we again confront the key question of the identity of the two terms of the metaphor and their interaction. In Lakoff and Johnson's (1980) terminology, Hausman's metaphor would be REAL MOUNTAIN IS PAINTED MOUNTAIN. This would imply that the REAL MOUNTAIN is understood or perceived in terms of the PAINTED MOUNTAIN. Elsewhere in his book, Hausman suggests that 'appreciators of Cézanne now see Mt St Victoire in a "Cézannish" way and in light of this can "go on" seeing in a "Cézannish" way other things in the world not imaged in any known Cézanne painting' (ibid.: 109). This is a legitimate claim: what is mapped from PAINTED MOUNTAIN on to REAL MOUNTAIN is something like 'the Cézanne-way-of-perceiving-a-mountain'. In that case the viewer, as Hausman points out, need not even be familiar with the real mountain. Although I am not sure that it makes sense to base this – in itself defensible – view on the interaction theory, I am prepared to give Hausman the benefit of the doubt here.

The second representational painting Hausman discusses is Vermeer's *Young Woman With a Water Jug*. In a manner analogous to his discussion of the Cézanne painting, Hausman identifies, with reference to the painting's title, the figure of the young woman with the water pitcher as 'one of the subjects or key meaning units' (ibid.: 151). Provisionally, then, the metaphor could be verbalized as REAL WOMAN IS PAINTED WOMAN. Hausman goes on to discuss several other components of the painting, such as the table and the window. He then explains, 'the point of this consideration of the painting thus far is to illustrate a way of interpreting the work in terms of the interaction of components so that one of the key extra-aesthetic meaning units is taken up as an image that is controlled aesthetically and that thus is transformed into a contrasting internal subject' (ibid.: 152). Apart from the PAINTED WOMAN there is, however, 'at least one other internal major term – that is, other than the extra-aesthetic woman-image – which helps compose the whole'. This other major term turns out to be 'space that is constituted by the spread of light over the carefully organized space of the room'. Hausman is aware that this is a controversial proposal. He realizes that

> the attempt to identify a second key term here is subject to [an] interpretation with which different interpreters might quarrel. However, it seems to me that there is clearly a second subject, something that helps account for the work's main substance, something that cannot be accounted for by noting exclusively the main subject of the figure of the woman as it interacts with other components. It is the control of another dominant factor that mobilizes the components interacting with the shape of the woman.
>
> (ibid.: 152)

The crucial question now is how this 'second key term' finds a place in the metaphor. What is its relation to the two terms identified earlier, REAL WOMAN and PAINTED WOMAN? Possibly, since Hausman sees no problem in having more than two terms in a metaphor, the resulting metaphor would run something like REAL WOMAN IS PAINTED WOMAN IS SPACE-AS-CONSTITUTED-BY-LIGHT. Now we get into serious trouble – in fact into the same kind of trouble that surfaced in Hausman's discussion of the plurality of terms in the Shakespeare metaphor examined earlier in this chapter. But whereas that metaphor was shown, with the aid of Lakoff and Turner's analyses, to be interpretable as in fact a metaphor embedded in another metaphor, the situation here surely is different. While postulating the metaphor REAL WOMAN IS PAINTED WOMAN is defensible, on the same grounds as REAL MOUNTAIN IS PAINTED MOUNTAIN in the Cézanne painting, expanding the metaphor into REAL WOMAN IS PAINTED WOMAN IS SPACE-AS-CONSTITUTED-BY-LIGHT is nothing less than baffling. The relation between the PAINTED WOMAN and the SPACE-AS-CONSTITUTED-BY-LIGHT is of an entirely different order than the relation between REAL WOMAN and PAINTED WOMAN, turning the 'metaphor' into nonsense. In no way can we say that either REAL WOMAN or PAINTED WOMAN is perceived, or experienced, as SPACE-AS-CONSTITUTED-BY-LIGHT. Of course, SPACE-AS-CONSTITUTED-BY-LIGHT may well be an important element in the overall aesthetic quality of the painting – but that is another matter altogether. Surely other elements contribute to that quality as well, which begs the question why Hausman decides that the third term is SPACE-AS-CONSTITUTED-BY-LIGHT and not, for instance, the PAINTING'S PIGMENT, CHOICE OF COLOUR, WOMAN'S POSTURE or whatever else might strike an observer of the painting as significant and contributing to the overall effect of the painting. If the importance of these or other aspects is granted, these would presumably be given a place as terms in the 'metaphor' as well. The consequence would have to be that in Hausman's approach there is in principle no restriction to the number of subjects that can metaphorically interact; and no criterion is given for what guides the selection of terms in the first place.

In his third and last (!) example, Hausman addresses the question of the metaphorical in non-representational painting. Considering Mondrian's *Painting 2: Composition in Gray and Black* (1925), Hausman admits that the absence of figurative components in the canvas might seem to make it difficult to identify its metaphorical terms. It does exhibit, however, 'at least three shapes that function as interacting subject terms' (ibid.: 155) – two rectangles and one square. They exhibit both interaction and tension, Hausman states. To be sure, 'other shapes enhance this interaction, but the key shapes functioning as major subject terms dominate the composition as a whole. The integration, then, is found in the equilibrium that pervades the composition without extinguishing the shapes' power to act with the tensions of imbalance, balance, and counterbalance' (ibid.). If Hausman wishes to suggest that, even in the absence of objects in the outside world (i.e., 'extra-aesthetic objects') that directly correspond to Mondrian's three shapes, there is something in that world that a Mondrian-way-of-seeing-shapes/colours transforms, I accept that this may be so – although again it is not clear why he needs Black's theory to make the point. The additional comments on tension and equilibrium refer to a use of these labels that is not even a remote echo of Black's strict terminology. Whatever value these observations may have in their own right, they have nothing in the least to do with an application of Black's interaction theory of metaphor.

Concluding remarks on Hausman

When all is said and done, the use Hausman makes of Black's interaction theory must be judged misguided. After identifying certain striking parallels between art and metaphor, Hausman enthusiastically applies elements from Black's theory to painting. The point, however, is that when he starts discussing Black's theory, he loses sight of the strict ways in which Black uses his terminology. Hausman extends the concept of 'interaction', which in Black obtains between primary and secondary subject, to a force which works between a number of components, both within and without a painting, and which somehow contribute to its artistic effect. He thus insufficiently distinguishes between the specific metaphorical interaction as proposed in Black and a more general influence mutually exercised by a wide variety of any elements that together form a whole. Aspects of the interaction theory (tension, interaction, resolution of tension) are stripped of their specific meaning, and loosely shown to obtain in painting. More specifically, Hausman invokes Black's theory to support the claim that great paintings make one see aspects of the real world in a different light. This results in metaphors of the type REAL X IS PAINTED X wherein the feature transferred from PAINTED X to REAL X seems to be the Cézannish, Vermeerish, Mondrianish, etc. way of looking at that reality. While the observation in itself is no doubt a relevant one, it seems hardly so shocking that it needs the underpinning of Black's theory. In short, whatever the merits of Hausman's views on the nature of (visual) art expressed elsewhere in his book, he has had to distort Black's interaction theory in an unacceptable manner to show its pertinence to art. Hausman's approach to Black's interaction theory therefore does little to further a theory of pictorial metaphor.

KENNEDY (1982)

More promising for the development of a theory of pictorial metaphor are a number of studies by John Kennedy, Kennedy (1982) being the most relevant for present purposes. One of the merits of the work done by this perception psychologist is his awareness that many rhetorical devices can have pictorial manifestations as well as verbal ones. Kennedy (1982) argues that there are standard modes of depiction, some of which he considers to be universal while others are culturally determined. These standard modes of depiction allow for what could be termed a 'literal' interpretation – in much the same way as literal language does. These modes are capable of being intentionally violated, resulting in some kind of anomaly. This anomaly will either be taken to be an error, or it will be taken to make a point. 'Where the anomaly is considered to be appropriate to make a point, without revising the standard canon ... the picture is taken to be using anomaly deliberately in a metaphoric manner' (1982: 590). Kennedy supports his claim that pictures can be metaphoric by presenting visual manifestations of fifteen figures of speech familiar from rhetoric, a selection of those presented under the heading 'technical terms' in Fowler (1926: 597 ff.). These devices are allegory, anti-climax, catachresis, cliché, euphemism, hendiadys, hyperbole, litotes, meiosis, metonymy, oxymoron, paronomasia, persiflage, personification, and prolepsis. Kennedy adds to this list 'allusion' and 'synecdoche'. For each of these seventeen devices, Kennedy attempts to find a pictorial example, which he subsequently interprets in terms of I.A. Richards's tenor/vehicle distinction (Richards 1965/1936: 96). Sometimes Kennedy substitutes the term 'treatment' for Richards's 'vehicle'. To give an idea of Kennedy's approach, here is his paragraph on 'anticlimax':

> *Anticlimax* is present when an event taken to be of major significance leads to one of inferior importance. In a depiction a large mural of a Greek temple with a crowd of priests and worshippers would be an impressive context, one offering an anticlimax if the small central figure were Alfred E. Neumann (familiar to eleven-year olds and college students as a fresh kid from *Mad* magazine). The contradiction involves an obvious anachronism; the tenor is the vast temple, the treatment is the annoying grinning kid. The contradiction deflates the setting, and it can be said to have appropriate 'grounds' if the idea is to indicate something is at fault in overdone, pompous ritual.
>
> (Kennedy 1982: 594)

I agree with Kennedy that the example he offers here contains some sort of anticlimax, but here surfaces a problem already encountered in the consideration of Wollheim's and Hausman's views: what is lacking is a discussion of the justification of identifying the temple as the tenor (primary subject) and Alfred E. Neumann as the treatment (secondary subject) of the anticlimax. It would have been illuminating to have had a discussion of how we know it is not the other way round.[12]

A more fundamental problem in Kennedy's article is the use of the 'tenor-vehicle/treatment' terminology itself. The alternation between 'vehicle' and 'treatment' may be a clue that the author himself did not feel fully at ease with it either. The loose way he applies the two terms suggests that a pair such as 'topic' and 'comment' would have been more appropriate. This suggestion for alternative terms is no pedantry, for Kennedy's borrowing of Richards's terms reveals a serious misunderstanding of Richards's deployment of the term 'metaphor'. Whereas Kennedy takes 'metaphor' as an all-inclusive term ('Metaphor [or trope] is a general term applying to many kinds of figures of speech' [ibid.: 593]), Richards uses the term in the far more restricted sense in which it is commonly used today: as one – albeit the most important – trope among others. Thus Kennedy either means something different by metaphor than Richards or he judges, mistakenly, that the tenor/vehicle distinction, which Richards himself only applies to metaphor in its restricted sense, can without further discussion be transferred to other tropes. As a result, Richards's vocabulary is too generally and hence imprecisely employed by Kennedy.

While Kennedy provides convincing pictorial examples of a great many rhetorical tropes, thus underpinning his claim that figures of representation can 'include both language and depiction' (ibid.), his theoretical discussion of them remains inadequate. His sometimes rather sweeping characterizations of the different tropes are excitingly suggestive, but call both for a more careful definition and description of their verbal origins, and for more detailed investigations into the pictorial manifestations that they can assume.[13] Black's warning not to consider 'all figurative uses of language as metaphorical, [in order not] to ignore the important distinctions between metaphor and such other figures of speech as simile, metonymy, and synecdoche' (Black 1979a: 20) is as pertinent in the realm of the pictorial as it is in the realm of the verbal. One of the problems with Kennedy's list is that he does not indicate what are the necessary and sufficient criteria for categorizing a certain pictorial phenomenon as a manifestation of a certain trope. Several of his examples could with equal justification have been categorized under a different label, as Kennedy himself realizes (1982: 596, 603).

This having been said, it should be pointed out that Kennedy briefly addresses, scattered over his article, several important issues that bear on the interpretation of a pictorial metaphor, or of a picture in general, and are thus highly pertinent to the development of a model of pictorial metaphor. Among the issues he raises are:

1 The importance of the fact that the viewer is able to 'sort out the relevant from the irrelevant [in a picture], and determine the governing principles, rather than accept all features equally' (ibid.: 604). This issue is closely connected, I would like to add, to the question of what the picture's creator intended to convey. Only if one has an idea what the creator of a picture aimed to achieve is it possible to distinguish between relevant and irrelevant details.

2 The question of how to assess the identities of the tenor (primary subject) and vehicle (secondary subject) in pictorial metaphor, and the grounds on which this distribution is based. In an illustration (ibid.: 590), Kennedy shows two pictures of a hybrid object that shares features with both a tree and a person. In one of them the tree-like features dominate, suggesting the metaphor TREE IS PERSON, while in the other the human properties prevail, giving rise to the metaphor PERSON IS TREE. This example reveals Kennedy's awareness that tenor and vehicle are not symmetrical and hence not reversible.

3 The influence of various aspects of context on the interpretation of pictures. Thus, Kennedy emphasizes the effects of cultural background on somebody's ability to interpret elements of pictures. 'Adult users of comic strips are probably now so enured [sic] to their use that it takes

research to bring to attention the fact that children in our own culture, and adults in other cultures, are mystified by them' (ibid.: 594). Moreover, cultural knowledge helps us to assess the identity of otherwise ambiguously depicted objects: 'The vague ship around a swashbuckling pirate is a sailing ship. The generalized boat under the fur-trapper is a canoe. The craft with Luke Skywalker in it is an X-wing fighter' (ibid.: 598. See also Kennedy 1985a: 58, 60). All of these issues will be examined at length in later chapters of the present study.

JOHNS (1984)

Like Kennedy, Johns aims to identify metaphorical devices in the pictorial realm and 'to examine metaphorical representation as a viable strategy for visually communicating abstract information' (1984: 291). She stresses the intentional character of metaphor and emphasizes that understanding metaphorical representations requires something she terms 'visual literacy' since 'communication relies on the "reading" of pictorial, typographic, and diagrammatic configurations and the ability to recognize those aspects that serve to convey information or participate in the constitution and perception of meaning' (ibid.). In order to analyse pictorial representations, Johns furthermore observes, it is first and foremost imperative to examine the interaction of the various parts within the configuration making up the picture. Starting from the thesis that 'metaphor's basic premise is the juxtaposition of familiar elements in unfamiliar ways, the connecting of ideas and things not previously connected' (ibid.: 292), Johns in her article identifies various types of what she calls 'visual metaphor', using forty-four plates (mostly of an artistic nature) to illustrate these types. Included in the list are such tropes as hyperbole, simile, metaphor, metonymy, synecdoche, personification, and allegory. A key aspect of these varieties of visual metaphor is that they contain one or more elements that have been 'appropriated' from their original context and 'reclassified' in the new context, thus generating new meaning – the latter in line with Black (1962), who is quoted with approval (ibid.: 293).

Johns's approach, informed by semiotic models, is in at least two senses identical to Kennedy's (1982). Her illustrations are as suggestive as his, but like him she uses the label 'metaphor' in its broad sense, that is, as virtually synonymous with the word 'trope' itself. Unfortunately, Johns only very summarily defines the various types of 'visual metaphors' as they are to be understood in their verbal manifestations before applying them to the phenomena in the plates she claims are pictorial variants of these types. The result is that the matches between the definitions and the pictorial applications remain rather impressionistic.[14] Because of the absence of a firm theoretical basis, it is difficult to generalize from the examples she gives.

DURAND (1987)

Durand, like Johns (1984) opting for a semiotic approach, aims 'to find a visual transposition of the rhetorical figures in the advertising image. In order to transpose the rhetorical figures to the visual field, a more formal definition of these figures was sought' (1987: 295). Durand distinguishes thirty verbal figures of speech, which he places into a grid pattern that is governed by the two axes of 'operation' (consisting of the following operators: addition; suppression; substitution; and exchange) and 'relation' (consisting of the subtypes identity; similarity of form/content; difference; opposition of form/content; and false homologies – the latter further subdivided into 'double meaning' and 'paradox'; see Table 3.1). Subsequently Durand provides pictorial counterparts to these verbal rhetorical figures, taken from advertising.

There are, however, various theoretical difficulties with Durand's proposals. A major problem is that Durand's definitions/descriptions of the rhetorical figures, undertaken before they are shown to apply to the visual material, is inadequate. Many figures are explained in hardly more than a single sentence and with little precision. Secondly it is unclear what criteria were used to decide which figures of speech were to be included in the grid. If 'rhyme' is allotted a place, then why not 'alliteration' and 'assonance'? Or are these latter to be seen as subsumed under rhyme? Do we have to deduce from the absence of 'simile' that Durand considers simile a subcategory of metaphor? And where are other tropes, such as for instance Kennedy's 'allegory', 'anti-climax', 'cliché', 'meiosis', 'persiflage', 'personification', and 'prolepsis'? Where is 'irony'? Several answers are possible. One is that (some of) these figures can be categorized under one of those identified under another name by Durand. Another is that these tropes according to Durand (but not according to Kennedy) have no visual counterparts. A third answer is that the figures did simply not fit in Durand's neat grid pattern. However this may be, the fact that Durand does not address these issues suggests that the scheme he developed has not been very thoroughly thought out.

The problems do not, however, stop at the stage of charting the verbal variants of the figures of speech identified. Their rationale, after all, is to provide a framework for transposing the rhetorical figures to the pictorial realm. But while the subsequent proposals for an application of the rhetorical figures to the pictorial realm are original and suggestive, little has been done to delimit the criteria justifying the decision to match specific labels with specific pictorial phenomena. Consequently, several transpositions from the verbal to the pictorial seem rather arbitrary. Although Durand nowhere explicitly addresses the matter, it transpires that there is no one-to-one correspondence between verbal and pictorial figures, so that the neat grid of verbal figures has to undergo extensive modification to fit the pictorial examples. This, in turn, results in a *different* organization of the

Table 3.1 Rhetorical figures in the advertising image

| Relation | Operation | | | |
	A Addition	B Suppression	C Substitution	D Exchange
1 Identity	Repetition	Ellipsis	Homeophore	Inversion
2 Similarity				
• of form	Rhyme	—	Allusion	Hendiadys
• of content	Comparison	Circumlocution	Metaphor	—
3 Difference	Accumulation	Suspense	Metonymy	Asyndeton
4 Opposition				
• of form	Anachronism	Dubitation	Periphrasis	Anacoluthon
• of content	Antithesis	Reticence	Euphemism	Chiasmus
5 False homologies				
• double meaning	Antanaclasis	Tautology	Pun	Antimetabole
• paradox	Paradox	Preterition	Antiphrasis	Antology

Source: Durand 1987: 296

pictorial parallel grid that needs to be established. For instance, after further subdividing his additive figures of similarity of form into eight categories (ibid.: 299, Table 2) to cover the pictorial variants of this verbal figure of speech, Durand indicates that the first, 'repetition', has already been discussed under 'additive identity' while the eighth, 'accumulation', 'is no longer a similarity figure' (ibid.: 301), the latter having been categorized under 'additive difference'. While as such this is no insurmountable problem, the virtual absence of an analysis, let alone justification of the modification makes the link between the verbal and the pictorial manifestations of the rhetorical figures rather tenuous. The link between verbal and pictorial figures is further weakened by the fact that the names of various figures from the grid ('anachronism', 'circumlocution', 'dubitation', 'tautology', 'periphrasis', 'euphemism', 'antimetabole') are never mentioned again, while, conversely, figures such as 'hyperbole', 'catachresis' (well-known figures in verbal rhetoric) suddenly crop up in the pictorial realm without having been explicitly identified in the verbal realm.

Furthermore, the grid might misleadingly suggest that the rhetorical figures are mutually exclusive and cannot co-occur or overlap. This is obviously untrue for the verbal tropes. Clearly, such figures as rhyme, periphrasis, anachronism, allusion, and pun can co-occur with a host of other tropes. The same holds true for the relationships between various pictorial examples Durand adduces. Arguably Durand's Figure 18, which shows a blown-up underground ticket and is treated under hyperbole ('The visual hyperbole shows an enlarged object' [ibid.: 311]), could also have been labelled a metonymy; after all the ticket metonymically refers to the underground as a means of transport. Another advertisement, for a bank (Durand's Figure 11), features two juxtaposed hands holding, respectively, a miniature apartment building and a cottage. The ad is used to demonstrate the pictorial counterpart of 'antithesis', but surely the diminutive size of the buildings exemplifies some other trope as well – perhaps 'understatement'. And since the bank finances, presumably, both types of houses, the two types are not merely contrasted but also compared, so that they could equally well have been discussed under 'similarity'. If and how pictorial tropes can co-occur is an issue left unexamined in the article.

Perhaps the wealth of examples paired to the weakness of the theoretical design can be explained by suggesting that in the last resort the voice of the ad-maker in Durand is stronger than that of the semiotician.[15] This idea finds support in the fact that he occasionally seems to address his fellow ad-makers, warning against the abuse of certain figures: 'Declining any structuration by the similarity relations, the figures of accumulation may be dangerous. They intend to create a feeling of number and of diversity, but in fact they may create a feeling of confusion, disorder, and chaos' (ibid.: 303). And discussing various types of antithesis he comments, 'such antitheses are dangerous, because they may devalue one such term of the opposition' (ibid.: 304). But be this as it may, while Durand's examples are evocative, and suggest what direction research into pictorial counterparts of various rhetorical figures could take, the theoretical basis of the model leaves much to be desired.

FORCEVILLE (1988)

Forceville (1988) is an early attempt of mine to found a model of pictorial metaphor on Black's interaction theory. The elaboration of Black's theory is short, and not in all respects fortunate:[16] it can hereby be considered to be supplanted by the exposition in Chapter 2 of this study. The representations I examined, like several of those discussed in Johns (1984) – which at the time of writing was not familiar to me – are Surrealist works of art. The choice of this corpus was justified in the following way:

> One of the central tenets of Surrealism was that ultimately all opposites (feeling vs. reason; beauty vs. ugliness; substance vs. spirit, etc.) are merely *apparent* opposites. In the last resort each two 'antitheses' are aspects of a deeper unity, and the Surrealists saw it as their task to show this unity. From this point of view, it is hardly surprising that metaphor, with its crucial characteristic of rendering one kind of thing in terms of another, could play an important role in bridging the seemingly irreconcilable opposites.
>
> (Forceville 1988: 151)

The ten works of art discussed all feature some sort of anomaly or tension, suggesting that the paintings contain an object, or objects, that is/are to be understood in terms of another object/other objects. Attempts are made in each case to establish the order of the terms of the metaphor by invoking various contextual factors. In some instances a definitive order, it is argued, can be established, while in others both an interpretation of the metaphor as A IS B and an interpretation as B IS A are defensible. In retrospect the analyses of the metaphors with an allegedly irreversible order are not fully convincing; even in these the terms can arguably be reversed. Another weakness of the study is the deliberate disregard of the titles of the art works under consideration. The pictures in themselves were already so bewildering that taking into account the puzzling Surrealist titles as well proved too much: after all, far from 'anchoring' the paintings/collages (Barthes 1986/1964: 30; see Chapter 4), they only multiply the pictorial mysteries – but this would seem to be no excuse for neglecting them. Noticeable, furthermore, is the emphatic statement that no attempts are made to give satisfactory *interpretations* of the metaphors identified (ibid.: 152).

These weaknesses in Forceville (1988) are revealing, and point out the way to a more satisfactory account. Since the Surrealist metaphors under consideration defy a decisive ordering of primary and secondary subject; since they are difficult or even impossible to interpret conclusively; and since the accompanying titles provide few clues to an interpretation, it seems unwise to try and base a model of pictorial metaphor on Surrealist art[17] – even though, conversely, the application of Black's theory may yield interesting insights into Surrealist works of art (see Forceville 1990). Apart from these illuminating shortcomings, the article appears to have two positive contributions to make. In the first place it suggests that the characteristic metaphoric tension between domains in the pictorial realm translates as a representation that is in one way or another a 'collage': one of the terms is 'alien' to the original representation. In terms of Johns (1984), it is taken from its original context and reclassified in the new context. Secondly, it argues that for an adequate understanding of a pictorial metaphor, text-external clues often need to be brought to bear on the representation. Put differently, the interpretation of a pictorial metaphor requires not only an understanding of the pictorial context and the (anchoring) verbal context, but also of 'the different kinds of knowledge invested in the image (practical, national, cultural, aesthetic knowledge)' (Barthes 1986/1964: 35), as well as of the conventions surrounding the *genre* to which the representation belongs. These contextual factors will be discussed at greater length in Chapter 4.

WHITTOCK (1990)

Although Whittock's *Metaphor and Film* focuses on metaphor in moving, artistic images, while the present study concentrates on static, non-artistic images, the book contains a number of observations that are pertinent to my concerns and therefore deserve closer attention. To begin with, for the concept 'cinematic metaphor' to be meaningful in the first place, a distinction should be capable of being made between the 'literal' and the 'figurative' – however awkward these labels are when the medium at stake is itself of a pictorial nature. That is, it should somehow be clear that a shot or a sequence should not be taken 'literally'. Can this distinction, which so clearly originates in the realm of language, be made for filmic images? With reference to Ricoeur (1977), Whittock argues that it can:

> The literal is merely what is current, or usual. With words, the literal sense is the one that is lexicalized. . . . One cannot, of course, have a lexicon of film images. But one certainly can have standard ways of filming things. When something is filmed in a standard manner, and nothing in the surrounding context of the shot indicates otherwise, our tendency is to accept the shot as primarily denotative. An image of a telephone depicts the object itself. Speaking in this way provides a means of defining a localized and marked cinematic metaphor as one where we realize a literal reading will not do.
>
> (Whittock 1990: 121)

The analysis of cinematic metaphor thus being deemed a legitimate enterprise, Whittock argues that his project is a double-edged sword. Apart from wishing to chart what the study of metaphor can contribute to the analysis and interpretation of films, Whittock correctly points out that 'film is a way of uncovering some fundamental properties of metaphor that a restricted focus on the verbal medium of literature runs the risk of neglecting' (ibid.: 4). In line with this view he endorses the idea that metaphor primarily takes place on a cognitive level and can manifest itself in different modes: 'An imaginative theory of metaphor . . . allows for the possibility of insight preceding utterance, and allows for different media giving their own form to that insight' (ibid.: 27; see also 116). The difference between media also means that cinematic metaphors are not necessarily amenable to adequate verbalizations. 'There is no reason to suppose that the effect of cinematic metaphors may be captured in words without loss, any more than there is for believing that verbal metaphors are reducible to literal exposition' (ibid.: 49).

As a first approximation to the model he will present, Whittock briefly argues that the Wittgensteinian notion of 'seeing-as' does not suffice to demarcate cinematic metaphors, since by definition any form of depicting involves a 'seeing-as'. What is needed in addition is 'interplicitness' – 'the mutual influence of disparate ideas or contexts upon one another, the interaction of old and new meanings together. Metaphor is a process of interplicit seeings as' (ibid.: 27). Of this notion of interplicitness, which as Whittock acknowledges is very similar to Black's interaction (ibid.: 145,

n. 25), various examples are given. Whittock cites Arnheim's (1958: 122–3) description of the famous scene in Chaplin's *The Gold Rush*, where the starving hero eats his boot as if it were the carcass of a fish, its nails as if they were chicken, and its laces as if they were spaghetti. Another example Whittock adduces is a scene in Fellini's $8\frac{1}{2}$, in which the hero, Guido, 'is dragged off by both arms to his calamitous press conference: His efforts to escape mimic those of a recalcitrant child' (ibid.: 31).

Whittock is aware of the importance of finding criteria to determine which of the two terms is the primary subject (tenor) and which is the secondary subject (vehicle) of a pictorial metaphor. He distinguishes two criteria: 'The stronger denotation, the one more fully present, will normally identify the tenor; the weaker or more suggested denotation will be that of the vehicle' (ibid.: 31). In more ambiguous circumstances, Whittock claims, the issue is resolved differently. He gives the example of the opening shot of a sequence in which it is initially unclear whether the scene is taking place in a bank or a church.

> But as the sequence unfolds it becomes clear that the action is taking place in a bank. The bank then becomes the tenor because it belongs to the level of main continuity. The custom, in film as in literature, is to situate the tenor in the plane of discourse or narration. If difficulties arise, it is usually a sign that we are faced with a more extended or complicated trope, such as allegory or double metaphor.
>
> (ibid.: 31–2)

These two criteria will prove to be pertinent in the analysis of metaphors in advertising, too, as will be argued in Chapter 6.

Whittock is also right in emphasizing the role of context for the analysis and interpretation of cinematic metaphors (ibid.: 12 *et passim*). He moreover realizes that the factors of time and place can affect the analysis and interpretation of metaphors. Having earlier introduced the term 'signification', which Whittock explains is roughly similar to 'meaning' or 'meaning as process' (ibid.: 145–6, n. 27), he observes:

> How audiences respond to cinematic tropes depends on their education, experience, and expectations. What at one date may be felt to be obscure and unsuccessful, several decades later may be lucid and modish. At any given time it is not possible to foresee what rhetorical strategies may be taken for granted in years to come. ... I am suggesting that many metaphors function through the signification of film images. Further, that signification is created not only by filmic context and the organization of that context but, more important, by life as people live and conceive it. Consequently, as the lived and living world changes, so the types of metaphor that films employ will change.
>
> (Whittock 1990: 40)

All this also entails, as Whittock discerns, that despite the 'high international currency' that films, as opposed to verbal texts, allegedly have, 'audiences often miss a great deal in a film made for another nation' (ibid.: 40). While this passage draws attention to the role played by those at the receiving end of the cinematic metaphors, that is, the film's viewers, Whittock also points out the varying extent to which the makers of the metaphors, let us say the directors, have actually succeeded in making a filmic metaphor explicit. Whittock argues that the director's intention alone does not suffice to identify metaphor. There should be manifest clues for a metaphorical interpretation of a certain cinematic phenomenon. 'Filmmakers, having rendered the object as they perceived it, will expect others to see it similarly. If they discover that others do not, they must acknowledge their failure, which is the failure to present the object in the aspect that they desired to show it' (ibid.: 28). Directors may thus simply fail to render adequately their vision in a metaphorical image. Whittock seems to refer to something different than these downright failures, however, when he briefly alludes to 'unstressed or subliminal metaphors'. These, I interpret, are cinematic phenomena that do not force the viewer to arrive at a metaphorical reading, but permit such a reading. Whether Whittock accepts this latter distinction or not, in any case he proposes 'when studying rhetorical devices to concentrate on those that proclaim themselves to be such or those that the filmmaker seems to be declaring as such' (ibid.: 50), and to call metaphors of this type 'marked' metaphors.

In his chapter 'Varieties of cinematic metaphor,' Whittock distinguishes ten cinematic subtypes of metaphor, with the following labels: explicit comparison (epiphor); identity asserted; identity implied by substitution; juxtaposition (diaphor); metonymy (associated idea substituted); synecdoche (part replaces whole); objective correlative; distortion (hyperbole, caricature); rule disruption; and chiming (parallelism) (ibid.). Each subtype on this list, for which Whittock does not claim exhaustiveness (ibid.: 68), is given a formal representation, discussed in some detail, and amply illustrated with examples from feature films. The one problem cropping up is by now familiar: it proves difficult, at times, to distinguish between various subtypes. Unlike Johns (1984) and Durand (1987), however, Whittock explicitly acknowledges the difficulties, although he is not overly troubled by them:

Some examples, though chosen to illustrate particular classes of metaphor, might well be interpreted in ways that indicate they should be placed in a different category. This should not worry us too much. We do not discern metaphors in order to categorize them but in order to profit from what they have to offer us: density of meaning intensely experienced. We knew the scheme adopted was at best a rough-and-ready one, as any taxonomy provided by a rhetorical theory of metaphor has to be. It will always fall short in mapping the subtleties of artistic function. Though inadequate, it does perhaps perform the service of apprising us of some strategies artists employ, and consequently of alerting us to watch out for future applications of them.

(Whittock 1990: 68)

Whittock is justified in de-emphasizing the importance of different ways of categorizing metaphors, of course, inasmuch as his primary aim is to show how an appreciation of the concept metaphor enhances a greater understanding of feature films. On the other hand, it somewhat detracts from the extent to which he is able to contribute to the theory of pictorial metaphor in general. This may be inevitable. The tension between wanting to elucidate 'texts' with the aid of theoretical models and wishing to develop theoretical models using 'texts' as illustrations is never fully resolvable. But in the present case, the matter has probably been further complicated, as Whittock himself suggests, by the artistic nature of the 'texts' under consideration (i.e., quality feature films). No model will ever be capable of mapping all the quirks and subtleties of the artistic mind. Consequently, an approach to pictorial metaphor that attempts to do more justice to theoretical requirements might do well to focus on a corpus of texts of a simpler, more straightforward kind. One way to curb complexities is to concentrate on texts whose intention can be established with a greater degree of certainty. Advertisements, whose primary function is to promote a product or service, fulfil this requirement.

SUMMARY

In this chapter, I have considered a number of studies that focus on pictorial metaphor, or on pictorial rhetoric more generally. Although they all, with varying degrees of success, contribute to a more all-encompassing theory of pictorial metaphor, none of them provide an entirely satisfactory model. An examination of their respective strengths and weaknesses, however, has yielded a number of criteria that have to be taken into account in the development of a better model. These criteria, which partly overlap, can be formulated as follows:[18]

1 For a pictorial representation to be called metaphorical, it is necessary that a 'literal', or conventional reading of the pictorial representation is felt either not to exhaust its meaning potential, or to yield an anomaly which is understood as an intentional violation of the norm rather than as an error. Inasmuch as the former type does not *force* the viewer to perceive the pictorial representation as a metaphor, an approach that aims to contribute to a theory of pictorial metaphor had best focus, for the time being, on representations that on a conventional reading would be anomalous.

2 Considerable confusion has arisen from the fact that the word 'metaphor' has both been used in the broad sense in which it is more or less equivalent with 'trope', and in a much more narrow sense in which it is

used as one trope among many others (albeit possibly the queen of tropes). Any model of pictorial metaphor should specify whether it claims to cover metaphor in the broad or in the narrow sense. An attempt to do the former is faced with two daunting problems. In the first place, the number of verbal tropes is vast and known under many partly overlapping names. Thus, one would have to find, or develop, a framework of verbal tropes that is sufficiently comprehensive and detailed both to accommodate a substantial number of them and to provide criteria to distinguish between them. Subsequently, one would have to find pictorial counterparts for these verbal tropes in such a way that these pictorial counterparts respect both intuitions about their verbal originals and maintain their distinctions in the 'translation' from word to image – and if this proves impossible, to adduce sound reasons why and how the framework of pictorial tropes differs from the corresponding verbal network. Since this is a task of intimidating proportions, it seems advisable, for the time being, to concentrate on 'pictorial metaphor' in the narrow sense.

3 An account of pictorial metaphor should show an awareness that a metaphor has two distinctive terms, one the primary subject or tenor, the other the secondary subject or vehicle, which are usually non-reversible. This entails that the transfer or mapping of features is from secondary subject (on)to primary subject, and not vice versa. The account must furthermore indicate by what mechanisms the identities of primary subject and secondary subject are established.

4 For the identification of the two terms of the metaphor, their labelling as primary subject and secondary subject, as well as for the interpretation of the metaphor, it is necessary to take various contextual levels into consideration. These contextual levels are partly text-internal, partly text-external.

In the following chapters a model of pictorial metaphor will be developed that takes these four criteria into account. The insight that it is important to be able to assess with a fair degree of certainty what is the *intention* of the maker of a pictorial metaphor (criterion 1) has resulted in a decision to assemble a corpus of *non*-artistic 'texts', namely advertisements. An advertisement has an unambiguous purpose: to sell or promote a product or service. If this central intention does not come across, an advertisement has failed. Advertising thus has a great commercial interest in having its intentions recognized and therefore provides a better corpus for the development of a model of pictorial metaphor than art, since whatever 'purposes' or 'intentions' an artist may have, they are seldom simple.

Black's interaction theory of metaphor meets the requirements of the criteria outlined under 2 and 3. His theory, as discussed in Chapter 2, yields three questions that will guide the investigations of those phenomena that I claim are best considered as pictorial metaphor: What are the two terms of the metaphor and how do we know? Which is the metaphor's primary subject and what its secondary subject and how do we know? What can be said about the feature(s) mapped from secondary subject on to primary subject? These deceptively simple questions, which I believe need to be asked of anything that purports to be a metaphor, will be addressed in detail in Chapters 6 and 7. However, before this task can be undertaken, it is imperative that the fourth criterion listed above, an examination of the various contextual levels bearing on the identification and interpretation of pictorial metaphors, is discussed in greater detail. This will be done in Chapters 4 and 5.

4 Advertising
Word and image and levels of context

INTRODUCTION

As stated at the end of Chapter 3, the images used to develop and elucidate the notion of pictorial metaphor in this book will be advertisements. There are at least two good reasons for focusing on advertising. The first is that it represents a 'text'-genre which is motivated by clear intentions; the second is that contemporary advertising contains many metaphors. I will briefly elaborate on these reasons.

If we approach an advertisement – or any other text, for that matter – we seldom do so innocently. The very fact that we know that what we see is an advertisement, and not a work of art, for instance, or a child's drawing, considerably helps shape our expectations about what it will communicate as well as our strategies for interpretation. In the case of advertising, there can be little doubt that the primary intention behind advertisements is to make people buy. Rossiter and Percy, for instance, describe advertising as a means of 'informing customers about products and services and persuading them to buy' (1987: 3). Similarly, Pateman points out that 'the point or purpose with which any individual advertisement is produced ... is, of course, to sell products', adding:

> It can be argued that it is only because of the genre assignment that we pick out certain formal properties as the *relevant* properties which then confirm or disconfirm our initial genre assignment. ... The relevant 'formal' properties of texts and images used in advertisements can only be *specified* on the basis of the recognition that they are being produced in advertisements.
>
> (Pateman 1983: 190)

In an article comparing two ads and a fragment of literary prose with regard to their grammatical, prosodic, and stylistic levels, Cook reaches a very similar conclusion as to the importance of genre. 'What I am suggesting then is that, in these ... texts, whereas an analysis of ling[uis]tic deviation and patterning reveals no difference between advertising and literary discourse, an analysis in terms of goals and plans reveals fundamental differences' (Cook 1990: 69).[1] Elsewhere Cook elaborates, 'ads exist to sell, and every member of contemporary industrial society – other than very young children – knows this. Once an ad is identified, such conative components as "buy our product" or "we recommend that" are understood by default' (1992: 171). The fact that advertising in the last resort always aims to sell a product has one other important consequence: 'Typical among the consumer's expectations about the text genre is that any evaluation of the commodity which the message might contain will always be positive' (Nöth 1987: 279).

These descriptions all pertain to commercial ads and ignore advertising (for instance by governmental bodies and political parties) that aims not at selling products or services, but rather at 'selling' ideas. Inasmuch as this last type of promotion, too, exemplifies fairly clear-cut intentions, it can for present purposes be included in the definition of advertising, and I will occasionally refer to non-commercial advertising. The importance of being able, for purposes of analysis, to assess the intentions of a piece of communication – whether it be an advertisement, a metaphor or indeed any text at all – can hardly be overrated. Roland Barthes was one of the first to realize the advantages of the clear intentionality inherent in advertising for elucidating the relations between word and image. In his classic article 'Rhetoric of the image' (to be discussed later in this chapter) he stated:

> We shall start by making matters considerably easier for ourselves: we shall study only advertising images. Why? Because, in advertising, the image's signification is assuredly intentional: it is certain attributes of the product which a priori form the signifieds of the advertising message, and these signifieds must be transmitted as clearly as possible; if the image contains signs, we can be sure that in advertising these signs are replete, formed with a view to the best possible reading: the advertising image is *frank*, or at least emphatic.
>
> (Barthes 1986/1964: 22)

I will come back to the aspect of intentionality in more detail in Chapter 5.

The second reason to use advertisements for an investigation of the principles underlying pictorial metaphor is that advertising is particularly rich in them. A moment's reflection reveals that this is in no way surprising. The aim of an advertiser is, as we have seen, to persuade a prospective client to buy (literally or figuratively) his/her product, service or idea. For this purpose he has only a limited amount of space (in printed advertisements and billboards) or time (in commercials). On the one hand, this limitation in time and space is a consequence of the fact that advertising is expensive. On the other hand, since people in the Western world are exposed to an enormous amount of commercial messages, an advertiser must try to have his/her ad noticed among numerous other ads and subsequently to create a maximally effective impact during the brief time span in which – if lucky – he has captured the consumer's attention.

Metaphors' deviation from conventional usage makes them attractive means to draw consumers' attention. Furthermore, one way of realizing the goal of making a claim for his/her product in a brief spatial or temporal span is for an advertiser to forge a link between the product and something that already possesses the characteristic(s) he desires to claim for the product. Now this closely echoes what happens in metaphor. If we recall Lakoff and Johnson's claim that 'the essence of metaphor is understanding and experiencing one kind of thing in terms of another' (1980: 5), the possibilities metaphor offers for advertising are obvious. Indeed Williamson's discussion of 'referent systems' in advertising can be unproblematically rephrased in terms of metaphor. Williamson argues that advertising borrows characteristics and affective values from ready-made, more or less structured domains of human experience and transposes these to the product advertised. These domains she terms 'referent systems'. 'This is the essence of all advertising: components of "real" life, our life, are used to speak a new language, the advertisement's' (1988/1978: 23), Williamson asserts, and as she later specifies, 'two systems of meaning are always involved: the "referent system" and the product's system' (ibid.: 43). Examples of referent systems that Williamson discusses at length, analysing a multitude of advertisements to explain this notion, are 'Nature', 'Science', 'Magic', and the world of film-star glamour. Vestergaard and Schrøder, in a passage inspired by Williamson (1988/1978), comment, 'the problem [the advertiser] faces is how to get the reader-consumer to associate the product with the desired image or quality; the solution is to picture the commodity juxtaposed with an object or person whose possession of the quality is obvious to the reader' (1985: 153). All this sounds familiar: here is given an explanation of something that was expounded, in greater detail and with different terms, in the studies by Black and Lakoff and Johnson examined in Chapter 2. What in the terminology employed by researchers working in the field of metaphor is the metaphor's secondary subject, vehicle, or source domain, is in Williamson's terms a referent system. In both cases, elements of the vehicle domain/referent system are transferred to, and adapted to, suit the target domain. And in the case of advertising this target domain is, or is connected to, the product advertised.

Advertisements, then, provide an excellent corpus for investigating more closely the phenomenon of pictorial metaphor. In order to facilitate the discussion of this type of metaphor, however, it will be necessary to distinguish a number of elements in the discourse situation of advertisements. To this end I will slightly adapt the communication model used in Vestergaard and Schrøder (1985: 16), who derive it from Leech (1974: 49), who in turn adapts it from Jakobson (1960: 353). The elements of which the model consists are message, code, channel, context, communicator and addressee. To emphasize that these elements do not reflect static, clearly separable roles, but dynamically interacting ones, the boxes' boundaries have been indicated by dotted rather than uninterrupted lines. Moreover,

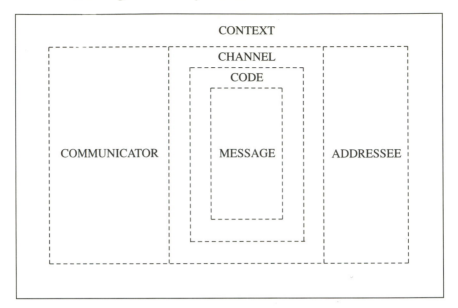

Figure 4.1 Jakobson's (1960) communication model

the roles played by the communicator and the addressee are too complex to discuss briefly here; they will be examined at length in Chapter 5. The other four will be investigated in the following sections.

THE WORD AND IMAGE ADVERTISEMENT TEXT

While in Jakobson's (1960) model 'message' is equivalent to 'linguistic message', the advertisements I will discuss have a multi-medial character. The advertising messages that are the focus of attention in this book all have both a pictorial and a linguistic component. The necessary presence of the former is self-evident: it would be difficult to talk about 'pictorial metaphor' without pictures. On the other hand, advertisements are very rarely of a purely pictorial nature. Even though current advertising trends reveal a clear shift from the verbal to the pictorial, a minimum of text – if only a product's name – is usually present. The advertisement 'messages' that will be examined, then, are 'word and image messages'. For one thing, this excludes radio commercials. But a further restriction has been made: the advertisements studied are of a static nature. This choice has been made for practical purposes. Printed advertisements and billboards need not be abridged, since they can be reproduced in their entirety and, more or less, in their original form.[2] This is not to say, of course, that pictorial metaphors do not occur in non-static advertisements such as TV commercials, but these can, by definition, not be satisfactorily transposed to print. Therefore, the medium of print is the 'channel' – to mention the second element from Figure 4.1 – via which the ads under scrutiny are conveyed. Printed advertisements and billboards are ideal for the analysis of word and image relations; they provide a complete word and image text in a very limited space/time span. One further subdivision must be made: the advertisements discussed will be either ads occurring in magazines/papers or billboard posters displayed on the streets and in public buildings. The most important difference between the two, for present purposes, is that in the latter the amount of verbal text is usually smaller than in the former. Unless specified otherwise, whenever I henceforth refer to 'advertising' or to 'ads' this label will include printed advertisements in papers and magazines as well as billboards.

Because of the dual nature of the word and image text, the question arises how the verbal and the pictorial actually relate to each other. In the next three sections I will have a closer look at this issue.

ROLAND BARTHES' (1986/1964) THREE KINDS OF MESSAGES

In his analyses of advertisements Barthes distinguishes between verbal and pictorial parts. Although the verbal part can be decomposed into two further components, i.e., the denotation and the connotation, as he acknowledges himself (1986/1964: 23), Barthes, somewhat confusingly, insists on treating the verbal part as conveying one message – the linguistic message. The linguistic message comprises everything expressed in language, whether it appears as a text, caption or headline in the image or outside it. Barthes distinguishes two functions the linguistic message may have in relation to the pictorial part: *relaying* and *anchoring*. In its relaying function, mainly manifesting itself, Barthes claims, in *sequences* of images such as films and comic strips, 'language ... and image are in a complementary relation' (ibid.: 30). In its relaying function, language is more important than in its anchoring function, because as relay it contains crucial information that is not present in the image. The anchoring function of language is, according to Barthes, more common. In this function the linguistic message guides the identification and the interpretation of the pictorial components of the image:

> The text *directs* the reader among various signifieds of the image, causes him to avoid some and to accept others; through an often subtle dispatching, it teleguides him toward a meaning selected in advance. In all these cases of anchoring, language obviously has a function of elucidation, but such elucidation is selective; it is a matter of a metalanguage applied not to the whole of the iconic message but only to certain of its signs.
>
> (ibid.: 29)

As far as the pictorial side of the advertisement is concerned, Barthes distinguishes between two aspects. First there is the 'connoted' or 'symbolic' image, which is the sum of – often discontinuous – signs which inhere in the image as a whole and in its parts, that is, all the associations evoked by it. Underlying this image, in a manner of speaking, is the second, 'denoted' or 'literal' image; it is 'what remains in the image when we (mentally) erase the signs of connotation' (ibid.: 31). This is the image in its innocent state, hypothetically seen before it is charged with the meanings of connotations. Although Barthes does not explicitly say this, I take it that the connoted and denoted messages of the image are in the same relation to each other as the connoted and denoted parts of the linguistic message. Let me elaborate on Barthes' text to make clear how I interpret him by giving an example of my own. The *word* 'apple' has as its denotation APPLE, (i.e., the concept 'apple') and among its possible connotations, say, 'being a fairly ordinary kind of fruit', 'keeping you healthy', 'being tasty', 'being the fruit with which the serpent seduced Eve, and Eve in turn seduced Adam', 'being the fruit of which Paris had to present a golden specimen to one of the goddesses Hera, Athena or Aphrodite, by his decision indirectly causing the Trojan War', etc. Similarly, a *picture* of an apple has the denotation APPLE (this is what Barthes calls the denoted or literal message) and the same range of potential connotations as the word 'apple'. This latter message of the picture is what Barthes calls its 'connoted' or 'symbolic' message. Just as a word cannot sustain a connotation without there being a denotation to which the connotation can attach itself, so there can be no symbolic message without a literal message in the picture. Conversely, it is almost impossible to look at a depicted object and be aware of its literal message without being simultaneously aware of (some of its) connotations, i.e., of its symbolic message. The connoted and denoted aspects of the image are therefore inseparable. As Barthes puts it, 'we never – at least never in advertising – encounter a literal image in the pure state' (ibid.: 31). The distinction between the literal message and the symbolic message is thus merely a theoretical one.

What will concern us here is mainly the relationship between the pictorial part of the message, consisting of Barthes' literal-cum-connoted messages, and the linguistic message (cf. Tanaka 1994: 1–4 for other critical comments). 'Anchoring' and 'relaying' are still useful concepts, but their appropriateness for the analysis of contemporary advertising requires some qualification. In the Panzani ad Barthes examines, he discusses the linguistic message in terms of its 'anchoring' function, and he suggests that this, indeed, is the function commonly applicable in advertising generally, while 'the relaying function is rarer (at least with regard to the fixed image)' (ibid.: 30). A first modification of Barthes' view is that a linguistic message may have a relaying function in addition to its anchoring role: surely many an advertisement that contains body copy is bound to convey information left unspecified by the image, for instance relating to the price and selling

points of the product displayed, and its non-visualizable qualities. But even
in an ad or billboard where such linguistic information is absent, the
situation is often not, or no longer, as simple as Barthes suggests.
Whereas in the early sixties Barthes' claim that the linguistic message
anchors the pictorial message may well have been true, the increasing
importance of the visual part of advertisements since that era has as one
of its consequences that the text no longer necessarily simply anchors the
image. Far more than at that time, there is now a complex interrelation
between the two. Let me try to link this changed situation to an element
of the Jakobsonian communication environment that has hitherto not
been mentioned – the 'code'. One of the problems of word and image
texts is that while for the former one can take recourse to the language
code, there is no precise equivalent of that in pictures – say, a pictorial
code. Whereas we have dictionaries and grammars which can help us
master the language code, matters are more difficult in the case of pictures. One of the great problems with analysing pictures is precisely that
there is no such thing as a rigorous 'grammar' of a picture. As Pateman
notes,

> Images are necessarily elliptical, for they have at most a few means of
> representing ... different kinds of conjunction .... It may be that they
> have a single means of representing all the different conjunctions,
> namely *spatial juxtaposition*. If this is so, then we are entitled to say
> that there is a visual 'syntax', but an impoverished one, relative to that
> of language.
>
> (Pateman 1980: 232)

Although this by definition precludes the possibility of a 'pictorial code' as
refined as that of language, modern, visually-oriented society has considerably increased our ability to 'read' pictures. Consequently, it would not, or
no longer, be quite right to consider the relation between verbal and
pictorial elements in advertising predominantly in terms of the former
anchoring the latter. Nowadays, the reverse situation obtains as well: the
text of an advertisement is often deliberately ambiguous or enigmatic – no
doubt to capture a viewer's attention longer than would otherwise have
been the case – and requires information supplied by the picture to solve
the riddle. Here one could say that the pictorial information to some extent
'anchors' the linguistic information as well as vice versa. Inasmuch as this
means that linguistic and pictorial information complement each other, we
should probably say that much contemporary advertising features 'relay'
rather than just (linguistic) 'anchorage'. This phenomenon can for example
be witnessed in a series of five different billboards for Smirnoff vodka
discussed in Cook (1988). In each, a picture is accompanied by a text that
partly varies per picture and is partly stable. The stable part is the second
part of the heading, 'with a dash of pure Smirnoff', and the pay-off:
'Smirnoff. Whatever you do with it, it's neat'. The billboard Cook discusses

in detail shows a man sitting on his covered balcony, relaxedly contemplat-
ing the rain outside, and sipping a cocktail that (we may assume) contains
Smirnoff. Next to him, a dog is being exercised on an indoor electric
walking machine. The heading runs: 'Walking the dog – with a dash of
pure Smirnoff'. Here the tension between the depiction of the dog being
exercised and the text 'walking the dog' is of such a nature that the picture
can be said to anchor the text as much as vice versa. While the text may be
an aid to understanding for the reader/viewer who might hesitate about
what the dog is doing (namely 'being walked'), and in that sense may
'anchor' the picture, it is simultaneously the picture of the dog running on
the walking machine that makes him decide on an unconventional interpretation of the verbal cliché 'walking the dog'.[3] We must bear in mind, then,
that in many modern ads text has a 'relaying' rather than merely an
'anchoring' function. However, since ads containing pictorial metaphors,
as we will see, tend to feature a 'problematic' picture, some linguistic
explanation is often needed to make sense of this picture. As it is the
pictorial metaphors in the ads and billboards that are of central importance
in this book, the concept of text anchoring image remains a serviceable
concept.

VERBAL ANCHORING AND RELAYING: FRANKLIN (1988)

One type of verbal anchoring that is of interest for the word and image
relations in advertisements to be discussed at length in Chapter 6 is that
which is found in the relation between art works and their titles. Thus,
Franklin observes that

> although titles may sometimes function simply as designators, they more
> often play a significant role in structuring meaning. In some cases, the
> structuring issues from the *focusing* (directive) or *integrative* function of
> the title, whereas in other cases, it involves a more *radical transformation*;
> such a transformation may come from resolving tension generated by
> initial 'distance' (or lack of fit) between apprehension of artwork and
> title.
>
> (Franklin 1988: 164)

It is to be noticed that Franklin's focusing function more or less corresponds
to Barthes' anchoring, while the transforming function is closer to Barthes'
relaying, the integrative function constituting something in between. Later
on in her article, Franklin specifically discusses the relation between work
and title in terms of Black's theory, and suggests that 'meanings of the title
phrase are "projected upon" the perceived artwork in just the way that
"associated implications" of the secondary subject are projected upon the
primary subject in Black's formulation' (ibid.: 169). Although this implies
that since they belong to different media, the inherent tension between
artwork and title is in itself sufficient to justify speaking in terms of

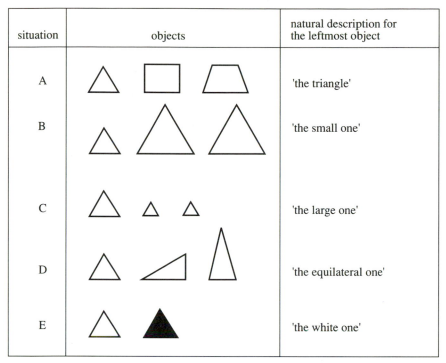

situation	objects	natural description for the leftmost object
A		'the triangle'
B		'the small one'
C		'the large one'
D		'the equilateral one'
E		'the white one'

Source: Bosch 1985: 146

Figure 4.2 The influence of pictorial context upon perception

metaphorizing, Franklin seems aware that in cases where the 'gap' between word and image is large, the concept of metaphorizing may be particularly apt: 'Where the bridging is novel rather than conventional, tension is heightened and resolution involves change (sometimes sufficiently radical to be termed "transformation")' (ibid.: 169–70). Franklin goes on to remark that in these cases, since the artwork is the object of focus, it is the meanings in the title that are projected upon the artwork rather than vice versa. As we will see in Chapter 6, the metaphorical relation that can obtain between a work of art and its title has parallels in the relation between visual and verbal elements in an advertisement, although the directionality of feature transfer is dictated by different considerations than in the realm of art.

PICTORIAL CONTEXT

In the preceding sections we saw in what sense text can help anchor a picture, that is, contribute toward its presumably intended interpretation. But it is not merely linguistic information that helps anchor elements in pictures; often that role is played by information in the same medium – that is by other pictorial elements. On a basic level this is demonstrated by the diagram (Figure 4.2) in Bosch (1985: 146), which is itself an adaptation of a diagram in Olson (1970). The left-most object we perceive as something that, had we been presented with it out of context, we would unhesitatingly describe each time as a triangle. However, the five triangles do not stand on their own, but are accompanied by different figures in each case, and these influence our perception of the triangle. Depending on the pictorial 'context', we 'see' the triangle differently, and this 'seeing differently' can be made explicit by our descriptions of it. The triangle can now be described as 'the small triangle'; 'the large triangle'; 'the equilateral triangle'; and 'the white triangle' respectively – or perhaps even 'the small one'; 'the large one'; 'the equilateral one'; and the 'white one'. The changing pictorial context, therefore, each time emphasizes different properties of the triangle – properties that can be made explicit by verbalization (see for further discussion of this type of diagram Olson 1970 and Bosch 1985). Briefly, the pictorial context of an object co-determines how we perceive that object. Of particular relevance for the development of a theory of pictorial metaphor are similarity judgments. As Bosch observes,

> If two things appear similar, or are even indistinguishable in one context, they may not only be easily distinguishable but even quite dissimilar in another context. And conversely, if two things are dissimilar or at least distinguishable in one context, there may be another context in which they are quite similar or even indistinguishable.
>
> (1985: 145)

An elegant illustration of the influence of pictorial context on similarity judgments is given by Tversky. In an experiment he provided two groups of 25 subjects each with one of the following sets of four schematically drawn faces (see Figure 4.3), which were displayed in a row. The subjects were instructed to subdivide them into two pairs. Tversky reports:

> The most frequent partition of Set 1 was c and p (smiling faces) versus a and b (nonsmiling faces). The most common partition of Set 2 was b and q (frowning faces) versus a and c (nonfrowning faces). Thus, the replacement of p by q changed the grouping of a: In Set 1 a was paired with b, while in Set 2 a was paired with c.
>
> (Tversky 1977: 342)

In a follow-up experiment, Tversky asked two different groups of 50 people which of the lower three faces most resembled the one at the top (the 'target') as presented in Figure 4.3. In the group confronted with set 1 a majority (44 per cent) found b most similar to the target a, whereas in the group confronted with set 2 a majority (80 per cent) found c most similar to the target a. That is, in the context of two smiling faces it is the non-smiling face that is seen as most resembling the neutral target face (set 1), while in

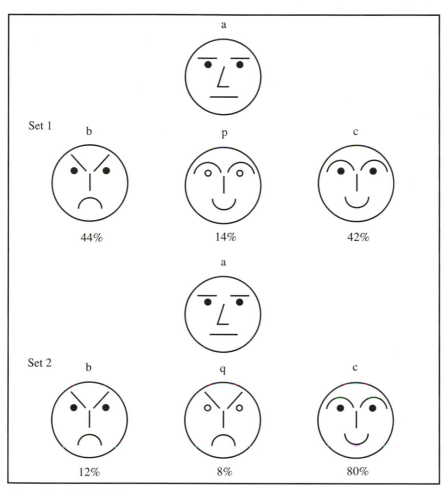

Source: Tversky 1977: 341

Figure 4.3 The influence of pictorial context upon similarity judgments

the context of two non-smiling faces it is the smiling face that is most like the neutral target face (set 2).

The reports of Olson and Tversky suggest, therefore, that just as verbal anchoring can affect the identification and interpretation of a certain pictorial representation, so can the presence of other pictorial stimuli. If we consider verbal anchoring in terms of verbal context, then what we have witnessed in this section is how pictorial context can have a very similar effect. Indeed, formulated more generally, contextual elements of any kind can be said to have an anchoring function, that is, to guide and constrain possible interpretations.

LEVELS OF CONTEXT

Hitherto I have considered the components 'message', 'code', and 'channel' from Figure 4.1. While the 'channel' can be objectively assessed, the components 'message' and 'code' – the levels that have traditionally received most attention in semiotic approaches – pose considerably more difficulties, as we saw. In Jakobson's original formulation 'message' equals 'verbal message', but the dual-media nature of the advertisements considered here necessitated a subdivision into verbal and pictorial elements and, accompanying that, the postulation of a linguistic and a (rudimentary) pictorial 'code'. Both the varying relations between these two codes and their unequal degree of precision already suggests that interpreting ads is by no means a simple application of 'codes'. Even the role of the linguistic code – that most refined of human codes – should not be overrated, specifically in advertising. Although a code is indispensable for the interpretation of most acts of communication, it is rarely sufficient. Many aspects of interpreting ads typically arise ad hoc and are therefore by definition not amenable to a code. It is in this spirit that Pateman, in a discussion of Barthes' Panzani analysis, criticizes the latter's denotation/connotation distinction, arguing that Barthes, 'fixing an image in a gaze, loses sight of the utterance in action' (1980: 235). Similarly, Cook points out:

> A weakness of the semiotic approach is its exclusive devotion to similarities, and then an air of finality once these similarities are observed, which blinds it to what is unique. Although it undoubtedly contributes to the analysis of an ad to see what it has in common with the myths of earlier cultures, or with other discourse types of its own period and place, or with other ads, there are also important elements which are unique in advertising, or in a given ad, as there are in any discourse type or instance of it. Under the influence of semiotics, academic thought has devoted its attention to those features of a phenomenon which allow one instance to be seen as equivalent to another; and in its analyses it has concentrated on those features to the detriment of others.
>
> (Cook 1992: 70)

These remarks can be read as a plea to pay more attention to the pragmatics of advertising. In terms of Figure 4.1, this entails a focus on the elements 'context', 'communicator', and 'addressee'. Leaving an extensive analysis of the communicator and the addressee in the discourse of advertising until Chapter 5, we are left with the factor 'context'. In practice, this category is supposed to cover anything of importance that is not captured by the other categories. As a matter of fact, that is a good deal. To complicate matters, I have already used the word 'context' to talk about word and image relations *within* the text. The problem is that the concept of context operates *beyond* the text as well; it simply depends on the focus of attention what is to be considered context. That means that context is by no means a stable factor. Indeed, it is also possible to subsume for instance 'channel', 'communicator', and 'addressee' under the label 'context'. This is what Cook does in his *The Discourse of Advertising*, although he uses different labels. In his model, 'discourse' is subdivided into 'text' and 'context'. Since 'text' is with due caution defined as 'linguistic forms, temporarily and artificially separated from context for the purposes of analysis', 'context' comprises the rest, including the pictures which in *my* account belong to the 'message' (Cook 1992: 1–2). All this need not unduly worry us. Different purposes inevitably entail different subdivisions in contextual levels. Ang's remarks on TV audiences' viewing behaviour are equally pertinent to the realm of advertising:

> 'Watching television' is always behaviour-in-context, a generic term for heterogeneous kinds of activities whose multifarious and shifting meanings can only be understood in conjunction with their contexts. Of course, 'context' itself cannot be reduced to a fixed number of 'background' variables, because contexts are indefinite, and indefinitely extending in time and space.
>
> (Ang 1991: 161)

The bottom line is simply that what is subsumed under the labels 'text' and 'context' respectively, and what contextual levels are to be distinguished, is bound to vary with the purposes of analysis.

For my own purposes it is useful to distinguish – indeed artificially – between contextual levels *within* the text (as I have done in the preceding sections) and those outside the text. A first level of context beyond the text that it makes sense to demarcate is the immediate, physical surroundings of the advertisement. In the case of printed ads these physical surroundings consist of newspaper or magazine articles and sometimes other ads; in the case of billboards, these surroundings can be manifold: a bus shelter, a railway station, a park, a blind wall . . . It will be obvious that the interaction between printed ads and surrounding texts is potentially bigger than that between billboards and physical surroundings. Printed ads, after all, have been deliberately placed in carefully selected papers or magazines, and one is, for instance, more likely to come across an ad for motorbikes in a periodical devoted to motorbikes than in a women's magazine. Since bus shelters, railway stations and parks are less subject to changes, active interaction between ad and physical surrounding is far more limited. Nonetheless, in principle physical context can influence the interpretation of the ad. A good example of this last type is the advertisement for the 'Vrije Universiteit, Amsterdam' that, since the early nineties, has appeared on tram 5, since line 5 actually has a stop in front of the main building of the Vrije Universiteit.

More important, however, are levels of context of a less physical nature. Thus, Barthes fleetingly refers to anthropological knowledge and, at length, to cultural knowledge. It is worthwhile to have a brief look at Barthes' mention of 'anthropological knowledge', which occurs in his analysis of the

Panzani advertisement. In order to interpret the pictorial elements of this ad for a pasta sauce, we must know 'what a tomato, a string bag, and a package of pasta are: however, this is virtually anthropological knowledge' (1986/1964: 25). This, surely, is a slip of the pen, for it seems likely that the proverbial pygmy, unfamiliar with Western civilization and, possibly, even with tomatoes, would be completely baffled by the picture. Thus, the knowledge required to interpret the pictorial element in the advertisement is *cultural* rather than *anthropological*. It is useful to distinguish between them. Inasmuch as all human beings need food and drink to exist; are in the habit of sleeping part of their lives; normally possess a head, two arms, two legs; and, when healthy, are capable of performing certain motor skills, etc., all explicit and implicit references to background knowledge pertaining to these facts invoke contextual knowledge of an anthropological kind.[4] Many other kinds of 'facts' are not human universals, but restricted to specific cultures or subcultures. For example, under what circumstances – if any – kissing and shaking hands, burping, whipping a criminal, etc. constitute acceptable or desirable behaviour is culturally determined, and reference to information of this kind therefore draws on knowledge of a cultural context. In analysing advertisements, cultural context is obviously of greater interest and relevance than anthropological context. While we cannot contrast human responses to animal ones since animals do not, as far as we know, respond to advertisements, it *is* possible to contrast advertisements from one culture to those of another. On the one hand we simply *must* consider to what extent many advertisements are embedded in a cultural context on penalty of not being able to interpret them; conversely, an analysis of the knowledge necessary to interpret a certain ad – as indeed of any act of communication – can reveal much about the (sub)culture in which it is embedded. This latter, of course, can be highlighted by misunderstandings that arise in cross-cultural transmissions of such discourses.[5]

One substantial sub-part of the cultural context, then, is an awareness of what Barthes called the 'code of connotation'. In his famous essay 'The photographic message' he explains,

> The code of connotation [is] apparently neither 'natural' nor 'artificial' but historical, or perhaps one should say 'cultural'; its signs are gestures, attitudes, expressions, colors, or effects endowed with certain meanings by virtue of the practices of a certain society. . . . Hence we cannot say that modern man projects into his reading of the photograph certain characterical or 'eternal' feelings and values, i.e., infra- or trans-historical feelings and values, unless we make it clear that signification is always elaborated by a specific history and society. . . . Thanks to its code of connotation, the reading of the photograph is therefore always historical; it depends on the reader's 'knowledge', just as if this were a matter of a real language, intelligible only if one has learned its signs.
>
> (Barthes 1986/1961: 16–17)

Another, no less important, aspect of the cultural code can be captured by what Abelson baptized 'scripts'. A script is defined as a 'coherent sequence of events expected by the individual, involving him either as a participant or as an observer' (1976: 33). Examples of scripts are: going to a restaurant; marrying; transgressing and ensuing (or non-ensuing) punishment; shopping; chatting up a girl/boy; negotiating a deal; decision-making . . . All these actions are characterized by a number of events (Abelson calls them 'vignettes', ibid.: 34) occurring in a more or less fixed order. Not all of the events necessarily occur; sometimes events change order; and in most scripts there are, at certain stages, certain alternatives available; nonetheless, in a given society, the variations a script tolerates are limited. Scripts, then, are a kind of blueprints that help people, often subconsciously, to decide how certain events are likely to unfold, and to evaluate events. It will be clear that the interpretation of texts, which after all usually describe events, requires the invocation of scripts. Apart from this general truth, the concept of scripts is of particular relevance for advertising texts. Abelson emphatically claims that 'attitude toward an object consists in the ensemble of scripts concerning that object' (ibid.: 41). We only need to substitute 'product' for 'object' and we have yet another view of what advertising attempts to do to a prospective client, namely, manipulate the scripts he or she brings toward the product.

SUMMARY

In this chapter I have elaborated on the two reasons why advertisements in general, and printed advertisements and billboards in particular provide ideal material for an analysis of pictorial metaphors. Moreover, I have adapted the Jakobsonian model of the communication situation with its six components – message, channel, code, context, communicator and addressee – and examined how four of these different 'slots' are filled in an advertising situation. An important difference from the conventional model is that the 'message' is not of a purely verbal nature, but constitutes a word and image text. The relation between these two media has been explored in terms of the Barthesian concepts of 'relaying' and 'anchoring'. The component 'context' has also been elaborated. It was argued that this category can be infinitely extended or subdivided according to the needs of the analyst and the text under scrutiny. For present purposes a subdivision has been made between verbal and pictorial context levels *within* the text, and physical, cultural, and anthropological knowledge levels *outside* the text.

Two components of the communication situation have not been discussed: communicator and addressee. In a sense they are the most important components since all the other components only matter in the light of the fact that in a communicative situation one more or less specified agent wishes to convey something to another more or less specified agent. Without a communicator and an addressee there is no communication in the first place; and all the other components are interesting only thanks to their existence. In particular, this has consequences for the role of context as sketched in this chapter. While code, channel and message are relatively stable factors in the communication situation, context is, as we have seen, a rather elusive one. The reason for this is that the factor context is more deeply affected than the other factors by who is the communicator and who is the addressee in a communication situation. This was very well understood by Sperber and Wilson (1986), whose account of the relation between communicator and addressee in a communication situation, and the consequences for the role of context, will be the subject of the next chapter.

5 Communicator and addressee in the advertising message

Relevance theory perspectives

INTRODUCTION

In Chapter 4 I investigated the levels of context obtaining in the word and image texts of advertising that are the concern of this book. Two elements from the well-known Jakobsonian communication scheme (Figure 4.1) were mentioned only perfunctorily: the communicator and the addressee of the message. Obviously, they are of crucial importance, since an act of communication always originates somewhere and is directed somewhere. An assessment of the respective identities of communicator and addressee is moreover an assessment that cannot, in practice, be separated from other aspects of a message, as the form a message takes is co-determined by who the communication partners are as well as by the nature of their relationship.

In this chapter the communicator and the addressee will be discussed with reference to Sperber and Wilson's 'relevance theory'. According to these authors, the guiding principle in the mental energy we expend in the process of communicating is the search for an interpretation consistent with the principle of relevance. In *Relevance: Communication and Cognition*, Sperber and Wilson argue that 'the principle of relevance is essential to explaining human communication' (1986: vii), and the very generality of the claim suggests applications beyond the realm of verbal communication that dominates Sperber and Wilson's own examples. Since the theory purports to account for the entire discourse situation, the roles of communicator and addressee are intimately linked, as will be shown, with the contextual levels discussed in the preceding chapter.

Sperber and Wilson's theory is not uncontroversial.[1] While its basic tenets are straightforward enough, its ramifications involve considerable complexities. The debate about the tenability of its various claims, and hence about its merits, is still in full swing, and not likely to be settled in the near future. The authors themselves admit as much: 'We are well aware that the view developed in *Relevance* ... is very speculative and, as it stands, too general to determine directly either specific experimental tests or computer simulations' (1987: 709–10). The present chapter has developed from the insight that Sperber and Wilson's theory, despite the shortcomings it may (yet) have, has a number of highly pertinent things to say that are applicable to the type of communication exemplified by advertising. In this sense, my approach to Sperber and Wilson's relevance theory is in the spirit of Pateman, who ends a review of *Relevance* with the following observation:

> I suspect that some of the interesting things [Sperber and Wilson] say about weak implicature, metaphor and irony could be treated as independent arguments by anyone who is not wholly convinced of the truth of the general theory, on which, undoubtedly, much more forceful criticisms will be brought to bear than those I have tried to articulate here.
>
> (Pateman 1986: 753)

SPERBER AND WILSON'S 'RELEVANCE THEORY'

The most valuable insights relevance theory has for a model of pictorial metaphor in advertising bear first, on the issue of the identities of the communicator/addressee(s) in an advertising message and second, on the distinction between strongly and weakly communicated aspects of advertisement messages. Furthermore the remarks Sperber and Wilson devote to metaphor deserve brief consideration. Since it is impossible to examine these issues without explaining how they are embedded in Sperber and Wilson's theory, I will begin by giving a summary of its general tenets, and gravitate towards what are, for my purposes, its most important elements. The summary in the following sections is mainly based on Sperber and Wilson (1986) and Sperber and Wilson (1987), the latter a précis of the former.[2] It makes no claim to being an exhaustive discussion of Sperber and Wilson's theory, and will only address criticisms of it when these immediately affect the use I want to make of its insights. That being said, I hope that, inasmuch as the applicability of a theory is one of the factors determining its failure or success, the present chapter contributes to the view that Sperber and Wilson's relevance theory is of crucial importance for the study of communication in its broadest sense.

A first approximation of relevance

In most acts of communication, Sperber and Wilson claim, two sub-parts can be distinguished. In the first place, there is the communicator's wish to communicate a certain message or, in Sperber and Wilson's terminology, a 'set of assumptions'.[3] This wish is called the 'informative intention' (1986: 29). Secondly, the communicator usually wants the audience, or addressee, to be aware of her[4] wish to communicate this set of assumptions: the communicator makes overtly clear that she wishes to communicate. The latter wish is labelled the 'communicative intention' (ibid.). Particularly in verbal communication it is often difficult to separate the two intentions. After all, as soon as someone starts talking to you in a familiar language both the informative and the communicative intentions are usually obvious: you understand the message (i.e., you recognize the informative intention) *and* it is mutually clear both to you and to the communicator that the latter *wanted* you to be aware that she deliberately and overtly tried to communicate the message to you (i.e., you recognize the communicative intention). A combination of these two intentions characterizes 'ostensive-inferential communication', which Sperber and Wilson describe as follows: 'The communicator produces a stimulus which makes it mutually manifest to communicator and audience that the communicator intends, by means of this stimulus, to make manifest or more manifest to the audience a set of assumptions' (ibid.: 63). Sperber and Wilson emphasize that the aspect of 'mutual manifestness' (captured in the communicative intention), which is what makes an act of communication 'ostensive', may be 'of little cognitive importance, but . . . is of crucial social importance' (ibid.: 61). This makes sense: there is a huge difference, socially speaking, between a situation in which a communicator just wants to get across a message to an addressee, and a situation in which she does not only want the addressee to recover the message, but also to make it clear to him that she wants him to be aware of her wish that he should recover the message. The difference can be illustrated as follows: imagine a noisy and busy cocktail party where Mary, behind Peter's back, says to someone, 'Peter is a fraud', hoping that Peter will hear but that he will be unable to identify her as the speaker. In that case she aims at having her informative intention, but not her communicative intention, recognized. On the other hand, if Mary, still at the cocktail party, addresses Peter and says, 'you are a fraud', she aims at having both her informative and her communicative intention recognized. Only in this last case is her informative intention *mutually* manifest; hence only this last case is an example of ostensive communication.

Now what is it that actually happens in communication? Sperber and Wilson argue that each communicator tries to affect – even if only marginally – one or more assumptions that the addressee entertains. For this to work, there must be some overlap between the network of assumptions of communicator and addressee. In earlier theories of communication, this overlap was conceived of in terms of 'mutual knowledge'. Sperber and Wilson, however, reject the notion of 'mutual knowledge' as implausible (ibid.: 15 ff.) and propose to replace it by the weaker notion of 'mutual manifestness'. They define: 'A fact is *manifest* to an individual at a given time if and only if he is capable at that time of representing it mentally and accepting its representation as true or probably true' (ibid.: 39). A fact can thus be manifest to an individual if it is perceptible in the immediate physical environment; but it can also be manifest when it is stored somewhere in his memory. This characterization, moreover, does not only hold for facts, but for all kinds of assumptions, whether true or false (ibid.), including beliefs, emotions, impressions, attitudes. If the set of assumptions that are manifest to an individual is defined as that individual's cognitive environment (ibid.), then it is possible to say that in any act of communication, a communicator attempts to affect the cognitive environment of the addressee (audience). For communication to take place, it is necessary that certain assumptions are manifest both to the communicator and the addressee, hence that they are mutually manifest. It is of course the task of the communicator[5] to ensure that the addressee activates the right kind of assumptions from the infinite number of assumptions that make up the latter's cognitive environment. If the communicator succeeds in her act of communication, this means that the addressee will make the new information interact with information already in his cognitive environment in one of the following ways:

a) he processes the new information in a context of old information and derives further information from this combination that was not derivable from either the old information or the new information alone;
b) he adopts certain new, or partially new, assumptions about the world in his cognitive environment – that is, he adds information to the store of information already in his cognitive environment;
c) he rejects certain assumptions about the world he had until that moment entertained as part of his cognitive environment – that is, he discards certain formerly held assumptions and replaces them by those of which he has just been made aware;
d) since assumptions are not necessarily either completely adopted or completely rejected, he may merely strengthen or weaken to a certain degree assumptions he already entertained, whereby it should be borne in mind that the strength or weakness of assumptions is to be considered in comparative, not absolute terms.

In all these cases, the communicator has succeeded in having an impact, an effect, on the cognitive environment of the addressee, since she has, in one way or another, and to however small a degree, altered the latter's cognitive environment. These effects Sperber and Wilson label 'contextual implications' (ibid.: 107 ff.).

In order to affect the addressee's cognitive environment, then, the communicator first assesses this environment and subsequently attempts to modify it by means of some stimulus. This stimulus can take a wide variety of forms: it may be verbal or non-verbal, an assertion or a question, a literal statement or a metaphor, a grimace or an under-the-table-kick-in-the-shin . . . *But whatever the nature of the stimulus, its interpretation by the addressee will be constrained and guided by the latter's awareness that his interlocutor is trying to be relevant to him.* The principle of relevance, Sperber and Wilson claim, is the quintessential criterion that rules communication. To begin with, it determines the nature of the *stimulus* chosen by the communicator:

she selects the stimulus that she thinks is the best she can provide in order to convey whatever it is that she wants to convey. Furthermore, the principle of relevance extends to the *context* in which that stimulus is to be processed by the addressee. The communicator, by choosing a particular stimulus, simultaneously activates the context in which the stimulus is to be processed, i.e., she increases the mutually manifest environment of herself and the addressee. To some extent the context may already have been established, for instance by the preceding exchanges between the two communication partners, or by the perceptual environment shared by them. But that context is continuously subject to change, if only because after each new exchange in a conversation between two people that exchange itself is added to the context. Often, moreover, a new remark made by one of the partners necessitates bringing into play additional contextual assumptions on the part of the listener. And, in accordance with what we have seen in Chapter 4, things do not necessarily end there, as Sperber and Wilson point out:

> A context in this sense is not limited to information about the immediate physical environment or the immediately preceding utterances: expectations about the future, scientific hypotheses or religious beliefs, anecdotal memories, general cultural assumptions, beliefs about the mental state of the speaker, may all play a role in interpretation.
>
> (ibid.: 15–16)

The choice of *what* contextual assumptions the addressee should bring to bear on the conversation, then, like the choice of the stimulus, is determined by the principle of relevance. Thus,

> it is not that first the context is determined, and then relevance is assessed. On the contrary, people hope that the assumption being processed is relevant (or else they would not bother to process it at all), and they try to select a context which will justify that hope: a context which will maximise relevance. In verbal comprehension in particular, it is relevance which is treated as given, and context which is treated as a variable.[6]
>
> (ibid.: 142)

The principle of relevance helps the addressee immensely: since he can be confident that the communicator has tried to be relevant, he is steered to the most plausible interpretation of the utterance, and can dismiss an endless number of alternatives that, theoretically, he could otherwise have processed as well.

Now how exactly are we to conceive of the notion of relevance? Sperber and Wilson define relevance as a combined function of effect and effort. Relevance increases to the extent that the information conveyed by the communicator has an impact on the cognitive environment of the addressee – that is, causes the addressee to modify his views of, or thoughts about, aspects of the world by adopting, rejecting, strengthening or weakening certain assumptions. Relevance is thus always a result of the interaction between a stimulus and the cognitive environment of the addressee. For relevance to obtain, a stimulus processed in a cognitive environment (context) should have a 'contextual effect': 'Having contextual effects is a necessary condition for relevance, and . . . other things being equal, the greater the contextual effects, the greater the relevance' (ibid.: 119). But since the processing of the stimulus costs energy, the benefits of the effects are always balanced against the effort it takes to process them. Relevance, then, decreases to the extent that the effort needed to interpret the stimulus is large. Consequently, relevance is always a function of a kind of cost-benefit balance.[7]

Sperber and Wilson postulate that each communicator aims at framing her message in such a way that the addressee will have to expend no more effort than necessary to process that message. In the situation where an addressee, processing an assumption in a context, achieves the best possible (but non-quantifiable) balance of effort against effect, he is said to have *optimally processed* that assumption (ibid.: 144). But when does the addressee know that he has hit upon the right interpretation? How many interpretations should he consider before deciding on the one he will take as the one intended by the communicator? Sperber and Wilson's suggestion is that the first interpretation of a message hit upon by an addressee that is consistent with the principle of relevance is the one intended by the communicator. This, to be sure, is one of the most daring and far-reaching claims in the book (for comments, see Adler 1987: 711, Morgan and Green 1987: 727 and Pateman 1986: 750). An important implication of this hypothesis is that it suggests why an addressee need not consider an infinite number of possible interpretations and then decide on the right one. This latter procedure would induce an enormous amount of effort, thus vastly decreasing relevance. The proposal is also intuitively plausible, since in the swift exchanges that characterize most oral communication, an addressee simply has not got the time to test an endless range of interpretations. It is useful to add that, as Sperber and Wilson emphasize in a reply to a comment on that score (Morgan and Green 1987) that the resulting interpretation is not necessarily *maximally* relevant, but merely *optimally* relevant:

> And what if the communicator intended an interpretation richer than the first interpretation consistent with the principle of relevance? Too bad. She should have eliminated that first interpretation one way or another; as things stand she will be misunderstood or, at best, only partially understood. One consequence of our approach is worth noting here. . . . When there is a series of richer and richer conceivable interpretations of a given stimulus, the right one is the poorest interpretation consistent with the principle of relevance.
>
> (Sperber and Wilson 1987: 747)

Relevance to an individual

One of the crucial insights of Sperber and Wilson is that the addressee of a specific message is not just anybody, but the particular person (although it could also be a machine or, as we will see later, a group of persons) to which the communicator wants to convey a particular message, at *that* particular moment, in *that* particular place, under *those* particular circumstances – the latter, of course being ever so many aspects of the context discussed in Chapter 4. The very fact that all these contextual factors must be taken into account means that 'relevance' never obtains objectively. Since time, place, and circumstances are ultimately less important than (or rather: subservient to) the identity of the addressee, the fact that 'relevance' is always 'relevance-to-somebody' and, even more specifically, 'relevance-to-an-individual' (see Sperber and Wilson 1986: 142 ff.) is vitally important. Sperber and Wilson are well aware of this and emphasize that 'we are the first in the literature to develop a concept of relevance *to an individual . . .* which is essential to our whole theory' (Sperber and Wilson 1987: 751). Given its centrality, this aspect of the theory receives surprisingly little attention in the 'Open peer commentary' in *Behavioral and Brain Sciences* (1987). It is to be noticed, incidentally, that Lakoff and Johnson (see Chapter 2), working in a very different tradition, similarly realize the importance of the question who is/are the addressee(s) of a message, although they use the concept 'meaning' rather than 'relevance' to make the point: 'Meaning is always meaning *to* someone. There is no such thing as a meaning of a sentence in itself, independent of any people. When we speak of the meaning of a sentence, it is always the meaning of the sentence to someone, a real person or a hypothetical typical member of a speech community' (1980: 184). The observation is reiterated by Johnson: 'Whether it be for human events or for words and sentences, meaning is always meaning *for* some person or community. Words do not have meaning in themselves; they have meaning only for people who *use* them to mean something' (1987: 177). Intentions, too, are central for Johnson: 'The key point for the theory of meaning I am advancing is that meaning always involves human understanding and intentionality. It is never merely an objective relation between symbolic representations and the world, just because there can be no such relation without human understanding to establish and mediate it' (ibid.: 178).[8]

To make all this more concrete, consider the present situation. If having finished reading this chapter you, the addressee, should be totally bowled over by what I, the communicator, have tried to communicate to you, say to the extent that you feel you must immediately read Sperber and Wilson's *Relevance*, completely revise the basic tenets of your own research project, or even abandon it altogether and train to be an accountant – then the effects of my message (that is: the effects that my message has on your cognitive environment) no doubt counterbalance the effort you have had to expend trying to understand my argument. As a consequence, in that case my message can be said to have a high degree of relevance. If on the other hand you think something like 'Boring, boring . . . '; 'This I already knew'; 'What nonsense!'; or 'What the hell is this author talking about?' it is obvious that the effort you have had to expend does *not* counterbalance the effects, so that relevance has been minimal or even non-existent. Whichever of the two responses better fits the situation, it should be realized that, as Sperber and Wilson claim, the *presumption* of relevance always applies (1986: 156 ff.). As a communicator I presume that my act of communication will have enough effects in the cognitive environment of those whom I envisage as my readers to make it worth their while to process my message. Simultaneously, I have framed my message in such a way that I presume you, the reader, will need to expend no unnecessary effort to recover it. To this end I have tried to establish a cognitive environment in which a number of assumptions is, or has become, mutually manifest. But while an act of communication always comes with the presumption of relevance, this does not entail that relevance is in fact always achieved. A message is relevant to the addressee if it triggers certain effects in his cognitive environment without costing undue energy to process it; if this does not happen, no relevance has been achieved – whereby it should be borne in mind that achieving relevance is usually no matter of simple success or failure, but one of degree. And since relevance is always relevance to an individual, this chapter may be relevant to some readers but not to others.

Strong versus weak communication

Another cornerstone in Sperber and Wilson's theory is the distinction they make between strong and weak communication. To understand this distinction, it is necessary first to deal briefly with another dichotomy they identify, namely between decoding and inferential processes of communication. In the first type, a message is encoded in a signal by the communicator, transmitted, and decoded by the addressee. The best-known code, of course, is that provided by the grammar and vocabulary of a natural language. The code model, however, cannot account on its own for communication processes; it is to be supplemented with, and in some cases supplanted by, inference. The signal as recovered by the addressee serves as the basis for a derivation of information that the addressee thinks the communicator has wanted to convey (i.e., of the informative intention). In Sperber and Wilson's own words, 'an *inferential process* takes a set of premises as input and yields as output a set of conclusions which follow logically from, or are at least warranted by, the premises. A *decoding process* takes a signal as input and yields as output a message associated with the signal by an underlying code' (1987: 698). The difference between the two is elucidated in the following exchange between Peter and Mary. 'Do you want some coffee?', Peter asks, and Mary replies, 'Coffee would keep me awake' (1986: 34). The language code allows Peter to establish that Mary has conveyed that coffee would keep her awake. However, this in itself is insufficient for him to decide whether Mary wants coffee or not. He has to activate certain contextual assumptions in order to make sense of her reply, and of course he is greatly helped by the certainty that Mary is trying to be optimally relevant. Thus, Mary intends Peter to process her reply in the context of his awareness that she does not want to go to sleep for a while, leading him to conclude that she could do with a shot of caffeine – or, alternatively, she wants him to process her reply in the context of his awareness that she wants to go to bed soon, leading him to conclude that she does *not* want coffee. The information that Mary wants (or does not want) coffee cannot be derived merely with the aid of the linguistic code, and has to be *inferred* by Peter by combining Mary's message with certain contextual assumptions. But why, one may wonder, does Mary not simply explicitly answer 'yes' or 'no', since that would cost less processing effort than the answer she gives now? Sperber and Wilson claim that the extra effort Peter needs to expend to process Mary's answer is justified by the amount of extra effect it brings about. Mary conveys more than simply that she does, or does not, want coffee; she simultaneously gives the reason for her wish to be served (no) coffee: she wants (or does not want) to go to bed soon – and this in turn gives Peter some ideas, for instance, as to how she envisages spending the rest of the evening. These ideas, if only tentative surmises, are to be seen as affecting Peter's cognitive environment. Hence a range of (potential) effects is triggered by Mary's answer that a simple affirmation or refusal would not have.

The preceding example also serves as an introduction to Sperber and Wilson's distinction between strong and weak forms of communication. The authors argue that in earlier models of communication there was a tendency to consider all communication as strong communication, i.e., a clearly identifiable assumption was either communicated or it was not. However, Sperber and Wilson maintain, much communication carries vague, suggestive assumptions that cannot be accounted for in terms of a binary model, while being nonetheless important. They have operationalized this notion by introducing the distinction between strong and weak communication.

Communicated assumptions are either 'explicatures' or 'implicatures'. Explicatures are assumptions that are explicitly communicated. More specifically, 'an explicature is a combination of linguistically encoded and contextually inferred conceptual features. The smaller the relative contribution of the contextual features, the more explicit the explicature will be, and inversely' (Sperber and Wilson 1986: 182). By emphasizing that the decoded information must always, to some degree, be combined with contextual information, Sperber and Wilson suggest that even explicatures must, in the last resort, be inferred. To illustrate the inference-part in the recovery of explicatures, Sperber and Wilson argue that when Mary says to Peter 'It will get cold', this utterance must in various ways be 'enriched' (ibid.: 181). Thus Peter must decide, among other things, what 'it' refers to (a corpse, a meal, or is 'it' simply a provisional subject?); how soon the future in which 'it' gets cold obtains (is it a matter of seconds, minutes, hours, weeks?); the propositional mood of Mary's utterance (is it a declaration or a question?); and its propositional attitude (an assertion? an ironical remark? a metaphor?). All these problems (reference-assignment, disambiguation, recovery of propositional mood and attitude) Peter solves by combining the assumptions of the utterance with relevant contextual information. In this case, the relevant contextual information may comprise, say, Peter's awareness of Mary having cooked dinner, of her seriousness, of his knowledge of intonation patterns. The end-product of all this inferencing is that it is mutually manifest that Mary intended Peter to infer, say, that 'the dinner will get cold very soon' (ibid.: 176–81). All this Sperber and Wilson count as part of the *explicit* content of Mary's original utterance. However, it is more than likely in the situation sketched above that Peter in addition infers that Mary wants him to come and eat dinner at once, and that it is moreover mutually manifest that it is this last derivation that makes it worth Peter's while to process the whole utterance. This last derivation, however, Sperber and Wilson claim, is of a different order than the earlier ones: it is part of the *implicit* content of Mary's utterance. This implicit assumption is called, following Grice (1975), an 'implicature'. Sperber and Wilson claim that 'the implicatures of an utterance are recovered by reference to the speaker's manifest expectations about how her utterance should achieve optimal relevance' (1986: 194). Since it is mutually manifest to Mary and Peter that it is the assumption 'Mary wants Peter to come and eat dinner at once' which makes Mary's utterance relevant, the assumption is *strongly* implicated. Assumptions that are strongly communicated *must* be processed by the addressee for the utterance to achieve relevance. Hence the implicature 'Mary wants Peter to come and eat dinner at once' is a strong implicature of Mary's utterance 'It will get cold'. By contrast, implicatures can be weak as well. To understand this difference more clearly, let us return to the situation where Peter asked Mary whether she wants coffee.

In the exchange about Mary's need for coffee, the particular situation is such that there is no doubt for Peter that Mary wants (no) coffee. If for convenience's sake we assume that Mary does not want to stay up very much longer, this means that by saying 'coffee would keep me awake', Mary strongly communicates the assumption 'No, I don't want coffee'. This assumption is thus a strong implicature: without it, the utterance does not achieve relevance. But she conveys more to Peter, for instance that she wants to go to bed soon, that she is tired and that hence he should not count on their making love before going to sleep, that she has no energy for difficult discussions, that perhaps she would like him to take over the task she is right now carrying out, etc. Mary need not have in mind precisely any of *these* assumptions, so she cannot be said to make any of them strongly manifest to Peter. But she intends Peter to entertain *some such* assumptions. These assumptions are thus made weakly manifest, since the validity for deriving them is not guaranteed as strongly as Mary's refusal to have coffee. In Sperber and Wilson's formulation, 'it is enough that the hearer should pay attention to some of these weaker implicatures for the relevance of the intended interpretation to become manifest' (ibid.: 197).

The distinction between strong and weak communication is important enough to justify a further example. Another exchange between Peter and Mary runs as follows:

Peter: 'Would you drive a Mercedes?'
Mary: 'I wouldn't drive ANY expensive car.'

(ibid.: 194)

Here, two assumptions are strongly implicated in Mary's reply. The first – that a Mercedes is an expensive car – is an *implicated premise*; the second – that Mary would never drive a Mercedes – is an *implicated conclusion*. The fact that Mary did not simply answer 'No', but forces Peter to expend additional processing effort by uttering a longer and more complicated sentence, means according to the principle of relevance that she communicates more than just that she would not drive a Mercedes. Peter might for instance supply other premises, such as that Cadillacs and Alfa Romeos are expensive cars as well, which would yield the implicatures that Mary would not drive a Cadillac or an Alfa Romeo either. These conclusions would be less strongly implicated than that Mary would not drive a Mercedes, but only slightly so. Now imagine, Sperber and Wilson ask, that Peter supplies the following premise:

Premise: People who refuse to drive expensive cars disapprove of displays of wealth.

This would then lead Peter to the conclusion that Mary disapproves of displays of wealth. Such a conclusion is considerably less warranted than that Mary would not drive a Mercedes. And Peter, reasoning that people who do not like expensive cars also dislike cruises, might even infer the implicature that Mary does not like cruises. This last conclusion, however, is very weakly implicated. To derive it, Peter has had to supply a premise which Mary almost certainly had not in mind when telling him that she would not drive any expensive car. This does not mean, however, that the conclusion is plainly invalid; it merely means that the responsibility for deriving it rests completely with Peter. These last observations lead to a crucial point: the more strongly an assumption is communicated, the more the communicator takes responsibility for having it derived by the addressee; the weaker an assumption is communicated, the more the addressee takes responsibility for deriving it. Certain utterances aim at triggering weak rather than strong implicatures. Sperber and Wilson give the name 'poetic effect' to 'the peculiar effect of an utterance which achieves most of its relevance through a wide array of weak implicatures' (ibid.: 222).[9]

Relevance and metaphor

Most of what Sperber and Wilson have to say specifically about metaphor bears only tangentially on the issues that are central to the present book. An aspect explicitly arising in their discussion of metaphor that *is* pertinent, however, is the gap between thought and language. Let me briefly expand on this aspect. The authors' remarks on metaphor are part of a passage in which they explain the difference between descriptive and interpretative dimensions of language use. They postulate that utterances can be used, as they often are in assertions, to represent the truth or falsity of some state of affairs in the real, or a conceivable, world, while for instance in the case of requests utterances represent *desirable* states of affairs. However, utterances need not only represent by virtue of being true or false of actual or desirable states of affairs; they can also be used to represent by resemblance, just like any other phenomenon. Direct quotations are the most obvious examples of utterances used to represent not what they describe but what they resemble; translations form another class; and summaries also represent by resemblance. Sperber and Wilson call the first type of representations, those that are true or false of states of affairs in the actual or a conceivable world, *descriptions*; and the second type of representations, those that represent other representations (particularly utterances) by resemblance, *interpretations*.

The authors argue that the reporting of speech or thought is the only generally acknowledged interpretative use of utterances. But interpretative use of utterances also plays an important role, they suggest, in speculative thinking: 'In scientific speculation too, inadequate or incomplete hypotheses are knowingly entertained, not as descriptions of the empirical phenomena under study, but as temporary representations of better hypotheses to come' (1986: 230). On a more fundamental level, however, Sperber and Wilson claim that any utterance represents something by resemblance, and hence interprets it, namely a thought of the speaker. Now on the basis of the code model, the relation between the utterance and the thought is seen in terms of identity, that is, the utterance is a literal representation of the thought. Sperber and Wilson, having rejected the code model as the sole explicative model of communication, see this assumption of literalness as too strong:

> We see verbal communication as involving a speaker producing an utterance as a public interpretation of one of her thoughts, and the hearer constructing a mental interpretation of this utterance, and hence of the original thought. Let us say that an utterance is an *interpretive expression* of a thought of the speaker's, and that the hearer makes an *interpre-*

tive assumption about the speaker's informative intention. It follows from our general account of inferential communication that an utterance should be an interpretive expression of a thought of the speaker's. However, we see no reason to postulate a convention, presumption, maxim or rule of literalness to the effect that this interpretation must be a literal reproduction. How close the interpretation is, and in particular when it is literal, can be determined on the basis of the principle of relevance.

(ibid.: 230–1)

It is on the plane linking utterance and thought that Sperber and Wilson locate metaphor. They elaborate:

> Let us say that an utterance, in its role as an interpretive expression of a speaker's thought, is strictly *literal* if it has the same propositional form[10] as that thought. To say that an utterance is less than strictly literal is to say that its propositional form shares some, but not all, of its logical properties with the propositional form of the thought it is being used to interpret. From the standpoint of relevance theory, there is no reason to think that the optimally relevant interpretive expression of a thought is always the most literal one. The speaker is presumed to aim at optimal relevance, not at literal truth.

(ibid.: 233)

Informally stated: a communicator's utterance can vary in the degree to which it resembles her thought. The greater the 'gap' between the two, the less literal the utterance. Optimal relevance will sometimes be achieved by a high degree of literalness, sometimes by a low degree of literalness.

It is to be noted that Sperber and Wilson's views on metaphor, although not worked out in any detail, have at least one important element in common with Lakoff and Johnson's, namely that thought and language are not simply identical. Lakoff and Johnson hold, to reiterate their crucial phrase, that 'metaphor is primarily a matter of thought and action, and only derivatively a matter of language' (1980: 153). Moreover, Lakoff and Johnson's central idea about metaphors is that they can manifest themselves in a variety of ways in language. These views are consistent with Sperber and Wilson's 'gap' between thought and utterance, a gap that is wider in metaphor than in literal use. An important *difference* between Sperber and Wilson's views on metaphor and those of Lakoff and Johnson is that the former seem to presuppose that thoughts are literal, in Lakoff's (1986) sense of Literal 3 (see page 28), whereas the latter contend that many aspects of human thinking are inherently metaphorical.

RELEVANCE THEORY AND BLACK'S INTERACTION THEORY

In what sense can Sperber and Wilson's relevance theory be mapped on to Black's interaction theory? In Chapter 6 I will examine in detail how

Black's theory covers pictorial metaphors, but at this stage it is useful to show how the interaction theory as applied to verbal metaphors can be enriched by Sperber and Wilson's insights. Instead of elaborating on Black's own example 'marriage is a zero-sum game', discussed in Chapter 2, let us take a fresh metaphor, 'museums are the graveyards of art', and look at it from the viewpoint of relevance theory.

To start with we would have to know who is communicating this utterance and who is the addressee. Let us suppose, for argument's sake, that it is addressed by a visitor in a museum to the person next to her, who happens to be looking at the same painting as she is. In this situation, the two people do not know each other, and the communicator thus can only make a very general assessment of the cognitive environment of her interlocutor. Since they are both in a museum, however, she can reasonably expect an interest in, and possibly some knowledge of, art on the part of the addressee. Let us further assume that communicator and addressee share a linguistic and cultural background.

The addressee, in Sperber and Wilson's model, trusts the communicator to have aimed at optimal relevance. The utterance in question being no more than a stimulus that gives the addressee some degree of access to the thoughts of the communicator, the addressee's search for the first interpretation consistent with the principle of relevance involves, we must assume, an assessment that there is a considerable 'gap' between thought and utterance on the part of the communicator, and hence that the utterance is not a literal, but, in this case, a metaphorical one.

Here let us return to Black's model. As we have seen in Chapter 2, in each metaphor one or more features from the domain of the secondary subject (the source domain) is/are mapped on to the domain of the primary subject (the target domain). This matching process involves the foregrounding, adoption or modification of certain features in the primary subject domain. In 'museums are the graveyards of art', the primary subject is 'museums', the secondary subject is 'graveyards'. Some features occurring in the source domain 'graveyards' that could be mapped on to the target domain 'museums' can be formulated as follows:

1a)   'graveyards contain dead bodies';
2a)   'graveyards have a solemn, but slightly unsettling atmosphere';
3a)   'graveyards are often maintained by local authorities';
4a)   'graveyards are sad and boring places';
5a)   'tombs in graveyards have tombstones';
6a)   . . .

After mapping on to the target domain, we get something like:

1b)   'museums are full of paintings by dead painters' or 'museums are full of art that is no longer alive';
2b)   'museums are places where one feels awed but also awkward';

3b) 'museums can survive only because local authorities pay for their maintenance';

4b) 'museums are sad and boring places';

5b) 'paintings in museums are always accompanied by little notices indicating title, name of artist, and dates of birth/death';

6b) ...

Since we do not know the addressee of the metaphor, we cannot be sure which of these projections, or which others, he will actually find relevant enough to process, nor in what order he will do so. Different addressees will to some extent vary in deciding which features are to be projected, and may come up with yet others. Projectable features that all or most addressees would agree on could be said to be strong implicatures of the metaphor; more idiosyncratically identified features would be weak implicatures. Although in the absence of a specified context, communicator, and addressee, it is difficult to assess what would be the strong implicature(s) of the metaphor 'museums are the graveyards of art', I would venture that one of the variants of 1b) is more strongly implicated than any of the other four. But whether this is correct or not, the interpretation of a metaphor is always subject to debate, and can never be exhaustively paraphrased. Inasmuch as the assumptions communicated (here: the features mapped from source on to target domain) are weak, let it be recalled, this means that the responsibility for deriving them lies with the addressee rather than with the communicator. Another aspect of weak communication should be mentioned here. As Sperber and Wilson point out, 'the more information [the communicator] leaves implicit, the greater the degree of mutual understanding she makes it manifest that she takes to exist between her and her hearer' (1986: 218). I want to argue that to some extent it works the other way round as well: using a stimulus that only achieves relevance through a wide array of weak implicatures, such as is the case with many metaphors, *creates* an atmosphere of mutual understanding. This is consistent with Cohen's emphasis on metaphor as a means to achieve intimacy between communicator and addressee:

> There is a unique way in which the maker and the appreciator of a metaphor are drawn closer to one another. Three aspects are involved: (1) the speaker issues a kind of concealed invitation; (2) the hearer expends a special effort to accept the invitation; and (3) this transaction constitutes the acknowledgement of a community. All three are involved in any communication, but in ordinary literal discourse their involvement is so pervasive and routine that they go unremarked. The use of metaphor throws them into relief.[11]

> (Cohen 1979: 6)

It seems clear moreover that an attitude, an emotional perspective, is built-in, in the metaphor 'museums are the graveyards of art'. Unless the further context of this utterance specifies otherwise, we (or rather: the addressee) will tend to assume that the speaker has wanted to convey a negative attitude concerning museums, since in our cultural encyclopedia graveyards have rather negative connotations.[12]

Further, some degree of 'matching' is required in the mapping of features from secondary on to primary subject. The 'dead bodies' from the source domain become either 'paintings by dead artists' or something like 'outdated paintings' after projection upon the target domain – the latter a reminder that sometimes different matches between source and target domains are possible. Similarly, the tombstones are transformed into the information-bearing labels that accompany museum paintings. Finally, although the list of mappable features is not a closed one, it is of course not arbitrary either. In other words, some features from the domain of graveyards will almost certainly *not* be mapped. The superstition that graveyards are haunted at night, for instance, seems difficult to transfer to the museum domain, as does the fact that graveyards tend to have yew trees and rectangular paths – although an inventive addressee could no doubt make sense even of these features. If he were to do so he would probably realize that their mapping is very weakly implicated and thus that he would have to take almost complete responsibility for that part of the interpretation.

The investigation of this example, then, shows that Sperber and Wilson's relevance theory is completely commensurate with Black's interaction theory of metaphor. In addition, it sharpens our awareness of the importance of the identities of communicator and addressee, while the distinction between strong and weak implicatures allows us to discuss in more precise terms the nature of the features mapped from secondary subject on to primary subject. I will come back to all this in Chapter 6. But first we will have to examine how relevance theory fares when confronted with advertisements.

RELEVANCE THEORY AND THE ANALYSIS OF ADVERTISEMENTS AND BILLBOARDS

The account of Sperber and Wilson's theory earlier in this chapter, although not exhaustive, provides a basis for exploring how their insights may help the study of pictorial communication – in the present case more specifically the analysis of (verbo)pictorial metaphors in advertisements. In view of Sperber and Wilson's claims that their theory applies to human communication in general, it should in principle work for advertising as well – at least inasmuch as advertising is a form of communication.[13] Let us consider the advertiser (who in reality is not an individual but a composite of, among others, the account manager, copywriter, art director and the advertising agency's client) to be the communicator of the advertisement. Any advertisement in itself embodies a bid for attention, and hence a communicative intention: 'Look at me, I have something to tell you that is worth your attention'. The advertiser's message, of course, comes with a *presumption of relevance* and the advertiser, like all communicators, wants to bring about changes (i.e., aims at triggering certain effects) in the cognitive environment of her addressee, and presumes that it is worth the effort of the addressee to process the stimulus. The addressee (i.e., the prospective consumer) may ignore this presumption by simply not looking at the advertisement or billboard. If he does look and process the message, he thereby recognizes the informative intention. *Recognition* of the informative intention with regard to a message boils down, I interpret, to *understanding* it, while *fulfilment* of the informative intention means *accepting* or *believing* it. Since one can understand a message without believing it, the informative intention can be recognized without being fulfilled. For ostensive communication to be successful it is enough if it is mutually manifest to communicator and addressee that the addressee has recognized the informative intention.

Obviously, as in other forms of communication, the advertiser has to provide a stimulus that activates certain assumptions from the cognitive environment of the addressee. Put differently, she must establish a mutually manifest cognitive environment. As to the message the communicator wants to get across, we saw in Chapter 4 that in commercial advertising the informative intention always boils down to some kind of positive claim about the product or service advertised. This awareness has far-reaching consequences for the way an advertisement is interpreted. It organizes the addressee's responses to all elements, verbal and non-verbal, in the advertisement, and it considerably narrows down the number of potential interpretations of an advertising billboard. In Sperber and Wilson's terms we could say that in advertising the communicator's informative intention is always heavily restricted by the circumstance that it has something to do with the selling of, and hence claiming something positive about, a product or service.

While an application of Sperber and Wilson's theory to advertising is promising, there are at least four important aspects in which this type of communication differs from the kind of communication that dominates *Relevance*: oral, linguistic communication between two persons in a face-to-face situation. These four aspects all relate to the fact that advertising is *mass*-communication, and are addressed by Sperber and Wilson either in passing or not at all. I will comment on each of them, and where applicable mention the consequences these characteristics have for the dichotomy between strong and weak communication.

1 *Non-co-presence in time.* In Sperber and Wilson's examples the communication partners are usually co-present in time, and usually alternate taking turns as communicator and addressee. In the case of printed ads and billboards this is obviously not the case: advertiser and audience are not simultaneously present, and the addressee cannot directly respond. This runs parallel with a shift from *oral* to *written* discourse, which has consequences for the question of reference. Ricoeur's observation about this

point, made in an essay on the distanciation of the literary text, is equally pertinent to billboards:

> In oral discourse, the problem is ultimately resolved by the ostensive function of discourse; in other words, reference is determined by the ability to point to a reality common to the interlocutors. If we cannot point to the thing about which we speak, at least we can situate it in relation to the unique spatio-temporal network which is shared by the interlocutors. It is the 'here' and 'now', determined by the situation of discourse, which provides the ultimate reference of all discourse. With writing, things already begin to change. For there is no longer a situation common to the writer and the reader, and the concrete conditions of the act of pointing no longer exist.[14]
>
> (Ricoeur 1981: 141)

One of the consequences of this circumstance is that there is no opportunity for immediate feedback. If an addressee has a problem understanding, say, a billboard message he has not, in principle, the chance to respond in such a way that the communicator can modify her earlier message. This means that the advertiser must think twice before sending her message: an unfortunate stimulus cannot be easily revoked or adapted.

2 *Number of communicators involved.* Most of Sperber and Wilson's examples pertain to a situation involving two people. In advertising, as in many forms of mass-communication, a composite communicator addresses a substantial audience that is moreover largely unknown, although this audience can theoretically be narrowed down to the advertiser's target group. Even so, the audience remains a fairly anonymous mass. This raises problems with respect to the question 'relevance-to-whom?'. In comparison with the one-to-one situation obtaining between Sperber and Wilson's Mary and Peter, the communicative problem is much more difficult, since the advertiser must be relevant not to an individual, but to a great number of individuals. Thus, unlike Mary, who in order to be relevant only needs to make an assessment of the cognitive environment of Peter (whom she moreover may know very well), the advertiser in order to be relevant must make an assessment of the cognitive environment of a large audience. Let us say, therefore, that advertisers' messages come with the presumption of relevance for their target groups.[15]

A specification of what this 'relevance-to-a-target-group' may consist of can be found in Beijk and Van Raaij. Although they do not refer to Sperber and Wilson's work, Beijk and Van Raaij (1989) emphasize a mechanism in the processing of advertisements by (prospective) consumers that is remarkably close to notions in Sperber and Wilson's theory. Firstly, Beijk and van Raaij's use of the notion of 'schemas' is very similar to Sperber and Wilson's 'cognitive environment'. Schemas, for Beijk and van Raaij, are coherent clusters of information stored in people's memory serving as 'interpretative frameworks' that predispose people to certain emotions and behaviour:

> They constitute a kind of dictionary for the interpretation of social events. Innumerable schemas are stored in memory. . . . Thus there are person-schemas . . . which contain verbal and non-verbal knowledge about important persons. Such a schema comprises for instance information about characteristics, physical appearance, status and typical behaviour of important persons. . . . Besides person-schemas, schemas about events and acts play an important role. Such schemas are sometimes called 'scripts' (Abelson 1976). . . . Since experiences that are relevant with respect to a certain schema are themselves incorporated in that schema, schemas are continually subject to change.
>
> (Beijk and Van Raaij 1989: 13–15)

Among the most important schemas stored in the mind, Beijk and van Raaij claim, is the 'self-schema'. This self-schema

> has been constructed out of experiences from the past . . . specifically out of those in which personal behaviour and the ways in which the external world has responded to this behaviour, plays a major role. The self-schema contains detailed information about the kind of person one is, thinks one is, or would like to be, with regard to various domains of behaviour. . . . Scripts of possible future situations are incorporated as well, [such as when] a person imagines certain future ways of behaving and other people's responses to that behaviour. . . . Products and services can also contribute to achieving those possible identities or avoiding undesirable ones. Information that bears upon the present or future 'self' is better remembered, more quickly identified, and more easily accessible in memory than information that is 'neutral' with respect to the 'self'. It is hardly too bold to suppose that all proffered information is first of all 'screened' for the significance it has for the 'I' or the 'self'. . . . An advertisement addressing the consumer personally is probably more effective than an advertisement containing more general information. . . . Activation of a self-schema apparently results in the establishment of a greater amount of associations and connections with the stimulus, and this in turn results in better storage and accessibility of the information.
>
> (ibid.: 15–17. My translations)

It will be clear that Beijk and van Raaij's account fits in well with Sperber and Wilson's: the advertiser, in order to communicate something to the (prospective) consumer, must by her stimulus activate certain schemas from the consumer's memory, that is, must trigger certain assumptions in his cognitive environment. Moreover, Beijk and van Raaij's claim that the predominant schema is the self-schema ties in perfectly with Sperber and Wilson's notion that relevance is always relevance to an individual.

The principle of 'relevance-to-an-individual' means that the advertiser should, ideally, make an assessment of the cognitive contexts of numerous people. Since these people are only known to her – if at all – in terms of her target audience, she is limited in the degree to which she can activate their cognitive environments (particularly their 'self-schemas'). While in the choice of her stimulus she can be reasonably sure of activating certain assumption schemas in her audience, assumption schemas that are characteristic of specific individuals are beyond her control. Hence she attempts to activate, in practice, some kind of common denominator in her target audience's cognitive environments. If anything is communicated beyond that, it will vary from individual to individual and is therefore, I propose, weakly communicated.

3 *Multi-media character of advertisements.* While the majority of Sperber and Wilson's examples of exchanges exemplify verbal utterances, the kind of advertisements examined in the present study usually feature a mixture of verbal and pictorial information. To the extent that advertisements contain visual information, we should realize, as Sperber and Wilson point out, that

> to varying degrees, all non-verbal communication is weak communication . . . one can never be sure which of a variety of assumptions made manifest by the communicator she herself actually had in mind. The set of assumptions which have been communicated can be defined in general terms, but the individual members of this set cannot be enumerated.[16]
>
> (Sperber and Wilson 1986: 175)

If advertisements contained only visual information, interpretation would depend very heavily on inference processes. However, they have a – usually rather limited – textual (that is: coded) component as well as a visual one. As we saw in Chapter 4, Barthes (1986/1964) argues that in advertising verbal information 'anchors' visual information: the former, that is, not only helps identify elements in the latter, but also restricts the number of interpretations it might give rise to. Even though Barthes's view had to be qualified in that particularly in modern advertising pictures may 'anchor' text as well as the other way round, text is still a vital element in making sense of an ad. The less verbal anchoring is present, we may deduce, the greater the range of interpretations that is possible. I will come back to this point in the experiment reported in Chapter 7.

4 *Ambiguity of the textual part of advertisements.* While Sperber and Wilson devote quite some attention to the issue of disambiguation, which they see as a standard part of the process of recovering explicatures, this all pertains to ambiguities that are meant to be resolved. They are rather silent, by contrast, on the issue of deliberate ambiguity. In fact, Morgan and Green (1987) argue that Sperber and Wilson's model cannot cope with deliberate ambiguity. Since in this model it is the *first* interpretation of a stimulus that

is consistent with the principle of relevance that is the correct one, after that the addressee stops interpreting. But how does this account explain the situation in which, Morgan and Green ask, a nasty Mozart remarks to his less gifted fellow composer Salieri about the latter's artistic products: 'I never thought music like that was possible', intending to be deliberately ambiguous between a compliment and a deprecation?

Sperber and Wilson respond to Morgan and Green's challenge by labelling Mozart's remark an example of 'layering':

> Deliberate ambiguity at one level can be used as a nonambiguous ostensive stimulus at another level. By putting Salieri in a situation in which he cannot tell whether he is being complimented or insulted, Mozart makes it manifest that there is much less mutual understanding between them than Salieri might wish. Moreover, Mozart does so in a manifestly intentional way: The failure of the first-level communication successfully communicates Mozart's sense of distance on a second level.
>
> (Sperber and Wilson 1987: 751)

Whether this is a satisfactory explanation of deliberate ambiguity or not remains to be seen. But while it may be a relatively rare situation in everyday communication, it occurs fairly frequently in the verbal part of advertisements. Pateman mentions the 'strategic exploitation' (1983: 200) of ambiguity in advertising, while Cook, in a section on the role of music in commercials, observes:

> Advertising favours any mode of communication which is simultaneously powerful but indeterminate in this way. This also applies to its use of language. ... For, although there are semantic meanings on which a certain agreement can be reached, any discourse also has connotations as elusive and as personal as those of music, and it is on the manipulation of these that advertising concentrates. To search advertising for fixed meanings and then to challenge them, as most critics and litigants do, is quite to miss the point, and to treat the discourse of advertising as though it were law, business or science – all of which aspire to more precise meanings.
>
> (Cook 1992: 45)

The deliberate indeterminacy of many advertisements, then, is another factor which enhances the derivation of weak implicatures.

Thus, from a relevance-oriented perspective, three of these four features of advertising (i.e., points 2, 3 and 4), I would like to suggest, share the important feature that they favour the triggering of weak implicatures. And as we saw in the section on strong versus weak communication, a crucial feature of weak implicatures is that the responsibility rests with the addressee rather than the communicator. Here, moreover, we can repeat Sperber and Wilson's observation about the link between implicitness and mutual understanding made with reference to metaphor (page 97), for it holds equally for advertising: a suggestive advertisement enhances the intimacy between communicator and audience.[17]

Could we go as far as to hypothesize that ads and billboards trigger *only* implicatures with various degrees of strength? I do not think so. An advertisement contains explicit information as well, thus yielding explicatures. We can here think of such information as prices, selling-points and certain other aspects of product information. And even billboards, which usually feature much less verbal information, at the very least contain the name or logo of the product advertised, which is an explicature. But can anything be said about the distinction between strong and weak *implicatures* in advertising? Although it is impossible to draw a clear-cut dividing line between strong and weak implicatures, as Sperber and Wilson themselves suggest (1986: 201), I postulate that there are two implicatures in any ad or billboard that are 'made so strongly manifest that [the addressee] can scarcely avoid recovering them' (ibid.: 197). They are 1) 'This is an advertisement for brand X'; 2) 'This advertisement makes a positive claim about brand X'. These two premises can be seen as consequences of the contextual influence exercised by the 'genre-assignment' discussed in Chapter 4. We will come back later to the significance of these strongly implicated premises.

TANAKA (1994)

In her recent study *Advertising Language: A Pragmatic Approach to Advertisements in Britain and Japan*, Tanaka, like me, proposes to analyse advertisements from a relevance theory-oriented perspective. While she does not explicitly address the question of how the mass-medial aspects of advertising affect Sperber and Wilson's model, based as it is mainly on examples of one-to-one oral, linguistic, synchronic communication taking place in one spot, as I did in the previous section, her account is largely commensurate with mine. One marked novelty, however, is her presentation of advertising as 'covert' as opposed to 'ostensive' communication. This novelty is theoretically important enough to warrant closer investigation.

Since Tanaka develops her notion of 'covert communication' in contrast with 'ostensive' or 'overt communication', it makes sense to return briefly to Sperber and Wilson's criteria for labelling communication as ostensive/overt. As we saw earlier in this chapter, ostensive communication requires that the informative intention be mutually manifest to both the communicator and the addressee. This 'mutual manifestness' is captured in the notion of a communicative intention. In normal circumstances, let it be recalled, a communicator does not only want to make the addressee aware of a certain set of assumptions (informative intention), but also wants to publicize this intention itself to the addressee (communicative intention). That is, the communicator usually wants to point out that the set of assumptions was deliberately made available to the addressee by the communicator. If both the informative and the communicative intentions are meant to be recognized, communication is ostensive or overt. By contrast, if there is no attempt to make the informative intention mutually manifest, there is no communicative intention, so that communication cannot count as ostensive. Tanaka (1994: 40) cites the following non-verbal example of non-ostensive information transmission, given by Sperber and Wilson:

> Suppose ... that Mary wants Peter to mend her broken hair-drier, but does not want to ask him openly. What she does is begin to take her hair-drier to pieces and leave the pieces lying around as if she were in the process of mending it. She does not expect Peter to be taken in by this staging; in fact, if he really believed that she was in the process of mending her hair-drier herself, he would probably not interfere. She does expect him to be clever enough to work out that this is a staging intended to inform him of the fact that she needs some help with her hair-drier. However, she does not expect him to reason along just these lines. Since she is not really asking, if Peter fails to help, it will not really count as a refusal either.
>
> (Sperber and Wilson 1986: 30)

Since Mary does not make mutually manifest the assumption that she wants Peter to help her, this is not ostensive communication, but a 'covert form ... of information transmission' (Sperber and Wilson 1986: 30). Tanaka employs this phrase to develop a distinction between ostensive and covert communication.

> *Ostensive communication*: an overt form of communication where there is, on the part of the speaker, an intention to alter the mutual cognitive environment of the speaker and the hearer.
>
> *Covert communication*: a case of communication where the intention of the speaker is to alter the cognitive environment of the hearer, i.e. to make a set of assumptions more manifest to [him], without making this intention mutually manifest.
>
> (Tanaka 1994: 41)

The 'covert' communicator thus does not publicize, i.e., make mutually manifest, her informative intention. Another example was Mary reviling Peter behind his back (see page 85). Tanaka claims that this situation often obtains in advertising, and gives two reasons for advertisers' predilection for covert communication. In the first place advertisers want to make the addressee forget that they are trying to sell him something (ibid.: 43); in the second place, the advertiser wants 'to avoid taking responsibility for the social consequences of certain implications arising from advertisements' (ibid.: 44). As examples of this latter type of implication Tanaka mentions references to taboo topics such as sex and snobbery (ibid.: 58).

Before commenting on Tanaka's proposal to regard advertising as 'covert communication' in some more detail, it is important to repeat a point made before, namely that belief in itself is not necessary for ostensive, or overt, communication. As Tanaka herself points out, 'it is possible for the hearer successfully to recover the set of assumptions intended by the speaker without actually believing them' (ibid.: 37). Neither is trust required for ostensive communication. As a matter of fact, 'cases of limited or non-existent trust in ostensive communication are not exceptional, and may even be the norm' (ibid.: 39). Hence, mistrust of the communicator, here the advertiser, is as such no barrier for ostensive communication. What bars advertising from being ostensive, Tanaka claims, is the lack of mutual manifestness of the informative intention.

In order to decide on the validity of Tanaka's approach, we must first assess what the informative intention of the advertiser is, that is, which set of assumptions she wants to make manifest to the addressee. Among the various ads discussed by Tanaka is a Japanese one for Haig whisky. She convincingly shows that apart from the mutually manifest message 'Haig whisky is more delicious than work', the sexual innuendo enhanced by the presence of a pretty woman in the accompanying picture simultaneously hints at the message 'Sex with me is more delicious than work'. The latter message, Tanaka claims, the advertiser 'conveys . . . covertly, leaving [her]-self room to deny any intention to communicate the sexual innuendo' (ibid.: 45). This example makes clear that while an ad may indeed fail to make certain assumptions mutually manifest (here: 'Sex with me is more delicious than work'), it simultaneously *does* make certain others mutually manifest (here: 'Haig whisky is more delicious than work'). Moreover, there are arguably assumptions that are mutually manifest in *each* advertisement: indeed, in the previous section I have claimed that, given modern Western man's familiarity with the genre of advertising, two strong implicatures of any advertisement identified as such are 'this is an advertisement for brand X' and 'this advertisement makes a positive claim about brand X'. That is, these assumptions are not merely manifest, but mutually manifest. This suggests that at least some of the assumptions that an advertiser intends to convey to an audience can be labelled ostensive, i.e., overt communication. A satisfactory definition of covert communication would thus have to accommodate the complicating factor that only *some* of the assumptions made available by the stimulus fail to be mutually manifest, whereas others are mutually manifest, hence overt.

There is another aspect in Tanaka's 'covert communication' that deserves further reflection. A major reason for an advertiser to indulge in covert communication, she argues, is the opportunity it provides to shift responsibility for the derivation of certain assumptions from herself to the addressee. This, of course, is precisely what happens in weak communication. As was discussed earlier in this chapter, the weaker an assumption is communicated, the more the responsibility for deriving it rests with the addressee. Would it be possible, then, to see the notions of covert communication and weak communication simply as variants of the same thing? Not really, it seems to me. Whereas in Mary's 'coffee would keep me awake' or 'I wouldn't drive ANY expensive car', Mary does not – at least in Sperber and Wilson's analysis of these utterances – necessarily have any ulterior motives in indulging in weak communication, the advertiser *does* have such motives. The advertiser exploits the possibilities of weak communication so as to hint at certain assumptions without being vulnerable to the accusation that she strongly backs them – after all they have not been made mutually manifest. Covert communication necessarily makes ample use of the possibilities of weak communication, but not all weak communication is covert communication. That being said, it is not difficult to imagine situations where Mary's utterances are less innocent than they are made out to be in Sperber and Wilson's analyses. Would Mary really not care which of a range of weak implicatures Peter derives? Or does she secretly hope that it is some rather than others? 'Coffee would keep me awake' ('Don't count on our making love this evening'). 'I wouldn't drive ANY expensive car' ('I am not the materialistic type – and thus the perfect lover for you'). Much apparently ostensive communication may comprise a lot more covert elements than Sperber and Wilson's analyses suggest.

SUMMARY

In this chapter I have taken a close look at Sperber and Wilson's 'relevance theory'. After a general, if partial, elucidation of that theory, it was shown to provide an enrichment of Black's interaction theory of metaphor. Particularly Sperber and Wilson's emphasis on the identities of the communicator and the addressee, and the distinction between strong and weak communication suggested useful refinements of Black's views. These two elements moreover were shown to converge in the crucial claim that relevance is always relevance to an individual. Subsequently, it was considered how Sperber and Wilson's theory could be adapted to advertising. Sperber and Wilson's book concentrates on oral communication between two interlocutors in a face-to-face situation, while advertising involves communication between a multiple communicator and a large audience in a situation that is characterized by non-co-presence of the interlocutors, a message that consists not merely of language but also of pictures, and is moreover often intentionally ambiguous. Although this shift to mass-communication necessitates some adaptations, as a whole Sperber and Wilson's model remains applicable. Tanaka's (1994) proposal to consider advertising in terms of 'covert' rather than 'ostensive' communication seems promising, though in need of further exploration. In at least one important respect her argument, although taking a different form from mine, leads to a similar conclusion: advertising makes abundant use of weak forms of communication.

6 Pictorial metaphor in advertisements and billboards
Case studies

INTRODUCTION

Let me very briefly recapitulate the most important insights we have gained hitherto. The essence of metaphor, as Lakoff and Johnson pointed out, is understanding or perceiving one kind of thing in terms of another kind of thing. A metaphor, then, consists of two 'things': a 'literal' primary subject and a 'figurative' secondary subject. Metaphor occurs first of all on the level of cognition, and can manifest itself on the pictorial as well as the verbal level – and possibly in yet other ways. Both the primary and the secondary subject of the metaphor can be envisaged as domains of meaning elements, ranging from verifiable facts to connotations, and including beliefs about and attitudes towards that subject. According to Black, in each metaphor one or more features of the domain of the secondary subject (the 'source domain') are mapped on to the domain of the primary subject (the 'target domain'). This mapping process involves the foregrounding, adoption or modification of certain features in the primary subject. There is thus a matching between elements from the source and target domains. The similarity between the two terms of the metaphor is not necessarily pre-existent, but is often created by the metaphor itself. The three crucial questions to be asked of anything purporting to be a metaphor are: (1) What are the two terms of the metaphor, and how do we know? (2) Which of the two terms is the metaphor's primary subject and which is its secondary subject, and how do we know? (3) Which features are projected from the domain of the secondary subject upon the domain of the primary subject, and how do we decide on these features? In answering all three questions various contextual factors must be taken into account. Moreover, it is important to realize who is the communicator of the metaphor and who is its addressee. The principle of relevance, as defined by Sperber and Wilson (1986), plays a vital role in assessing the interpretation of the metaphor.

In this chapter I will propose that Black's theory can be used to develop an account of pictorial metaphor, and show how this can be done.

CASE STUDIES: METAPHORS WITH ONE PICTORIALLY PRESENT TERM (MP1s)

Consider Figure 6.1,[1] in which the foregrounded object is a shoe. We see immediately that there is something odd about this shoe: it is located in a place where we would not ordinarily have expected it. Since we trust that the communicator of this message, the advertiser, is trying to be optimally relevant, we expect that the odd position of the shoe is not a mere whim. We realize that the shoe is depicted in a place where we ordinarily would have expected something else, namely, a tie. Therefore this shoe is not merely a shoe but also suggests the concept TIE. Put differently, the viewer is invited to understand and perceive the phenomenon SHOE not in its usual, 'literal' sense, but in terms of the very different phenomenon TIE. Since understanding and perceiving one kind of thing in terms of another is the essence of metaphor (Lakoff and Johnson 1980: 5), we can regard the SHOE/ TIE relation as a metaphor. The metaphor can be verbalized as SHOE IS TIE.

Three questions immediately arise. First, how do we know at all that the second term of the metaphor is TIE and not something else? After all, the TIE is not even visible. This becomes clear when we consider Figure 6.2, a doctored version of the advertisement. Even with the help of the text ('Regardez mes chaussures!' – 'Look at my shoes!') we would not be able to identify the second term of the metaphor. Indeed, in this picture we cannot even say that what we have here *is* a metaphor, since there is no (suggestion of a) second term. Thus it is thanks to the pictorial context that we can establish which is the absent term of the metaphor. Black's creativity theory here is entirely applicable: the similarity between the two terms is not pre-existent but – with the aid of this specific context – created. At this stage we have answered the first of the three questions that need to be asked of anything that purports to be a metaphor, i.e., what are the two terms of the metaphor?

The second question is, how do we know that the metaphor is SHOE IS TIE rather than TIE IS SHOE? This question pertains to the identification of the metaphor's two terms: what is the metaphor's primary subject and what is its secondary subject? Here we have a problem which at first sight might seem to be characteristic of pictorial metaphors, since the elements in pictures are not linearly perceived in the way a sequence of words is. And it is this linearity which is such a great help in the distribution of primary and secondary subject in the case of verbal metaphors. After all, in the type of verbal metaphors which theorists usually cite, the examples are one-line metaphors of the paradigmatic 'A IS B' type, in which the term mentioned first invariably is the primary subject and the second the secondary subject. This might lead us to think that all verbal metaphors feature this neat, linear order, with its simple distribution of primary subject and secondary subject. But this is not always the case. Christine Brooke-Rose, after observing that 'most equations with the copula put the proper term before

Figure 6.1 Source: Advertising agency: Publi-Est/Gerstenhaber + Cie.

Figure 6.2 Source: doctored version of Figure 6.1

the metaphor [= secondary subject]', gives the following counterexample from Spenser's *Amoretti*: 'That ship, that tree, and that same beast am I' (Brooke-Rose, 1958: 117–18). Here the secondary subjects (ship, tree, beast), are mentioned *before* the primary subject 'I'. The form of the verb 'to be' employed, however, here is an additional clue – absent in pictorial meta-phors – as to the order of the terms: the form 'am' indicates that the subject cannot be but 'I'. But of course the presence of a form of the verb 'to be' is by no means indispensable. As the examples 'rusty joints' and 'the brook smiled' (see Chapter 2) show, verbal metaphors may well occur without a form of 'to be' and hence often require closer analysis before their primary and secondary subjects can be identified as such.

Returning to the pictorial metaphor of Figure 6.1 we realize that in the absence of the kind of information that in the paradigmatic verbal 'A IS B' cases usually suffices to assess the order of the terms (linearity and grammati-cal clues), the key device in determining this order in its pictorial counterpart has to be a different one, namely context. Context here has to be taken in a wider sense than above, where we invoked the pictorial context to determine the second, pictorially absent, term. Invoking the immediate pictorial con-text of the shoe, i.e., the male torso-and-shirt-and-jacket, helps little to determine the *order* of the terms. But if we extend the context to include an assessment of the *genre* in which the metaphor occurs, this problem is solved. Here it is the awareness that the picture-cum-text we are looking at is an advertisement and that the advertisement is one for shoes rather than for ties which guides the viewer's distribution of primary subject and secondary subject as SHOE IS TIE instead of TIE IS SHOE. Of course the three shoes depicted on the right, as well as the verbal reinforcement of the product to be sold ('La chaussure en beauté'; 'Shoes at their most beauti-ful'), steer the addressee into assessing that this is an advertisement for shoes. Hence it is the combination of the understanding of the wider pictorial-cum-verbal context and the classification of the picture as an advertisement that is responsible for the distribution of primary subject and secondary subject.

The third point to be made with reference to this metaphor is the matter of feature transfer. What feature(s) is/are projected from the domain of the secondary subject (TIE) upon the primary subject (SHOE)? Helped by (1) the general awareness that the communicator is trying to be optimally relevant; (2) the more specific awareness that this is an advertisement and hence that the communicator has the intention of making a positive claim for the product advertised; and (3) the even more particular verbal reinforcement 'La chaussure en beauté', the viewer presumably will take the metaphor to hint that the feature transferred can be formulated as 'non-functional beauty'. More informally phrased, the interpretation could be something like: 'Clerget shoes are so beautiful that it would be a shame to wear them on your feet, where they are hardly noticeable; rather, you ought to wear them proudly, well in view, on the spot where you normally wear your favourite tie'. In line with what relevance theory predicts, subtle variations of this interpretation are possible, and to be expected: after all, metaphors allow room for a measure of idiosyncratic interpretation – that is, 'weak implicatures'. Thus, one could also interpret as follows: 'In the uniform of the businessman – his suit – the tie is conventionally the item of clothing that allows him most to express his personal taste. By using the metaphor SHOE IS TIE, Clerget now exhorts (prospective) buyers to consider Clerget shoes as another opportunity to express personal taste'. But what happens, one might wonder, if this advertisement is seen by somebody for whom TIE does not at all evoke positive connotations – say by an anarchist or a punk who regards the wearing of ties as a despicable concession to a disgustingly capitalist society. The issue is, in fact, very similar to one that Black raises about the connotations evoked by the concept WOLF in people confronted by the metaphor MAN IS A WOLF (Black 1962: 40). As Black warns, the metaphor would no doubt be understood very differently by people living in a culture where wolves are seen as embodying reincarnations of dead humans. That is, if one wished to express the idea that man is cruel, aggressive, bloodthirsty etc. in such a culture, the metaphor 'man is a wolf' would be inappropriate. The same applies here. If the advertiser wished to convey to an anarchist that Clerget shoes are beautiful, enable one to express one's personal taste etc., then the present metaphor would be a rather unfortunate choice of stimulus. However, it seems probable that the anarchist does not exactly belong to the advertiser's target group anyway, so that this is not really a problem: the advertiser is not trying to be relevant to anarchists . . . But now substitute for the anarchist, a persistent critic might object, a businessman who considers ties awkward, unnecessary and irritating pieces of clothing. Surely *he* belongs to the target group of the advertisement? Admittedly, this is more problematic. But although the advertiser here risks the loss of a potential customer, the chances are considerable that the businessman will realize that in the (sub)culture in which he works, ties are generally considered to be beautiful, enabling one to express personal preference etc., rather than as awkward pieces of clothing. In this respect, this particular businessman is in a situation similar to biologists confronted with the metaphor 'Richard is a gorilla'. The biologists are aware that in Western culture gorillas are considered to be aggressive animals, and although from their own expert knowledge of gorillas they know this to be factually wrong, they nonetheless understand the metaphor to mean 'Richard is aggressive' rather than 'Richard is a nice, peace-loving man' (see Searle 1979: 102).

All this can be reformulated in terms of two important insights of Sperber and Wilson's relevance theory. First, 'relevance is always relevance to an individual' (Sperber and Wilson 1986: 142 ff.), and unless that individual happens to be oneself, one can never be completely clear about the relevance of a message to a specific individual. Second, given a shared (sub)cultural background, a group of addressees confronting this advertisement are likely

Table 6.1 The selection of mappable features in a pictorial metaphor

Primary subject			Secondary subject
SHOE	IS	TIE	
Piece of apparel			— Piece of apparel
With an elongated form			— With an elongated form
			— ...
			← Worn primarily for aesthetic purposes
			← Piece of clothing in a businessman's outfit that allows for personal taste
			← ...
			✕— Made of cloth
			✕— Can be folded
			✕— ...

to agree on at least part of the interpretation. This part, which then constitutes the message's 'strong implicatures' can be complemented by more idiosyncratic 'weak implicatures' in the interpretation of specific individuals (see Chapter 5, 'Strong versus weak communication', p. 90).[2] We can now, analogous to the scheme in Chapter 2 (MAN IS WOLF), render the situation as follows: 'Being a piece of apparel' is a feature that occurs in the domains of both SHOE and TIE. Moreover, the two objects have, at least when displayed in two dimensions and seen from the right angle, roughly the same elongated form. Hence these features can be said to be conventionally shared features – although the similarity of form would probably not readily occur to a viewer outside the present context, at least not more readily than the similarity between ties and other oblong things. And further reflection might reveal yet more shared features. Apart from these 'pre-existent' features of similarity, the features 'worn for aesthetic purposes only' and/or 'being the only piece of clothing in a businessman's outfit that reveals personal taste' are metaphorically projected upon the primary subject SHOE, and hence momentarily 'transform' the primary subject. Besides these features, relevance theory predicts, yet other features might be seen as projectable by some, but not all, addressees. Finally, even allowing for varieties in interpretations among individuals, there are certain features of TIE that seem not to be mappable on to SHOE – such as 'being made of cloth' and 'foldable'.

Similar reasoning can be applied to Figure 6.3. As in Figure 6.1, there is something odd in this advertisement. We see what seems to be sweetcorn in a wine-glass, which is not a normal place for sweetcorn to be in. By contrast, we would ordinarily expect to find wine in a wine-glass. The sweetcorn in the wine-glass, then, is a deviation from what is expected, that is, from convention, from 'literal' use, and suggests we have a metaphor here. In this metaphor the second term of the metaphor

Figure 6.3 Source: Advertising agency: Beverly-Markagri, Groupe 'Publicis'

is WINE, which we can identify thanks to the pictorial context (the glass itself; the typical position of the hand holding the wine-glass), although WINE is of course also verbally reinforced ('L'Appellation très contrôlée'). The verbal anchoring, however, also requires us to revise our original assessment of the yellow things in the glass as (just) sweetcorn. The pay-off – the line of text underneath the picture – 'Des semences pour l'agriculteur exigent' ('seeds for the exacting farmer') suggests that the sweetcorn should not primarily be understood as food, but as seeds (which in turn yield food). The order of the terms can be inferred from the fact that the advertisement is for sweetcorn seeds rather than for wine, that is, the viewer is invited to perceive sweetcorn seeds in terms of wine rather than wine in terms of sweetcorn seeds, yielding the metaphor SWEETCORN SEEDS ARE WINE. It is to be noticed that the pay-off makes clear that this ad is not aimed at consumers of sweetcorn, but rather at farmers. This circumstance affects the nature of the features projected from WINE upon SWEETCORN SEEDS. Whereas to a potential consumer of sweetcorn the pertinent features would have been something like 'made of high-quality grapes', 'having a delicate taste', 'preciousness', 'deserving respectful treatment', the fact that the ad is aimed at farmers to some degree changes this. For one thing, the product advertised is no longer specifically sweetcorn seeds, but seeds in general. For another, the farmer is no doubt primarily interested in making a profit.

Thus, projectable features may include 'contributing to the prestige of the farm as yielding first-rate products', and 'increasing the possibilities of making a profit'. The identity of the addressees, here farmers, clearly affects the interpretation of the metaphor.

The lofty connotations of WINE are also exploited in Figure 6.4, a Dutch billboard for Grolsch beer. A Grolsch beer bottle in a cooler is accompanied by the text 'Op een dag . . .' ('One day . . .'). The Grolsch beer bottle is depicted as lying in a cooler. Since beer bottles are not normally kept in coolers, there is an anomaly in this picture that invites a metaphorical reading. By being located in a cooler the beer bottle is presented in terms of a bottle of white wine or champagne. The advertiser assumes that the addressee is aware of the white-wine/champagne-in-the-cooler convention, as well as of the two strong implicatures I postulated in the previous chapter as inhering in any billboard (here: (1) this is an ad for Grolsch beer; and (2) something positive is claimed about Grolsch beer). The advertiser expects that these assumptions, together with many others,[3] will be part of the cognitive context of the addressee, and that they will be activated. The addressee is thus expected to process the metaphor as GROLSCH BEER IS CHAMPAGNE/WHITE WINE. The metaphor can now be said to have been identified, and two of the three crucial questions pertaining to metaphor answered.

Now we come to the third question: what feature(s) or connotation(s) is/are mapped from the domain of the secondary subject CHAMPAGNE/WHITE WINE on to the domain of the primary subject GROLSCH BEER? What, in other words, are the *relevant* features of CHAMPAGNE/WHITE WINE in this situation? The addressee, having established that the metaphor is GROLSCH IS WHITE WINE/CHAMPAGNE, presumably will search the domain of white wine/champagne for positive features or connotations that can be projected upon the domain of GROLSCH BEER. Thus, in our Western cultural context, white wine/champagne (at least the variety that deserves a cooler) is a high-quality drink; it is to be drunk with appreciation; growing grapes and bottling them as wine or champagne is a process that takes time and expert knowledge; drinking champagne connotes festivity, etc. Again, this list of mappable connotations is not a fixed one: an individual addressee does not necessarily process all of them, and alternatively may come up with others. In Sperber and Wilson's terms, the metaphor triggers a wide range of weak implicatures. Even though not all addressees will pick up precisely the same connotations, the general direction in which the addressee's inferences are steered is clear enough: some positive aspects associated with white wine/champagne are to be projected upon Grolsch beer. At this stage it may be added that the experienced Dutch billboard watcher is helped by the verbal (i.e., anchoring) context. He knows that it is an abbreviated form of the original slogan: 'Op een dag drink je geen bier meer, maar drink je Grolsch' ('One day you will no longer drink beer, but you will drink Grolsch'). This particular billboard was part of a series of billboards and commercials for

Figure 6.4 Source: Advertising agency: FHV/BBDO

Grolsch, all aimed at positioning Grolsch as a premium beer rather than just-your-average-man's brand. Previous exposure to the casually chic yuppie atmosphere of the commercials helps an addressee realize that the connotations pertaining to white wine/champagne that are particularly relevant in this context are those that have to do with white wine/champagne's quality, exclusiveness, etc.[4]

In the examples discussed, the primary subject of the metaphor coincided with the product advertised, and this product is visually present in the advertisement. This is hardly surprising since one would expect an advertiser to make some sort of claim about her product, and the primary subject is the term of the metaphor about which something is predicated. Moreover it makes sense that an advertiser should want to depict her product, if possible. These appear not to be isolated examples. Let me briefly touch upon a number of similar examples. Figure 6.5 is perhaps more difficult than the preceding ones. It may be rendered verbally as PETROL NOZZLE IS GUN. Again, I propose, we realize that PETROL NOZZLE is the primary subject because it is metonymically closer to the product advertised, Volkswagen, than GUN is. To state that the feature transferred from GUN to PETROL NOZZLE is simply 'capable of killing', while appropriate, is not quite satisfactory. The metaphor needs further specification: the posture of the man holding the NOZZLE against his temple suggests that he is on the verge of committing suicide. It would already be more suitable to say that the feature transferred from GUN to NOZZLE is 'being a potential instrument of suicide'. Nonetheless, we have not yet sufficiently interpreted the metaphor. After all, we expect the advertiser to be optimally relevant to us, and at this stage we can still say, 'So what?'. We also must take into account the rest of the advertisement, that is, the text, which can be translated as 'Or else buy a Volkswagen'. We are to adduce the knowledge from our cognitive environment that cars run on petrol and that petrol is poured into a car via a petrol nozzle. The anchoring verbal text suggests that the man in the picture is the owner of a car that is *not* a Volkswagen. From all this, the viewer is to deduce that the man is unhappy with his present car, even so unhappy that he is on the verge of committing suicide. If he buys a Volkswagen, however, his troubles will be solved. Have we now sufficiently interpreted the metaphor, and the way it functions in the broader context of the advertisement? In terms of relevance theory we can say that in return for our 'effort' we have now received some cognitive 'effect'. This effect could be formulated as the awareness that Volkswagen claims that if we buy one of their cars, we avoid a lot of the kind of troubles that owners of

Figure 6.5 Source: Advertising agency: DDB, New York

other cars have. I suspect that most people will volunteer an interpretation similar to this one. If this intuition is correct, then it is warranted to call this interpretation a *strong* implicature of the advertisement as a whole. In the previous chapter it was argued, however, that word and image texts, and ads in particular, often encourage the derivation of weak implicatures as well. In the present case, I would say that *for me* the metaphor is open to further elaboration, that is, I feel I have not finished adapting the relevant features from the domain of the secondary subject GUN to the domain of the primary subject PETROL NOZZLE. The presumed unhappiness of the owners of non-Volkswagens can be further narrowed down: after all it seems likely that their sorrow has something to do with the petrol itself. Since my knowledge of the world tells me that one thing car owners are often unhappy about, in connection with petrol, is its high price, I am inclined to interpret the metaphor PETROL NOZZLE IS GUN more specifically, in the present context, as suggesting that non-Volkswagen owners are unhappy about their cars because these cars use up so much costly petrol – which constitutes a marked difference with respect to Volkswagens. Undoubtedly, to some viewers/readers this may seem far-fetched. If so, this implicature is to be labelled as a weak rather than a strong one.

Figures 6.6 and 6.7 are obviously part of the same campaign. The metaphors can be verbalized as TICKET IS DECK CHAIR; and TICKET IS SKI JUMPING SKIS respectively. The tickets metonymically refer to the airline company that issues them. But what is the feature of DECK CHAIR and SKIS that is projected upon TICKET? Again, the overall cultural context and the context within the advertisement help to answer this question. As part of the relevant overall cognitive context we bring to bear on this ad the fact that airline companies transport people from one place to another, and that these trips are usually either for business or for holiday purposes. The destinations are given verbally ('Les Antilles', 'Genève'), and the types of activity (sunbathing and skiing) are associated with holiday relaxing rather than with the hustle and bustle of business travel. Finally, the pay-off 'Air France, Vacances' reinforces the idea of 'holiday'. All these contextual factors suggest the connotation 'holiday' of DECK CHAIR and SKIS – although I venture that a picture of a deck chair will even in complete isolation evoke the connotation 'relaxation' or 'leisure' in most (Western) people. This is less clearly the case for the skis, since in isolation, or in different contexts, it could also have the connotation 'high-level sports achievement'. One could even argue that if presented on its own this latter connotation of SKI JUMPING SKIS would be the more likely one, since the kind of skiing done on such skis may well be primarily reminiscent of contests. Why, then, did the advertiser not depict the more common 'leisure time' skis? Well, probably because that would have meant depicting the Air France ticket in two clearly distinguishable parts, which in turn might have suggested the ticket had been torn – and *that* might have evoked undesirable associations of brokenness, incompleteness, damage ... But of course all this is not in

Figure 6.6 Source: Advertising agency: HCM

Figure 6.7 Source: Advertising agency: HCM

order, since the metaphor TICKET IS SKI JUMPING SKIS *does* appear in a context which clearly steers our interpretation in the 'right' direction. The context so forcefully directs our interpretation, in fact, that we easily disregard the fact that ski jumping skis are not prototypical holiday skis at all.

Consider another example of pictorial metaphor. Figure 6.8 (originally in black and white) is a Dutch billboard for one of the leading Dutch newspapers, *de Volkskrant*. The (hardly readable) pay-off can be translated as 'de Volkskrant – the most informative morning paper of the Netherlands'. The picture features an alarm clock where the hammer has been substituted by a steel nib, yielding NIB and HAMMER as the two terms of the metaphor. How do we know whether the metaphor is NIB IS HAMMER or HAMMER IS NIB? The strong implicatures I postulated as inhering in any billboard steer the addressee to NIB IS HAMMER: this is an ad for newspapers, and a nib is metonymically closer to 'newspaper' than an alarm clock's hammer. Notice, incidentally, that the fact that this is an advertisement for a newspaper is conveyed only by the pay-off, that is, by a textual component. Which features from the domain of the hammer are transferred to the domain of the nib? Now there is not really much that is transferred from the little piece of metal called a hammer in itself to the little piece of metal called a nib. The metaphorical coupling between nib and hammer only serves to 'tap' the two domains involved. It was already assessed that the nib metonymically refers to writing. More precisely it refers to the press, and even more precisely to *de Volkskrant* – the latter two specifications being due to the anchoring text. The hammer, on the other hand, metonymically refers to the alarm clock and is itself the part of it that is responsible for the noise. The connotation of the hammer/alarm clock that is transferred can thus be described as 'causing somebody to wake up'. In the mapping on to the domain of *de Volkskrant*, this connotation must be adapted, since a newspaper does not *literally* wake one up: the search for an interpretation consistent with the principle of relevance helps the audience realize that *de Volkskrant* somehow makes one wake up *figuratively*, alerts one to events in the world, arouses one from the fake world of dreams, etc. Once the 'bridge' between the domains of the primary and the secondary subject has been established, it is possible to expand on the mappings. Thus, one could remark on the fact that the alarm clock depicted is an old-fashioned one compared to the modern digital types. Now the feature 'being old-fashioned' in itself can have both positive and negative connotations. In its positive interpretation we understand 'being old-fashioned' as suggesting high quality, a refusal to give in to the fads of the day, reliability, etc. Negatively interpreted, 'being old-fashioned' suggests low quality, rigidity, a refusal to yield to modern insights and improvements. I would predict that the two genre-bound, strong implicatures of any advertisement ('this is an advertisement for brand X'; 'this ad makes a positive claim for brand X' – see page 104) favour the former interpretation of 'being old-fashioned' – although a

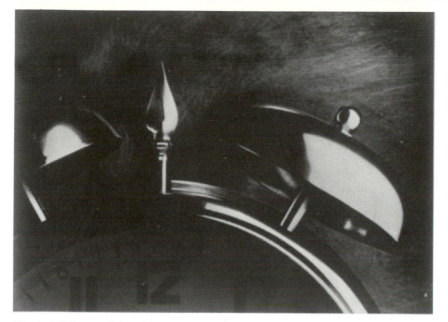

Figure 6.8 Source: Advertising agency: PPGH/JWT

subversive reading (see pages 189ff.) would reverse this. Of course the feature 'being old-fashioned' – and no doubt there are others – is less strongly implicated. The anchoring textual element 'morning paper', incidentally, is relevant here in a specific sense, since alarm clocks are associated with mornings rather than evenings. This, then, would be an example where pictorial information to some extent anchors verbal information as well as vice versa: thanks to the picture, the otherwise neutral word 'morning' is foregrounded.

In the pictorial metaphors considered hitherto, the primary subject each time was either the product itself or something that metonymically referred to the product. Moreover, this primary subject was each time *pictorially represented* (SHOE, SWEETCORN SEEDS, BEER BOTTLE, PETROL NOZZLE, TICKET [2x], NIB respectively), while the secondary subjects were *not* pictorially represented, but univocally suggested by the context (TIE, WINE, CHAMPAGNE, GUN, DECK CHAIR, SKI JUMPING SKIS, HAMMER respectively). As we saw, this is in no way surprising: most advertisers like to have their product visually represented in their ads. It is thus tempting to formulate a rule based on this: in a pictorial metaphor where only one of the two terms is visually represented while the identity of the other is suggested by the pictorial context, it is the visually represented term that is the metaphor's primary subject. Such a rule would help us routinely assess the distribution of primary and secondary subject. However, while in the majority of cases this is indeed what happens there are exceptions. Consider Figure 6.9. In this billboard for Dunlop tyres we see instead of the expected TYRES the unexpected LIFE BUOYS. We know TYRES to be the other term of the metaphor because of the relevant pictorial context – the car. The order of the terms is inferred from the name of the advertiser, 'Dunlop tyres' (the advertisement is for tyres, not for life buoys), so that the verbalization of the metaphor is TYRES ARE LIFE BUOYS. The feature projected from secondary subject upon primary subject is 'providing safety'. The rest of the pictorial context, the rather grim weather, suggesting storm and rain, possibly allows us to label the feature projected even more specifically as 'providing safety against water'. If so, this illustrates the familiar Blackian theme that often a degree of adaptation or translation is involved in the projection of features from secondary upon primary subject. The water in which a LIFE BUOY would provide safety is, say, a sea; the water against which TYRE would be a safeguard is rain.

This example differs in one important respect from those discussed above: it is here the secondary subject of the metaphor instead of the primary subject that is pictorially rendered. This unusual billboard – unusual precisely because the advertiser has dared to dispense with visually representing the product or something metonymically related to it – proves that the visual representation of a term does not automatically lead to its being accorded primary subject status. What *does* make us decide, then, that TYRES is the primary subject of the metaphor? To some extent the answer seems to be the anchoring verbal context 'Dunlop tyres'. In a larger sense this can of course be phrased in terms of the principle of relevance. Knowing that this is an ad for Dunlop tyres we realize that Dunlop wants to make a claim for tyres in terms of life buoys rather than the other way round.

Figure 6.10 is a German ad for a well-known brand of genever (Dutch gin). In a scene with what seem to be a number of typical Amsterdam houses along a canal, one of the houses has been replaced by a bottle of gin. The heading can be translated as 'Finally in Germany, too, old house?' Since the ad is for gin, the verbalization of the metaphor would be, in its most basic form, BOTTLE OF GIN IS HOUSE, or in a more detailed version, BOTTLE OF DUTCH GIN IS OLD DUTCH HOUSE. For an interpretation of the metaphor, a closer look at the body-copy is required. The body-copy runs, in approximate translation:

> Clear, savoury, strong. For one hundred and fifty-four years the Dutch have jealously guarded it. Now it is available in this country as well: Holland's number one gin, Oude Bokma Genever. Prosit, Cheers.[5]

The picture not only suggests the typical Dutchness of the genever, but also the virtual impossibility of 'rausrücken', (literally: 'taking [it] out'), these two features both being exploited in the transfer from 'typically Dutch canal house' to 'bottle of Dutch gin': just as you find this kind of house only in Holland, so you find this kind of drink only in Holland; just as it is

Figure 6.9 Source: Advertising agency: Abbott Vickers/SMS Ltd.

(virtually) impossible to 'take out' a house from a row of city houses along a Dutch canal, so it is quite something that at long last Bokma is exported outside Holland. Notice that the verbal context plays an important role in the assessment of which feature(s) is/are to be mapped from secondary subject on to primary subject. Incidentally, for a Dutch – or should I say Amsterdam? – viewer (who, of course is *not* the intended addressee of the message!) there may be something oddly conflicting about the typically Amsterdam setting and the fact that the genever is distilled in Leeuwarden, the capital of the Northern province of Friesland. Information about this latter fact is given verbally, on the bottle's label. But the (German) audience that is the envisaged addressee for the ad would presumably not be aware of these niceties, so that this would not jar. Alternatively, it could be argued that, as in TICKET IS SKI JUMPING SKIS (Figure 6.7), the fact that the metaphor occurs in an ad, and hence triggers all kinds of expectations to do with this *genre*, prepares addressees to ignore certain inconsistencies.

Having now examined several advertisements presumed to contain a pictorial metaphor, we can conclude that they all fit Black's theory. In each case it proved possible to answer the three questions deemed crucial for establishing metaphor, i.e., which are the two terms, what is their order, and which feature(s) is/are projected from secondary subject upon primary subject. We can thus summarize the metaphors verbally (see Table 6.2).

Some general observations must be made. First, as we saw, the feature(s) mentioned here as projected is/are often not the only possible one(s). The

Figure 6.10 Source: Advertising agency: Baums, Mang und Zimmermann, Düsseldorf

Table 6.2 Primary subjects, secondary subjects and projected features in pictorial metaphors

Figure	Primary subject	Secondary subject	Projected feature(s)
6.1	shoe	tie	'not functional but designed for aesthetic purposes'
6.3	seeds	wine	'high quality'; 'yielding first-rate products'
6.4	beer bottle	champagne	'high quality'
6.5	petrol nozzle	gun	'being potentially lethal'
6.6	ticket	deck chair	'holiday/exoticness'
6.7	ticket	skis	'holiday'
6.8	nib	hammer	'waking up'
6.9	tyre	life buoy	'providing safety'
6.10	genever bottle	old house	'typically Dutch'; 'difficult to transport'

ones given here can be understood, I hypothesize, in terms of Sperber and Wilson's *strong* implicatures. Besides these strong implicatures there is potentially a whole range of implicatures that are interpreted by some people only, or even by a single perceiver – and thus should count as *weak(er)* implicatures. And even the allegedly strong implicatures to a considerable extent depend on the cognitive context shared only by people with the same (sub)cultural background.

A second aspect we should be alert to is that, in order for these pictorial metaphors to be amenable to discussion, they had to be 'translated' into language. Since there is no perfect, 100 per cent fit between the pictorial and the verbal, a translation might meet with objections. One way in which I have tried to forestall objections is by omitting any adjectives, preferring, for example, SHOE IS TIE to SHOE IS BEAUTIFUL TIE. Obviously, the latter formulation already shows a degree of *interpretation* of the metaphor. By translating the pictorial metaphor into bare A IS B form, however, I think the rendering of the metaphor is fairly uncontroversial. Even so, discussion as to how precisely the two terms of the pictorial metaphor are to be labelled remains possible. It is furthermore to be noted that the metaphors have been verbalized as NOUN IS NOUN. This stands to reason: after all, the primary and secondary subjects encountered were all physical objects, and hence capable of depiction. But this should not be taken to mean that the pictorial metaphors preclude actions, typically associated with verbs. As we have seen, the two objects/nouns involved in the metaphor in turn trigger considerations of what one can do with the objects involved, or what they themselves can do. The depiction of a gun suggests the possibility of killing or committing suicide; skis are connected to skiing; an alarm clock's hammer with making a noise, waking up – and all these actions associated with the secondary subject are candidates for metaphorical mapping on to the target domain.

At this stage I have established that in all but one of the metaphors hitherto discussed the pictorially present term of the metaphor is the primary subject; that the primary subject is, or metonymically refers to, the product advertised; that the pictorially absent term is unambiguously suggested by the pictorial context; that if the pictorial context should leave us in doubt as to which term is the primary subject and which the secondary subject, we need only *one* element from the next layer of context to resolve this doubt, namely, a realization of what the product is; and finally that there is a projection of identifiable and nameable features from the source domain upon the target domain, although – in accordance with the insights of relevance theory – not all features will be seen as transferrable with equal strength, nor will precisely the same features be deemed transferrable by all addressees.

CASE STUDIES: METAPHORS WITH TWO PICTORIALLY PRESENT TERMS (MP2s)

Hitherto I have examined advertisements containing metaphors in which only one term of the metaphor was pictorially present. There are also advertisements, however, which contain metaphors that feature both terms pictorially. Figures 6.11 and 6.12 show fairly straightforward examples. In Figure 6.11 we easily recognize the two terms of the metaphor as EARTH and CANDLE, both of which have been partially depicted. There is no pictorial context which might help us establish beyond doubt the order of the terms, so we have to consult the anchoring verbal context to decide which of the terms is the primary and which is the secondary subject. The heading itself ('We extract energy from the earth as if it were inexhaustible') and the information (in small print at the bottom) that the authority which, in 1976, commissioned this warning advertisement was the Dutch Ministry of Economic Affairs suggest not only that EARTH is the primary subject of the metaphor, but also supplies the feature mapped from the secondary subject CANDLE on to the primary subject EARTH: 'providing an exhaustible amount of energy'.

Figure 6.12 (originally in black and white), a Dutch advertisement of the late seventies, provides another fairly clear example. Both terms have been depicted, the BRICKS in their entirety, the EARPHONES only partially, namely, in the electrical cord and the part of the earphones that goes over the man's head. The EARPHONES refer to the product advertised and thus occupy the primary subject position, leaving the secondary subject position for the BRICKS. The metaphor, then, is EARPHONES ARE BRICKS. The heading translates as 'Most earphones have one big disadvantage', reinforcing the feature transferred from secondary subject to primary subject – heaviness. Notice that the primary subject's referent is obviously earphones of a kind that are *not* promoted by the manufacturer. This example proves therefore that a primary subject can also refer *antonymically* to the product advertised.

The metaphor in Figure 6.13 belongs to the same series of advertisements as those in Figures 6.6 and 6.7. As, however, part of the Indian headdress is pictorially present in the small part dangling beside the Indian's ears, this metaphor, unlike the other ones, is strictly speaking a metaphor with two pictorially present terms (from now on abbreviated as MP2). Note that INDIAN HEADDRESS does not at all, in itself, connote 'holiday'; it is the verbal context which activates or rather creates this connotation. Furthermore the secondary subject in Figure 6.13 connotes 'holiday' only for a certain audience, say a European, adult audience living in the latter half of the twentieth century. This shows once more that pictorial metaphors, like their verbal counterparts, are embedded in, and dependent on, a cultural context.

In a billboard for *de Volkskrant* (Figure 6.14, originally in black and white) from the same series as Figure 6.8, we see a bunch of keys with one key that deviates from the rest, since it does not end in a bit but in the by now familiar nib. The metaphor would here be NIB IS KEY. The concept KEY evokes a domain that contains connotations such as 'lock', 'locked space', 'space that one is not allowed to enter', 'guard', 'private property', etc. With a key one can gain access to a space that otherwise will remain closed and, vice versa, with a key one can deny access to others. Thus it is the feature 'enabling one to open a space that otherwise remains closed' that is central in the concept KEY and seems to be amenable to projection upon the target domain NIB (itself, as we saw, metonymically linked to 'de Volks-krant'). As so often, the matching process between source and target domain requires a degree of adaptation. Again, the anchoring text provides help in this process. Thus the 'closed space' from the source domain in the target domain becomes, presumably, 'information that is difficult to obtain' or 'information that some people try to suppress'. Unlike the earlier Volkskrant metaphor (Figure 6.8), the present one features (elements of) *both* terms pictorially: both the KEY and the NIB are partially depicted. As was observed with reference to Figure 6.8, it is the text that reveals the name of the product advertised and hence supplies the primary subject of the metaphor ('de Volkskrant'), but it also thereby helps steer the interpretation of the metaphor. This can be gauged by imagining the text to be replaced by 'Amnesty International'. Precisely the same picture would then lead to a rather different interpretation. The awareness of the reader – either already existent or enhanced by an extension of the anchoring text – that Amnesty encourages people to write letters of protest to authorities in countries that are known to imprison and torture critics of the regime could then lead to an interpretation like: 'Writing letters could help release political prisoners'.

The last example of pictorial metaphor to be discussed in this section is a British billboard. It will be instructive first to consider the doctored, incomplete version in Figure 6.15. Perhaps at this stage it is already possible to identify to some extent the two terms of the metaphor: PARKING METER and ?DYING/?DEAD/?SICKLY CREATURE, but I suspect no addressee coming fresh to this version of the billboard would be able to decide on their order, let alone determine what features are projected from secondary

Figure 6.11 Source: Advertising agency: McCann-Erickson

Figure 6.12 Source: Advertising agency: KVH/GGK

Figure 6.13 Source: Advertising agency: HCM

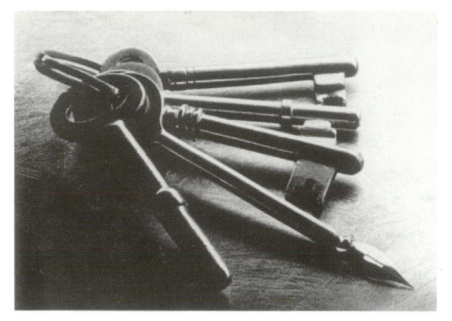

Figure 6.14 Source: Advertising agency: PPGH/JWT

subject upon primary subject. Once the addressee is informed that the heading inscribed above the pictorial hybrid is 'Starve a meter',[6] this verbal foregrounding of METER might lead to the hypothesis that PARKING METER is the primary subject of the metaphor. Furthermore, the anchoring imperative 'starve' suggests that the creature is dying rather than ill or already dead. The metaphor would then run PARKING METER IS DYING CREATURE. Even at this stage the metaphor does not yet make sense. Why should the meter be starved? What is this an advertisement for? The complete version of the billboard helps out (Figure 6.16). Once it is clear that the billboard was commissioned by the London Underground, the addressee is capable of understanding the ad as a whole. What features are projected from the domain of DYING CREATURE upon that of PARKING METER? From among the numerous features that cling to the concept DYING CREATURE (many of them, again, culturally determined) the principle of relevance here induces the addressee to select the crucial one that if a creature is not fed, it dies – an interpretation that is reinforced by the reference to 'starving'. Projected upon the domain of PARKING METER, giving or withholding food is transformed into giving or withholding coins. A parking meter, after all, 'feeds' on coins. There may, of course, be other features but, as always in metaphors, not all of them are projectable. A feature in the domain of DYING CREATURE that is probably *not* intended for projection is 'evoking pity'. Since the communicator is London Underground, it is not

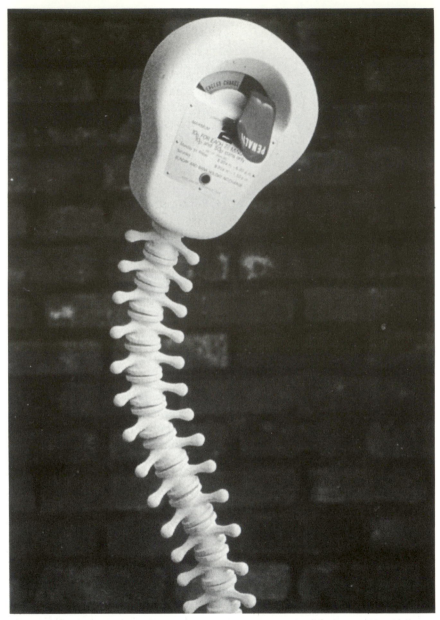

Figure 6.15 Source: doctored version of Figure 6.16

likely that she wants her addressees to feel pity for an object that is metonymically associated with her great competitor, the car. Analogously to Figure 6.12, incidentally, the primary subject of the metaphor is metonymically associated with something that is emphatically *not* advertised. Here too, then, the primary subject refers contrastively to the product advertised.

IS THERE A FUNDAMENTAL DIFFERENCE BETWEEN MP1s AND MP2s?

In the preceding sections, I made a distinction between pictorial metaphors with one pictorially present term (MP1s) and those featuring (parts of) both terms (MP2s). But to what extent does this reflect a clear-cut division? Let us look once more to, for instance, Figures 6.1, 6.4, and 6.11, and test whether these MP1s could be reconceptualized as MP2s, that is, as metaphors featuring (parts of) both terms. I would argue that in the case of SHOE IS TIE we would have to take recourse to a strained rendering like MAN'S TORSO-WITH-SHOE IS MAN'S TORSO-WITH-TIE; GROLSCH IS CHAMPAGNE would be rephrased as COOLER-WITH-GROLSCH IS COOLER-WITH-CHAMPAGNE; and TYRES ARE LIFE BUOYS could be 'transformed' into WHEELS ARE LIFE BUOYS. As this would mean that now the MAN'S TORSO-WITH-SHOE, the COOLER-WITH-CHAMPAGNE and the WHEEL are (partially) depicted, and hence that both terms of the metaphor are pictorially present, we would have to say that the metaphors belong in the MP2 category.

Now I have stated before that the verbalizations employed are no more than approximations designed to render into language what is presented pictorially, and that other formulations are therefore conceivable. Here, however, we are talking about something different than minor variations in the wording chosen to render the pictorial metaphors. The two verbalizations reflect different ways of *experiencing* the metaphors under consideration. The issue is, 'what belongs to the metaphor, and what belongs to its context?' The question whether one of each of the pairs quoted above is a more adequate verbalization than the other is therefore by no means a trivial one. If the answer is negative the entire distinction between MP1s and MP2s is irrelevant; but if we feel that one verbalization is a more appropriate characterization of what we 'perceive' than another, this tells us something about the ways we channel our perceptions into categories and concepts.

I cannot adduce decisive evidence, but I contend that in all three cases the alternative formulations suggested seem to miss the point of the metaphor: what matters in the advertisements is the shoe rather than something like 'man's torso-with-shoe'; Grolsch beer rather than Grolsch-in-a-cooler; the tyre rather than the wheel (the advertiser promotes *tyres*, not wheels). Thus it appears to make sense to stick to the original verbalizations.

When re-examining the metaphors which were classified as MP2s, we discover that, conversely, these are technically open to conversion into MP1s. Thus, the MP2 EARTH IS CANDLE (Figure 6.11) could also be rendered as UPPER PART OF EARTH IS UPPER PART OF CANDLE, and EARPHONES ARE BRICKS (Figure 6.12) as EAR-COVERING PARTS OF EARPHONES ARE BRICKS. In the case of the Indian headdress advertisement (Figure 6.13) we might opt for the rephrasing TICKET IS UPPER PART OF INDIAN HEADDRESS. Here again, however, I maintain that the original verbalizations render the metaphors more adequately, since the alternative verbalizations draw attention to irrelevant information. I will therefore tentatively conclude that although often different verbalizations are available to render the pictorial metaphors, there is one 'privileged' plane on which the two terms/concepts most meaningfully interact.

Confirmation of the idea of a privileged plane can be found in Lakoff's notion of 'basic level' categorization (1987: 37ff. *et passim*), which will be briefly addressed here. Drawing on research done in a wide variety of fields, Lakoff concludes that in their categorizing activities, people psychologically favour the levels that are in the *middle* of taxonomic hierarchies. It is on this level that people most immediately interact with their environment. For instance, people find the (basic level) category CHAIR more immediately useful than either the superordinate category FURNITURE or the subordinate category KITCHEN CHAIR. Similarly, the category DOG would be more directly important than either the categories ANIMAL or TERRIER. Lakoff approvingly cites the findings of Berlin and his colleagues with reference to the identification of this intermediate level of categorization:

– People name things more readily at that level.
– Languages have simpler names for things at that level.
– Categories at that level have greater cultural significance.
– Things are remembered more readily at that level.
– At that level, things are perceived holistically, as a single gestalt, while for identification at a lower level, specific details (called *distinctive features*) have to be picked out to distinguish [between different species].
                                    (Berlin *et al.* 1974, paraphrased in Lakoff 1987: 33)

Although the preferred verbalizations of the pictorial metaphors discussed cannot be characterized as typically belonging to the *middle* of a taxonomy, we have something very similar here. First, the privileged namings indeed tend to be both more intuitively and linguistically simpler than the rejected alternatives. MAN'S-TORSO-WITH-TIE is undoubtedly less often – if at all – used as a unit than TIE, and is correspondingly more difficult grammatically: a simple noun versus a noun phrase containing two modifications. Second, the preferred levels reflect categories that have greater cultural significance. The unit MAN'S-TORSO-WITH-TIE is a less striking cultural one than TIE. The latter is a far more common topic in social intercourse than the former. Third, and of particular importance where depiction is concerned, TIE is presumably seen as an entity, a holistic structure, a gestalt-like unit, while MAN'S-TORSO-WITH-TIE is not. Similar reasoning holds for EARPHONES versus EAR-COVERING PART OF EARPHONES; CANDLE versus UPPER PART OF CANDLE; INDIAN HEADDRESS versus UPPER PART OF INDIAN HEADDRESS; GROLSCH BEER BOTTLE versus GROLSCH BEER BOTTLE-IN-COOLER. And what about TYRE versus WHEEL? Are these not more or less equally basic? Here, I would

Figure 6.16 Source: Advertising agency: Foot, Cone & Belding

contend, the general idea of privileged, basic levels is complemented by the notion of relevance already indicated: the ad is one for TYRES, not WHEELS.[7]

To further support the claim that the subdivision into MP1s and MP2s is a valid one, it may finally be added that the distinction has a parallel in verbal metaphors, namely in the opposition between *metaphor in praesentia* and *metaphor in absentia*. Ricoeur (1977: 186) gives the examples 'Jim is an ass' and 'What an ass!'. In the first sentence both primary subject and secondary subject are given; in the second sentence the primary subject is not given and must be recovered from the context. There is one crucial difference between the verbal metaphor in absentia and the MP1 metaphors examined above, however: whereas in the verbal specimens it is the primary subject that must be recovered from the context, in pictorial ones, as we have seen, this is usually the secondary subject.

But does a comparison between Figures 6.6, 6.7 and 6.13, and between Figures 6.8 and 6.14 not make the entire subdivision seem trivial? According to my classification Figures 6.6, 6.7, and 6.8 contain MP1s, while Figures 6.13 and 6.14 contain an MP2 just because a part of the secondary subject INDIAN HEADDRESS (in Figure 6.13) and of KEY (in Figure 6.14) happens to be pictorially present. But it is clear that the advertisements (and the metaphors they contain) are based on the same idea. Granting all this, we are nonetheless left with one important technical difference between MP1s and MP2s. Whereas in MP2s no contextual features (pictorial or verbal) are necessary to establish the identity of the two terms of the metaphor, in MP1s contextual features are indispensable to establish the identity of one of the terms, namely the pictorially absent term of the metaphor. This, of course, is no different from the situation in verbal metaphor. In Ricoeur's 'Jim is an ass' both terms are given, and no context is needed to assess the identity of each of them, whereas in '[What an] ass!' situational context is needed (in effect: information that provides an answer to the question who the exclamation 'Ass!' is referring to) to make this ass(!)essment. I propose therefore that in their most plausible verbalizations some metaphors have one pictorially present term, while others have two pictorially present terms, and thus that neither of the categories can be incorporated into the other.[8]

CASE STUDIES: PICTORIAL SIMILES

In the three previous sections a distinction was made between pictorial metaphors with one pictorially present term (MP1s) and those with two pictorially present terms (MP2s). In the former type one of the terms (usually the secondary subject) is itself pictorially absent but unambiguously suggested by the pictorial context. In the latter type the two terms are conflated into a hybrid phenomenon pictorially featuring parts of both terms. But this dichotomy does not exhaust the possibilities.

Consider Figure 6.17. It features a picture, part of a German advertisement for swimwear, in which a girl in a bathing suit and a dolphin are depicted next to one another, in mid-air, apparently in the process of diving into the water. The positions of girl and dolphin are strikingly similar; moreover, the resemblance between the dolphin's smooth skin and the girl with her well-fitting bathing suit is emphasized by the identical angle of light on both of them; and one can perceive a further, less emphatic similarity between the dolphin's fin and the girl's hair sticking out. But the similarity is not just physical: dolphins are known to be good swimmers and to leap up from the water. These various aspects of resemblance invite the viewer/ reader to equate girl and dolphin in much the same way as in the MP1s and MP2s discussed before. Slotting the two terms in the metaphorical primary and secondary subject positions is no problem either: since the picture is part of an advertisement, and the text informs us that the ad promotes swimwear, relevance theory predicts that the bathing-suit-wearing girl is a more probable candidate for the primary subject position than the dolphin. Features that qualify for mapping from the domain of DOLPHIN on to the domain of GIRL are 'smooth skin' (adaptable to 'bathing-suit-as-second-skin' or 'perfect fit' in the target domain), 'beauty and elegance', and 'naturalness'.

Figure 6.17 is not an isolated example. The same line of reasoning can be pursued for Figure 6.18, which appeared in a Dutch magazine. Here the two phenomena juxtaposed are BUTTERFLY and WATCH. Since Lassale watches are the product advertised, WATCH is the primary subject and BUTTERFLY the secondary subject. At least one of the features projectable from BUTTERFLY to WATCH is suggested in the pay-off: 'The profile of elegance'.

Although Figure 6.19, a Dutch ad, is more complicated, it seems to me that it should be ranked together with the preceding figures. The pay-off can be translated as 'But we have Dommelsch [beer]', and the two terms compared are BEER CRATES and GREAT WALL OF CHINA.[9] The primary subject, here metonymically associated with the product advertised, is BEER CRATES, whereas GREAT WALL OF CHINA is the secondary subject. It is to be noticed in this advertisement that it is the *dis*similarities as much as the similarities that count here, as the contrastive 'but' of the text emphasizes. One of the features of GREAT WALL OF CHINA that is projected upon DOMMELSCH BEER is probably 'famousness', 'prestige', and/or 'national pride'. Dutch Dommelsch beer, we can interpret, resembles the Great Wall of China in having (or deserving?) a similar kind of national fame, prestige or pride. Simultaneously the dissimilarity between GREAT WALL OF CHINA and DOMMELSCH BEER is stressed: Holland cannot boast an architectural project as renowned as the Chinese Wall. It is to be added that the idea that the Dutch should not lose any sleep over that ('well, so what – after all we have good, typically Dutch Dommelsch Beer') plays an important role in the dissimilarity.

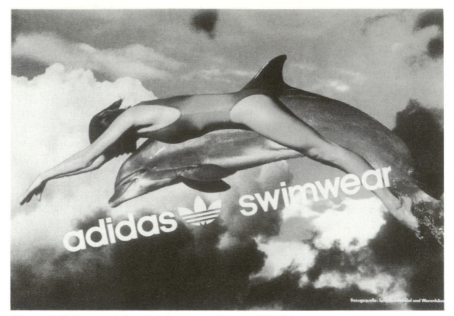

Figure 6.17 Source: Advertising agency: Young & Rubicam

The three advertisements discussed in this section, then, can be analysed in the same way as the MP1s and MP2s investigated earlier. Nonetheless they differ in a technical manner from both MP1s and MP2s. Let us first consider more precisely how they are distinguishable from MP1s. The label MP1 was reserved for metaphors where one of the terms was pictorially absent but unambiguously suggested by the pictorial context. Stripping the ad of all pictorial context made it impossible to infer what the non-depicted term of the metaphor was. In the examples considered in this section, however, both terms have been pictorially rendered, and I contend that the two terms would be seen as similar even if the entire pictorial context were to be eliminated. Hence it would be inappropriate to subsume these examples under the label MP1.

In MP2s, on the other hand, parts of each of the two terms of the metaphor have been depicted; both remain identifiable even if both the pictorial and the verbal context were to be removed. That holds for our present examples, too. But there is one important difference: all the examples labelled MP2s consist of hybrid phenomena that were nonetheless perceived as a single object. The two objects were, in one way or another, physically integrated into a single gestalt. In Figures 6.17–6.19, on the other hand, the two phenomena compared are clearly separate entities.

Since the examples discussed in this section are technically different from MP1s and MP2s, they deserve a label of their own. One attractive possibility

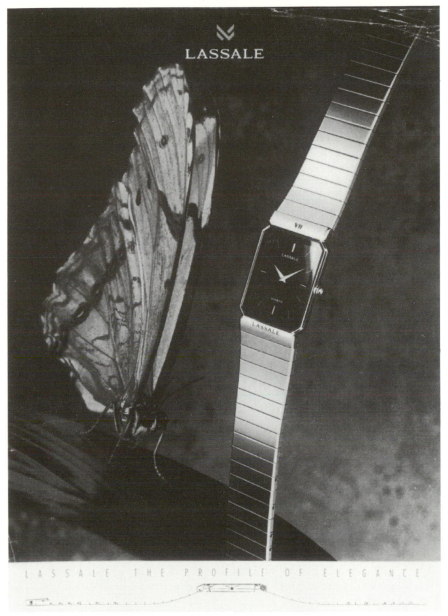

Figure 6.18 Source: Advertising agency: Campaign Company

Maar wij hebben Dommelsch.

Figure 6.19 Source: Advertising agency: Noordervliet & Winninghoff/Leo Burnett

is to call them 'pictorial similes'. In the following paragraphs I want to explore whether this suggestion can be formally supported. For the label 'pictorial simile' to be acceptable, the phenomena in Figures 6.17–6.19 should somehow correspond to MP1s and MP2s in a way analogous to the correspondence between verbal simile and verbal metaphor. Let us consider whether establishing this analogy is warranted.

The paradigmatic verbal metaphor takes the form 'A IS B'. However, as the examples 'the brook smiled' and 'rusty joints' (Chapter 2) showed, a form of the verb 'to be' is not necessarily literally present in a verbal metaphor. Thus, the two metaphorical terms are connected by TO BE on a cognitive rather than, necessarily, on a verbal level. Put differently, on a cognitive level a metaphor always takes the form 'A IS B'. But as was argued in Chapter 2, the same holds for verbal simile: on a cognitive level, the verbal simile 'A is like B' has the same form as verbal metaphor – A IS B (see Wheelwright 1962: 71; Ortony 1979: 188–9; Cooper 1986: 143; Kittay 1987: 17–18; and Lakoff and Turner 1989: 133 for similar views on the fundamental sameness of metaphor and simile). This leaves uncontested, however, that there is a difference between the *manifestations* of verbal metaphors and similes: the latter are expressly signalled by the occurrence of certain phrases (e.g., 'like', '(such) as'), whereas these are absent in verbal metaphors. Hence, the question whether it makes sense to label Figures 6.17–6.19 'pictorial similes' depends on whether they can be said to exemplify a pictorial counterpart of this verbal 'like' and any effects that this 'like' may have on interpretation. Now while the precise relationship between a verbal metaphor and its corresponding simile is by no means a foregone conclusion, the following observations have been made about their differences:

A simile is weaker than its corresponding metaphor. In a short passage on metaphors and similes, Black notes:

> To call, 'Poverty is a crime,' a simile or comparison is either to say too little or too much. In a given context of utterance, 'Poverty is like a crime' may still be figurative, and hardly more than a stylistic variant upon the original metaphorical statement. . . . But to suppose that the metaphorical statement is an abstract or précis of a literal point-by-point comparison, in which the primary and secondary subjects are juxtaposed for the sake of noting dissimilarities as well as similarities, is to misconstrue the function of a metaphor. In discursively comparing one subject *with* another, we sacrifice the distinctive power and effectiveness of a good metaphor. The literal comparison [= simile!] lacks the ambience and suggestiveness, and the imposed 'view' of the primary subject, upon which a metaphor's power to illuminate depends.
>
> (Black 1979a: 31–2)

Similar views are expressed by Ricoeur (1977: 47), Miller (1979: 222), Indurkhya (1992: 27) and Glucksberg and Keysar (1993: 406).

Metaphors suggest a stronger fusion between primary subject and secondary subject than similes. Verbrugge, rejecting the idea that the difference between a metaphor and its corresponding simile is merely stylistic, hypothesized that

> The metaphor form seems more likely to evoke an imaginal experience in which the topic's [i.e., primary subject's] identity is transformed, while the simile is more likely to evoke a process of comparison in which the roles of the two terms are relatively equivalent. If so, the frequency of experiencing fanciful transformations should be greater in response to metaphors than to similes.
>
> (Verbrugge 1980: 108–9)

Verbrugge's intuitions were validated in the experiment he subsequently conducted to test subjects' reactions to metaphors ('A IS B') and their corresponding simile forms ('A is like B'): 'Ceteris paribus, the metaphor form is more likely to evoke a fanciful, directional transformation in which two identities are partially fused' (ibid.: 118).

Thus, similes are considered as weaker and more explicit, as well as to invite fusion between primary subject and secondary subject to a lesser extent, than their corresponding metaphors. To be sure, these characteristics can be seen as aspects of the same underlying intuition. Metaphors are experienced as stronger than similes because the short-cut of the metaphorical 'is' constitutes a less explicit and hence more surprising link than the simile's 'is like'; the metaphorical 'is' to a greater degree suggests transformation of the primary subject by the secondary subject than does simile's 'is like'.

While similes can thus be distinguished from metaphors, they have also often been distinguished from ordinary, literal comparisons. Ortony, who subscribes to the view that metaphors and similes are essentially similar, discusses the difference between similes and ordinary similarity statements in terms of non-literal versus literal comparisons. Juxtaposing 'encyclopedias are like dictionaries' and 'encyclopedias are like gold mines', he argues that in the former the two terms of comparison ('encyclopedias' and 'dictionaries') share high-salient predicates[10] while the latter do not (Ortony 1979: 193). That is, in literal comparisons the two terms would independently of one another evoke a number of the same high-salient predicates (in the present example for instance: 'are a source of information'; 'often appear in the form of a book', etc.) while in non-literal comparisons (similes) they would not. Ortony summarizes:

> In a comparison, 'A is like B', if high-salient predicates of B are also high-salient predicates of A, then the comparison is a literal one and the two referents will be judged as being 'really' similar. If a high-salient predicate of B is a less-salient predicate of A while there are high-salient predicates of B that cannot be applied to A at all, then we have a simile.

If no high-salient predicate of B can be applied to A then the comparison is either uninterpretable, or nonsense (if there is a difference).[11]

(ibid.: 194)

By this criterion, 'encyclopedias are like dictionaries' is a literal comparison, while 'encyclopedias are like gold mines' is a non-literal comparison or simile.[12] Kittay, discussing the difference between comparing the Church to a hippopotamus and comparing the Church to the State reaches a similar conclusion:

Literal comparison takes place within fixed, common, or given categories, for example, when hippopotami are compared to elephants – a comparison within the category of large mammals – or when the Church and the State are compared – a comparison within the category of authoritative and powerful institutions. But comparisons in metaphor and simile cross categorial boundaries.

(Kittay 1987: 18–19)

And Indurkhya, using Ortony's examples, discusses the difference between simile and literal comparison in terms of the degree of unconventionality involved: 'In applying "dictionary" (and its related concepts) to encyclopedias, the degree of unconventionality is much less than in applying "gold mines" to encyclopedias' (Indurkhya 1992: 27).

The crucial question now is whether, and if so how, these observations about verbal similes are translatable to the visual realm, and more specifically to the phenomena in the three advertisements considered in this section. I think that such a translation is possible. In the first place, there is a juxtaposition of the two terms rather than a fusion. In each case, both terms have been pictorially depicted in their entirety, thereby *inviting* rather than *forcing* the viewer to experience one in terms of the other. This clearly contrasts with the MP1s and the MP2s analysed in the previous sections. In MP1s one of the terms (usually the primary subject) physically takes the place of the other term, the latter having a 'ghost-like' presence thanks to the surrounding pictorial context. In MP2s, the two terms have been indeed literally fused into a single hybrid, a 'gestalt'. In both these types, it seems warranted to state that the two terms are in a relation of 'identity', whereas in the case of the type examined in this section the two terms are literally 'juxtaposed'. With some exaggeration one could claim that while the MP1s and the MP2s constitute a spectacularly violent fusion, Figures 6.17–6.19 are better characterized as gentle, explicit comparisons.

However, precisely because of this greater explicitness, it is necessary to establish whether Figures 6.17–6.19 do not, perhaps, simply display the pictorial equivalent of so-called 'literal comparisons' rather than of similes. In Ortony's terminology, the question can be reformulated as whether the mapping involves high-salience predicates from the secondary subject that are not already high-salience predicates of the primary subject. Only if the answer is affirmative is the label 'simile' more appropriate than the label 'literal comparison'. Let us consider Figures 6.17–6.19 in the light of this question. In Figure 6.17, the features identified as among those that are mappable from the domain of DOLPHIN on to the domain of BATHING-SUIT-WEARING GIRL can be rephrased as the predicates 'has a smooth skin', 'displays beauty and elegance', and 'is a natural swimmer'. Are these predicates that would have been spontaneously evoked if Figure 6.17 had occurred without the depicted dolphin? The question is a difficult one, and only permits a tentative answer. Given the fact that the picture as a whole is an advertisement for swimwear, it is certainly possible to defend the claim that some, or all, of these predicates are high-salient ones of the depicted BATHING-SUIT-WEARING GIRL, that is, predicates that would have been elicited even without the DOLPHIN. On the other hand, even if this is correct, at the very least the salience of these predicates is increased by the presence of the DOLPHIN. Thus, for instance the aspect of the 'perfect fit' of the bathing suit would not have been so prominent without the comparison with the DOLPHIN. Moreover, it seems to me that the element of surprise caused by the juxtaposition of BATHING-SUIT-WEARING GIRL and DOLPHIN is mainly due to the fact that we do not ordinarily put GIRLS, not even BATHING-SUIT-WEARING GIRLS, in the same category as DOLPHINS. Hence the comparison crosses categorical boundaries, which, as we saw, is Kittay's criterion for distinguishing metaphor and simile from literal comparison.

Similar reasoning can be applied to the comparison between WATCH and BUTTERFLY in Figure 6.18. Even though in this latter ad the WATCH may in itself evoke the predicate 'is elegant', a predicate which is moreover spelled out in the pay-off, the comparison could still be qualified as a simile rather than as a literal comparison: not only have categorical boundaries been crossed, but the predicate 'is elegant' acquires a special meaning thanks to the presence of the BUTTERFLY. The notion of elegance is the specific one associated with a butterfly, which is a different kind of elegance than that suggested by, say, a dolphin, a fashionable dress, or a brilliant combination in a chess game. Moreover, the secondary subject BUTTERFLY suggests related but different predicates as well, such as 'is beautiful'; 'is vulnerable'; 'is lightweight', etc. – which are not necessarily already high-salient predicates of the Lassale watch.

Figure 6.19, finally, also juxtaposes two phenomena that are not conventionally grouped together. The decision what predicates are mapped from GREAT WALL OF CHINA on to BEER CRATES is complicated, as discussed, by the element of *dis*similarity between the two. If we opt for 'having/deserving fame', then surely this is a predicate that is low-salient or even non-existent in the domain of (DOMMELSCH) BEER CRATES and hence its prominence or even introduction in the target domain is the result of a mapping from the source domain GREAT WALL OF CHINA.

It seems to be warranted, then, to understand the juxtaposed phenomena in Figures 6.17–6.19 in terms of pictorial simile rather than in terms of 'literal' pictorial comparison. However, further research into this distinction, both theoretical and empirical in nature, is necessary. Among the aspects that deserve consideration are the following:

1 To corroborate and refine the analysis of Figures 6.17–6.19 as pictorial similes, it will be helpful to locate and investigate pictorial phenomena, whether in advertisements or in other types of images, displaying a type of comparison which is more appropriately called a 'literal' comparison.
2 The question needs to be asked to what extent the pictorial medium itself affects decisions about the '(non)literalness' of a comparison. While the verbal comparison 'a bathing-suit-wearing girl is like a dolphin' may, due to the fact that the two terms belong to different conceptual categories (i.e., the human versus the animal), be fairly uncontroversially classified as a simile rather than a literal comparison, rendering this comparison in a picture emphasizes prominent *physical* similarities that would not readily occur to a *reader*. The pictorial variant is more appropriately verbalized as '*This* bathing-suit-wearing girl is like *this* dolphin.' As a consequence at least some pictorial comparisons might well strike one as more 'literal' than their verbal counterparts. That is, the importance of ad hoc physical, visual similarity in a pictorial comparison may well overrule the importance of conceptual dissimilarity in its corresponding verbal one. This points to a deeper problem, namely that the concept of 'similarity' itself is as yet insufficiently charted. Gentner is quite right in claiming that studies of metaphor and analogy need 'to make finer differentiations in the notion of similarity' (Gentner 1989: 230).

I want to close this section with two proposals. The first can be made with reasonable reassurance: the phenomenon in the three advertisements discussed in this section is technically different enough from MP1s and MP2s as examined in previous sections to allow this phenomenon a label of its own. The second is to choose for this category a label already familiar from the realm of verbal tropes, namely 'pictorial simile'. This more far-reaching proposal, however, will require further theoretical and empirical substantiation and research.[13]

DISCUSSION

What other observations can be made when we survey the small corpus of pictorial advertisement metaphors and similes investigated? First, a degree of physical similarity between primary subject and secondary subject is often involved. It must be realized, however, that even this physical similarity can only to a limited extent be said to be 'pre-existent'. In several instances, the primary subjects have been bent, folded, cut, rearranged, or modified by other techniques in order to *create* (physical) similarity with the secondary subject. But physical resemblance is by no means a *conditio sine qua non* for pictorial metaphors. For instance, there would seem to be very little intrinsic physical similarity between a nib and the bit of a key (Figure 6.14) or between a watch and a butterfly (Figure 6.18). Thus, when intrinsic physical similarity is largely or entirely absent, identification of the terms, of their order, and of the projected feature(s) depends completely on contextual features. In many cases *location* is a more important factor than physical resemblance. It is because we expect a bit at the end of a key that we are able to establish the correspondence between primary and secondary subjects in the ad referred to. In some cases, however, physical resemblance plays a rather important role. Thus, in Figure 6.9, it seems vital that lifebuoys are round. If lifebuoys happened conventionally to have been square, the advertisers would no doubt have rejected the idea of creating the metaphor TYRES ARE LIFEBUOYS, since square tyres strongly evoke the undesirable connotation of 'not-rolling'. Similarly, the visual effect of the metaphor in Figure 6.10 depends to a considerable extent on the fact that the Bokma bottle, like the houses, is square rather than round.

Second, the role the pictorial metaphors play in the advertisements in which they appear varies widely. In some cases there is a fairly far-fetched relation between the metaphor itself and the message conveyed by the advertisement as a whole. An example is provided by Figure 6.5, where the metaphor (PETROL NOZZLE IS GUN) requires the complement of the verbal message ('Or else buy a Volkswagen') before the advertisement as a whole can be understood. The same holds for Figures 6.12 and 6.16. These advertisements are similar in depicting an undesirable situation and verbally suggesting that this unpleasantness can be avoided by choosing the product advertised instead. But for instance in Figures 6.1 and 6.4 the pictorial metaphor captures the essence of the advertisement message as a whole ('Clerget shoes are so beautiful you ought to wear them proudly where you ordinarily wear your tie'; 'Grolsch beer is as good and prestigious as champagne').

Although it is impossible to quantify the importance of the anchoring role of the text in each case, it is evident that the advertisements investigated differ considerably in the extent to which the text is necessary to clarify the purpose for which the pictorial metaphor in each advertisement was used. In those advertisements where the anchoring function of the text is not very strong, that is, where the textual message reinforces rather than directs or curbs the pictorial message, the pictorial metaphor comes close to being able to stand on its own. Thus I suspect that such ads as Figures 6.1 and 6.4 constitute cases which could be understood even without the anchoring text. Let us try to imagine them without any text and thus without knowing what the name of the product is. There would appear to be two potential clues left to establish the order of the terms. In the first place, as we saw, in many MP1s the present term is, or refers to, the product advertised, and hence constitutes the primary subject. In the case of Figure 6.1, the shoes depicted on the right hand reinforce this idea. However, it was clearly shown in Figure 6.9, where it was the absent term which referred to the product advertised – and hence was the primary subject – that this 'rule' does not work in all cases. But we have a second potential clue. For in most cases only one of the two possible variants A IS B and B IS A makes any sense. If we consider again Figures 6.1 and 6.4, reversing the terms as ?TIE IS SHOE and ?CHAMPAGNE IS GROLSCH, it would in the present (i.e., advertisement) context be difficult to find properties which could be mapped from secondary subject on to primary subject.

It is clear, however, that the ability to sort out the order of the terms presupposes the realization that the metaphors under consideration are part of an advertisement. After all, a particular pictorial metaphor, when displayed in a pop-art collage rather than in an advertisement, might have to be processed with reversed terms. Imagine that we encounter the SHOE/TIE metaphor in a very different context, for instance as an artistic collage in a series where in each collage the tie has been substituted by a different 'alien' object, e.g., a parking meter, a candle, or a genever bottle. The metaphors would in that case probably be understood as TIE IS SHOE; TIE IS PARKING METER; TIE IS CANDLE; TIE IS GENEVER BOTTLE, that is, with TIE in primary subject position. To test these hypotheses, however, empirical research is inevitable.

Surveying the whole corpus of pictorial metaphors and similes hitherto investigated, then, we can state that it is immediately clear (i.e., before consulting the text[14]) to the viewer which the two terms of the metaphor/simile are. In fact, it is only because he recognizes the terms (whether simultaneously present or not) that the viewer is aware of something odd or striking. In this respect, there is no contrast with verbal metaphors – *mutatis mutandis* the following observation by Novitz holds for pictorial metaphors as well: 'It seems plain enough that we can only recognize that an utterance is a metaphor if we know that it should not be taken literally; and this, of course, requires familiarity with the literal meanings of at least some of the words and phrases deployed in the utterance'. Novitz proceeds: 'Equally obvious is the fact that we cannot understand or be appropriately affected by a metaphor unless we are acquainted with the literal meanings of the terms within it' (Novitz 1985: 101). For present purposes we would have to reformulate this last phrase as '. . . unless we are acquainted with the way in which the terms are conventionally used'. Although pictures are certainly more 'international' than words, an understanding of the terms of a pictorial metaphor requires knowledge of the cultural background in which the metaphor is embedded. Looking at Figure 6.13, people from a radically different culture might very well be at a loss because they would be unfamiliar with the concept INDIAN or else associate entirely inappropriate connotations with it – that is, inappropriate for understanding the metaphor.

Finally, I would like to touch briefly on a matter which, although important, has hitherto barely been touched upon. In the previous sections,

I discussed the language-component in the advertisements primarily in its function of 'anchoring' the image and the pictorial metaphor contained in it. On close inspection, however, it transpires that in a number of advertisements there is some sort of *formal* resemblance between the pictorial metaphor contained in it, and some part of the anchoring text, usually the heading. We can witness this phenomenon for instance in the Air France advertisements (Figures 6.6, 6.7, and 6.13). The recurring slogan in these advertisements is: 'Air Fr*ance* Vac*ances*', with an obvious rhyming pattern. I argued that in each of the three advertisements it was the feature 'exoticness' or 'holiday' from the secondary subject – whether DECK CHAIR, SKIS or INDIAN HEADDRESS – which was projected upon the primary subject TICKET. I also claimed that the ticket metonymically referred to the airline company issuing them: Air France. We can now see that the metaphorical relationship between TICKET and its three secondary subjects, the ticket being physically represented in terms of something else, has a verbal parallel in the slogan's phrasing. That is, the pictorial resemblance between ticket and deck chair, skis and Indian headdress respectively, is echoed in the verbal resemblance of *Air France – Vacances*. This observation should serve as a reminder that the overall effect of an advertisement can depend on considerably more than only the pictorial metaphor it contains.

CASE STUDIES: VERBO-PICTORIAL METAPHORS (VPMs)

In the previous sections a distinction was made between MP1s (or pictorial metaphors *in absentia*), MP2s (or pictorial metaphors *in praesentia*) and pictorial similes. In all three types, the two terms were pictorially represented or unambiguously suggested by the pictorial part of the advertisements. However, we can distinguish yet another major variant of pictorial metaphor, namely the variant in which one of the terms is rendered pictorially and one is rendered verbally. Let us consider a number of these verbo-pictorial metaphors (VPMs) more closely.

A first example (Figure 6.20) is provided by a Dutch ad for Venco liquorice with the heading 'het zwarte goud' ('black gold'). We need not waver between possible ways of naming the pictorial term; it cannot but be 'liquorice' as there is nothing else pictorially represented. Since LIQUORICE and BLACK GOLD cannot be equated in a literal relationship, the relationship, to make sense, must be a metaphorical one. The next question is, what is the primary subject and what is the secondary subject? Since LIQUORICE rather than BLACK GOLD is the ad's concern – the product the addressee has to be informed about – it is clear that we are invited to conceive of LIQUORICE in terms of BLACK GOLD rather than of BLACK GOLD in terms of LIQUORICE. We can verbalize this metaphor, then, as LIQUORICE IS GOLD, or LIQUORICE IS BLACK GOLD. Having identified the two terms of the metaphor as well as assessed their order, we now have to determine what is or are the feature(s) projected from secondary upon primary subject. It is possible, of course, simply to focus on GOLD, with as its outstanding property 'being valuable' – this being one of the dominant connotations of GOLD – and consider the adjective 'black' to have been added solely because of its appropriateness to liquorice. I suspect, however, that for many viewers/readers the collocation 'black gold' evokes more specific connotations. Both in Dutch and in English, the phrase in one of its senses refers, metaphorically again, to coal, and the ad obviously exploits this idea: the physical resemblance between the liquorice and the structure of coal is reinforced by the way the liquorice has been depicted. In this second reading, the property projected from coal upon liquorice draws on the notion of coal as a valuable natural resource. In both readings the crucial property projected from the secondary subject BLACK GOLD upon the primary subject LIQUORICE remains 'being valuable'. Supposing that many viewers/readers will bring to bear the connotations of the 'black gold-as-coal' on their interpretation of the metaphor, it might at first seem strange that the makers of the ad apparently did not worry about the fact that 'coal' also has the property of 'inedibility', which is a rather negative one in this context. (Incidentally, it is probably partly for this reason of avoiding unwanted connotations that the Dutch slogan for a long-running campaign promoting milk was 'Melk, de witte motor' – 'Milk, the white motor' – rather than the more logical 'Melk, de witte benzine' – 'Milk, the white petrol'. After all the idea is that the human body 'runs' on milk, much as a machine (a car?) runs on petrol.) But this apparent carelessness about the negative connotation of inedibility in the liquorice ad is explained away when we consider who are the addressees of this advertisement. The group of addressees is not the general consumer: one would not be likely to have come across this advertisement in a national newspaper, or on a billboard out on the streets. This ad appeared in a trade journal for retailers who had to be persuaded to stock 'Venco liquorice' with the promise that it would yield them a huge profit. Hence, the property 'being valuable' of the BLACK GOLD is far more relevant than the property of 'inedibility' in this situation. Although the body-copy of the advertisement gives some clues as to the target group, at least as important a hint comes from another contextual factor: the journal in which it appeared. Once more we here have evidence for Sperber and Wilson's claim that relevance is always relevance to an individual.

Another example of VPM is found in Figure 6.21, with a heading which could be rendered as 'Instead of dating'.[15] The complete body-copy runs, translated:

> With a BMW motorbike you know what you've got. And with a date that remains to be seen. Of course dating someone [or: a date] can be very attractive. But so is a BMW motorbike.
>
> If, however, you are really looking for a long-lasting relationship, what could be more reliable than a BMW motorbike? A BMW motorbike is what you could call the very opposite of a dayfly.

Figure 6.20 Source: Advertising agency: Young & Rubicam

Figure 6.21 Source: Advertising agency: PPGH/Moussault

For one of its strong points is its life expectancy. It lasts for years. Without ageing quickly. And without high maintenance costs. They are machines of almost indestructible quality.

Moreover, they are comfortable. The rider controls his machine. And not the other way round. What is noticeable is the sense of peace when you're riding on a BMW. You will discover that you are not the only one who wants to ride on a BMW.

That becomes particularly apparent when you find out about the very high trade-in value if you sell it. But that won't happen until much later. First make a test-ride at your BMW dealer's. A date can wait. *BMW makes riding marvellous.*

It seems to me that this intriguing advertisement allows for at least two constructions of the metaphor that it contains. The body-copy suggests that instead of a lover one had better opt for a BMW motorbike. Thus, the metaphor can be provisionally verbalized as BMW MOTORBIKE IS LOVER. Let us first establish the age and gender of the addressee of this 1984 advertisement. Since the reader/viewer is addressed as 'je' rather than as 'u' (the latter the polite form in Dutch; cf. French 'tu' versus 'vous') the addressee is presumably young. Furthermore, although it cannot be definitively proven, I would guess that the addressee is male: the motorbike depicted was typically one ridden by young men rather than women. If we assume this to be correct, then the metaphor's secondary subject LOVER could be narrowed down in either of two ways. The first one is BMW MOTORBIKE IS (MALE) FRIEND. If we take into account that until very recently homosexuality was still too much of a taboo to be openly acknowledged in advertising, we can further hazard the guess that a homosexual reading was not intended (although not impossible). In that case, the background assumptions for this male addressee-oriented ad might be sketched as follows: a young man is always faced with the choice between spending his time with his girlfriend and 'going out with the boys'. In this ad, the BMW is presented as the male friend, to be preferred to a girlfriend, the advantages of the former being elaborately sketched in the body-copy.

However, there is another, and more probable, reading: instead of going out with his girlfriend, the male addressee is invited to explore a similarly exciting, quasi-sexual relationship – the relationship with a BMW motorbike. In this reading the motorbike becomes a kind of rival girlfriend, yielding the metaphor MOTORBIKE IS GIRLFRIEND.[16] The body-copy, then, exploits a number of alleged features from the relationship between the young man and his would-be girlfriend, which are then projected upon the relationship of the young man and his BMW.[17] Remarkably, however, after the opening paragraphs there are almost no further explicit references to the source domain of (relationship with a) girlfriend, but a lot to the target domain of (relationship with a) motorbike. From a metaphorical point of view, this is curious: ordinarily, if a metaphor is used, this is to present the primary subject in terms of the secondary subject, necessitating projections of features from the domain of the secondary subject that transform, or highlight, features in the domain of the primary subject. Here, however, soon after its introduction, the domain of the secondary subject seems to be largely ignored, whereas the target domain is apparently extensively explored on its own. Now this could well mean that the source domain has done its work, and is no longer necessary for further elucidation of the primary subject. The metaphor simply has been exhausted. But although the rest of the body-copy can indeed be read as independent of the metaphor, it is difficult to escape the sensation that the metaphor has not been altogether abandoned – not least because the penultimate line once more refers to the source domain ('A date can wait').

I want to suggest that, in the reading BMW MOTORBIKE IS GIRLFRIEND, after the establishment of the metaphorical correspondence between the two domains, the reader is surreptitiously invited to go on supplying correspondences in the remainder of the text. This, in fact, boils down to something odd: whereas normally the source domain is exploited in order to build up the target domain, here what happens is the reverse. What makes this hypothesis plausible is that it indeed proves *possible* to do this, and hence that there is the hint that the metaphor *could* also be read the other way round – as GIRLFRIEND IS MOTORBIKE: 'For one of its strong points is its life expectancy. It lasts for years. Without quickly ageing. And without high maintenance costs'. (Supply something in the GIRLFRIEND domain like: 'You never know how long a relationship with a girl will last. Moreover she ages (quickly) and it is a costly business to entertain a girlfriend'.) Later on we read that 'the rider controls his machine. And not the other way round'. (Supply something like: 'Girlfriends are always nagging, they always want you to do this, expect you to do that ...') Moreover, 'you will discover that you are not the only one who wants to ride on a BMW'. (Supply: 'Your friends are jealous that you make love to your girlfriend'.) Even the phrase that BMWs have a 'very high trade-in value' is suggestive: 'If you end a relationship with a girl, that's it, but the BMW can be sold and hence does not leave you empty-handed'. If I am right in claiming that such a mapping from the domain of BMW motorbikes on to the domain of girlfriends is suggested, a person processing this mapping is temporarily exploring the metaphor GIRLFRIEND IS MOTORBIKE.[18] It may be observed that due to this latent reversibility,[19] the central metaphor of this very clever advertisement yields a rather offensive image of the concept GIRLFRIEND.

I am aware that the constructions and interpretations of the metaphor in Figure 6.21 may be regarded as far-fetched by some people. Inasmuch as they are idiosyncratic, they will have to count as weak implicatures of the message. But even if only some of my interpretations are granted plausibility, this already suggests that the contextual factors that must be taken into account exceed the limits of the page on which the advertisement is printed. Such considerations as the gender of the addressee and the gender of the would-be LOVER are to a considerable degree suggested by (sub)culturally determined norms and values pertaining to role models. Time is a relevant factor here. What was still (barely?) acceptable in 1984 might well be considered not done today.

In light of this it is interesting to consider Figure 6.22 (original in black and white), a much more recent advertisement for BMW (April 1991), which exploits the same basic idea, but simultaneously introduces a significant variation. Figure 6.22 has as its pictorial part the latest BMW model, but the heading now can be translated as 'This is a personal ad'. The body-copy runs, in free translation:

Disagreeable as this way of making contact may be, here he is, the new BMW K75 RT, hoping to get to know you. That's maybe a slightly unusual way to begin, but there's a reason for it. After all, he is sporty and quite good-looking, even though we say so ourselves. He owes his strong, dynamic character to the three-cylinder engine that even at as far as 3000 revolutions per minute can deliver eighty per cent of the torque.

The K75 RT loves travelling, as his aerodynamically designed fairing

Figure 6.22 Source: Advertising agency: PPGH / JWT

shows. But the motorbike is not only the touristy type. You will often meet him in sports circles as well.

That's why he has carved out a truly brilliant career with the police. For he is not just fast, but also solid and reliable.

The K75 RT is not a drinker. Few others are as economical when it comes to petrol. Moreover he knows when to stop. After all he can come equipped with the special BMW-designed anti-blockage system (ABS) for motorbikes.

He is open to new influences. To give an example, the K75 RT is the first motorbike that can be fitted with a catalytic converter specially developed by BMW.

All in all this attractive type (see photo) is the ideal travelling companion to explore new horizons with.

Please reply immediately, at the address of your nearest BMW dealer.
The new BMW K75 RT.

Here the verbalization of the metaphor would be something like BMW MOTORBIKE IS (PROSPECTIVE) PARTNER. The tone of the ad has considerably changed; the sexually charged macho atmosphere of the earlier ad has here given way to a more open approach, geared to people who see a relationship more as a partnership than in terms of dominance and possession. Moreover, the ad can be read as being aimed at women as much as at men, while there seems to be room for a homosexual reading as well. This no doubt is as much a consequence of changing ideas about the relationships between men and women (and between men and men, women and women) as of the possibility that BMW have discovered that they can increase their sales by appealing to a wider audience.

In the next example of VPM (Figure 6.23), the headline consists of a warning: 'The biggest market for new products'. The pictorial part shows a specimen of the type of dustbin used at the time in Holland. Since the advertisement is one from a marketing agency recommending its own market-research to potential customers, the metaphor can be verbalized as MARKET IS DUSTBIN. The property projected from DUSTBIN upon MARKET is obviously 'used to throw rubbish in'. This metaphor is similar to the TYRES ARE LIFEBUOYS one (Figure 6.9) in that here, too, it is not the primary subject but the secondary subject which is depicted. While in TYRES ARE LIFEBUOYS this could be considered a rather daring move, here it was probably a decision flowing from sheer necessity: after all, it is very difficult to *depict* the concept MARKET. But be this as it may, we have to conclude that just as was the case in purely pictorial metaphors, the question which term is depicted and which is not yields no unfailing criterion for the distribution of primary and secondary subject in a verbo-pictorial metaphor.

Another example of VPM (Figure 6.24) is a highly complex one, showing once more how much a full understanding of advertisements can be dependent on the cultural context. What we see here is a condom in a half-opened

Figure 6.23 Source: Advertising agency: J. Walter Thompson

packet, and underneath it the slogan 'a clever tip from the NVSH'. The NVSH ('Nederlandse Vereniging voor Sexuele Hervorming'), it should be explained, is an institution advocating sexual reform and giving advice on all sorts of sexual matters. Whereas nowadays it leads a fairly dormant life, in the late sixties and early seventies it was a well-known and controversial institution. The heading, which can be translated as 'What about putting on a coat before you go to church?', suggests that condom and coat should be equated[20] – but all this in itself is not sufficient to understand the metaphor, and hence the ad. One has to know that there is an expression in Dutch slang which translates as 'to leave church before the singing' ('voor het zingen de kerk uitgaan') and in a sexual context means 'withdrawing the penis before ejaculation' (i.e., coitus interruptus), usually in order to avoid impregnation.[21] Only when one is aware of this does it become clear that, just as a coat provides protection against rain, a condom prevents another sort of liquid from penetrating. Thus, the metaphor can be verbalized as CONDOM IS COAT. Notice that the feature projected from COAT upon CONDOM is 'protecting against unwanted liquid', and that the aspect of who benefits from this protection cannot be projected: the hypothetical 'churchgoer' is the one who benefits in the literal expression, while it is the 'destination' of the condom-user who benefits (i.e., is 'protected from unwanted liquid') in the metaphorical expression. It also transpires that one should not go too far in mapping features from secondary subject on to primary subject: obviously one is not supposed to derive the more general metaphor WOMAN IS CHURCH. Finally, given the allusion to the expression 'to leave church before the singing' with its connotation of avoiding pregnancy, it is clear that this advert promotes condom-use as a means to avoid pregnancy rather than sexually transmitted diseases. Since nowadays condom-use is increasingly associated with reducing the risk of contracting sexually transmitted diseases, particularly AIDS, this advertisement (1982) recognizably bears the stamp of the pre-AIDS era.

Figure 6.25 is a Dutch billboard for Artis, the Amsterdam zoo. The metaphor can be verbalized as ORANG-UTAN IS MONA LISA. It is intriguing to consider what is/are the features projected from MONA LISA upon ORANG-UTAN. Connotations of MONA LISA that come to mind are for instance 'famous painting', '(supposedly) beautiful woman', 'the often discussed enigmatic smile'. All of these can be adapted to be somehow attributable to the primary subject ORANG-UTAN. Moreover, once the bridge between the domains of primary and secondary subject has been built, it is possible to extend the correspondences to ZOO IS MUSEUM. The principle of relevance, at least, seems to allow this. The implied exhortation could then be something like: 'The zoo is as much worth visiting as a museum' and/or 'The famous Mona Lisa is on display only in a far-away museum; you need only to travel a short distance to come to Artis to see an equally famous/beautiful/interesting/ . . . specimen'. Moreover, the word 'live' in the pay-off perhaps suggests an opposition: 'The Mona Lisa is only a *representation* of a woman: if you come to Artis you will have a chance to admire a *real*

Figure 6.24 Source: Realization: Hans Haselaar, Wim Ubachs, Roel Salomons

Figure 6.25 Source: Advertising agency: FHV/BBDO

monkey.' As for instance in Figure 6.19, the *dis*similarity between primary
and subject thus may play a role as well as the similarity.

Figure 6.26 is an advertisement for BAT tobacco, with the heading 'Die
weiße Geliebte', 'the white lover'. The metaphor here is CIGARETTE IS LOVER.
Like in the first BMW advertisement, the domain of LOVER, more specifically, girlfriend (since the 'Geliebte' is female – 'Sie'), is mined for connotations that are subsequently to be mapped on to the cigarette. The body-copy
begins, translated:

> She entices and makes so many people happy. Gives them happiness,
> gives them pleasure. And in many ways. You can work with her, have a
> good time with her, dream with her. . . . The white lover is very adaptable,
> but simultaneously creates her own kind of atmosphere . . .

Here the features to be mapped on to the primary subject CIGARETTE are
explicitly given in the body-copy of the advertisement.

A final example of VPM to be given here is Figure 6.27 which, despite its
English heading, is a Dutch billboard. The metaphor in it is BOTTLE OF MOBIL
MOTOR OIL IS INTRAVENOUS DRIP. As usual, the primary subject is the term
depicted. The secondary subject, however, is not given verbally as 'drip': rather,
the text 'Intensive Care' is one of the elements belonging in the source domain
of the concept DRIP. In combination with the visual resemblance between the
BOTTLE OF MOBIL MOTOR OIL and a DRIP – itself reinforced by the position of the
BOTTLE and the way the liquid is depicted as pouring from it – the domain of the
secondary subject is sufficiently identified. It is thus enough that the two
domains as such are identified. Once this has been done, it is no problem to
match the corresponding elements in the two domains. Part of the interpretation of the metaphor could thus be, 'Mobil motor oil is the life-blood of
one's car'. This last example also serves to show that the subdivision into
pictorial and verbo-pictorial metaphors is not an absolute one. In principle,
a simple test can be devised to determine whether a metaphor is a pictorial
or a verbo-pictorial one. If one were to delete *all* textual material from an
advertisement, and the two terms of the metaphor could still be identified
(even if their order might not be capable of being established), then the
metaphor in question is a pictorial metaphor or simile. In a VPM, deleting
all text results in disappearance of the metaphor. In the metaphors discussed
in this section, removing the text leaves only a depicted object which is just
itself: liquorice, a dustbin, a motorbike, a condom, a cigarette, an orang-
utan. . . . In terms of Barthes's distinction between the anchoring and
relaying functions of text *vis-à-vis* the picture with which it occurs (see
Chapter 4), the text in VPMs has a strongly relaying function. However,
the example of MOBIL MOTOR OIL IS DRIP is less clear-cut. Arguably, the
bottle of Mobil Oil has been depicted in such a way (bottom-up, with a
slow stream that suggests a thin plastic tube) that even without the text
'Intensive Care' some viewers might be reminded of a drip. Inasmuch as
this is true, the metaphor in this billboard borders on being an MP1.

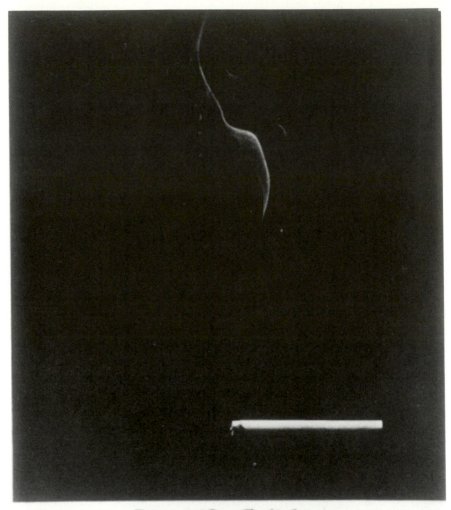

Figure 6.26 Source: Advertising agency: HSR & S

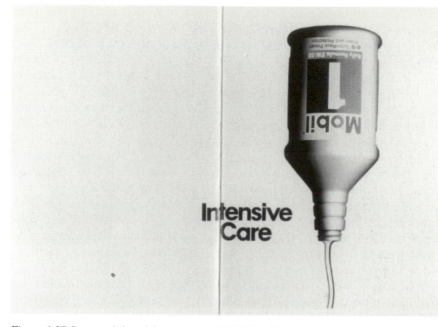

Figure 6.27 Source: Advertising agency: DDB Needham

MORE DISCUSSION

Some more general remarks can be made about the verbo-pictorial meta-phors analysed in the previous section. In the first place, both magazine advertisements and billboards were examined. But there is a difference in the way these two types of advertising are perceived. Obviously, a billboard needs to be taken in at a glance. While there is the possibility, indeed probability, of a viewer being repeatedly exposed to the billboard, each time he is confronted with one the duration of exposure is presumably fairly brief. In a printed ad, the chances are that a reader will spend rather more time. This difference no doubt accounts for the fact that most billboards make sparing use of text, while printed advertisements often contain more verbal information. In terms of the VPMs identified, however, this does not make much difference, since the verbally rendered term (usually the secondary subject) appears in the heading or in the pay-off. While in billboards it is up to the viewer/reader to interpret the metaphor for himself, printed advertisements often provide (partial) interpretations in the body-copy, as we have seen for example in Figures 6.21, 6.22 and 6.26. But even in these latter cases it is possible to arrive at a rudimentary interpretation purely on the basis of picture + heading/pay-off.[22]

Another aspect that deserves commenting on is the role of the *pictorial* context in VPMs. In the examples discussed, it is noticeable that pictorial context is either completely absent, or neutral in nature, which is a marked contrast with MP1s. This makes good sense, of course, since in MP1s the pictorial context is absolutely necessary for the identification of the second term of the metaphor. As the second term of the metaphor is simply physically absent, it is only thanks to the pictorial context that its identity can be recovered, as a comparison between Figures 6.1 and 6.2 made clear. The absence or neutrality of context in most verbo-pictorial metaphors can be largely explained by the fact that the pictorial part of the advertisement is needed to identify only one of the metaphor's terms, the other term being identified by the text. From this perspective one could hypothesize that the ads' makers feel that any pictorial context would only have distracted attention from the pictorially rendered term – and since this term is usually the product itself, it makes good commercial sense to focus entirely on that term. Notice that almost the same argument holds for MP2s: here both terms are rendered pictorially, so that no pictorial context is necessary to identify them. However, both in Figures 6.12 and 6.13 there *is* pictorial context in the form of the man's unhappy face and the Indian-cum-sky-scraper respectively – contextual features that help establish the features 'big disadvantage' (Figure 6.12) and 'holiday' (Figure 6.13). In the simile in Figure 6.19, too, pictorial context contributes to the assessment of what features are projected from secondary upon primary subject. Pictorial context could have been used in VPMs in a very similar manner to suggest one or more projectable features. As we will see in Chapter 7, absence or neutrality of context is probably a characteristic of the specimens of VPM that happen to be considered here, rather than a general characteristic of this type of metaphor.

SUMMARY

In this chapter a number of magazine advertisements and billboards were discussed with reference to the (verbo)pictorial metaphors they were claimed to contain. It was shown that Black's interaction theory of metaphor was applicable to these metaphors, and that their interpretation was guided by Sperber and Wilson's (1986) relevance theory. The three central questions that in the close of Chapter 3 were argued to be crucially important for the determination whether something should be termed a metaphor could all be satisfactorily answered with regard to the phenomena in these advertise-ments. A consideration of various levels of context (verbal, pictorial, cultural) was shown to be essential for the answerability of Black's three questions. Moreover, the fact that the similarity between the two terms of the metaphors usually was a result of the metaphor rather than the other way round corroborates Black's creativity thesis: the similarity between the two terms of a metaphor is often *created* rather than pre-existent. Four sub-types of pictorial metaphor were distinguished, classification depending on the nature of the second term (usually the secondary subject):

1 *Pictorial metaphors with one pictorially present term (MP1s)*. Here the second term is not depicted, but unambiguously suggested by the pictorial context. Removal of the pictorial context results in the disappearance of the second term, and hence in non-metaphor. In most cases the pictorially present term is, or refers metonymically to, the product advertised. Removing the verbal context does not usually affect the identification of the two terms[23] – although it may problematize their characterization as primary and secondary subject respectively.

2 *Pictorial metaphors with two pictorially present terms (MP2s)*. Here parts of both terms are pictorially represented, resulting in a hybrid phenomenon perceived as a single gestalt. Removal of the pictorial context – if present in the first place – still allows the reader/viewer to identify both terms. Removing the verbal context again does not affect the identification of the two terms, although it may problematize their characterization as primary and secondary subject respectively.

3 *Pictorial similes*. Here both terms are pictorially represented in their entirety. Removal of the pictorial context – if present in the first place – still allows the reader/viewer to identify both terms. Removing the verbal context again does not affect the identification of the two terms, although it may problematize their characterization as primary and secondary subject respectively.

4 *Verbo-pictorial metaphors (VPMs)*. Here one of the terms is rendered textually, while the other is rendered pictorially. Removal of pictorial context – if present in the first place – does not affect the identification of the two metaphorical terms. Eliminating the text results in the disappearance of one of the terms, and hence in non-metaphor. In most cases the pictorial term is, or metonymically refers to, the product advertised.

In Chapters 4 and 5 it was claimed that identification and interpretation of the metaphors do not take place solely on the basis of the image and text itself, but are also partially dependent on the identity of the communicator and addressee of the advertisement text, as well as the (sub)cultural context in which the advertisement features.[24] Various metaphors discussed in this chapter were shown to be directed not at the general public, but at a specific target group. Metaphors are often designed to communicate to these specific sub-groups. Relevance theory provides us with several clues in this respect. The awareness that the advertiser is attempting to make a positive claim for the product or service advertised is one factor constraining the possible interpretations of a pictorial advertising metaphor. Within these constraints, the interpretation of the metaphors cannot be definitively and exhaustively given. It seems probable, however, that certain interpretations will be agreed upon by more addressees than other interpretations. These can be understood in terms of Sperber and Wilson's strong and weak implicatures respectively. As in all communication, the communicator of a commercial message, the advertiser, must make an assessment of the cognitive context of her addressees. The choice of metaphor, as well as the interpretations it allows, are hence partly determined by the target audience an advertiser envisages.

The interpretations of the metaphors in the present chapter were by and large my own – although numerous people commented on them in lectures and during presentations at conferences. It would be of interest to obtain more detailed insights into the question how advertisements are interpreted by various individuals. In the next chapter, we will have a close look at the results of an exploratory experiment in which some forty people were asked to respond to three IBM billboards all containing a (verbo)pictorial metaphor.

7 Individuals' responses to three IBM billboards

An exploratory experiment

INTRODUCTION

In Chapter 6 a number of advertisements and billboards containing a (verbo)pictorial metaphor or simile were discussed. While the interpretations offered of these metaphors were intended to be at least plausible, an element of subjectivity on the analyst's part was inevitably involved. The reason why it was nonetheless justified to discuss and interpret the ads as I did, so the argument runs, is that various contextual factors constrain the number of possible interpretations. But even if the validity of this justification is accepted, the question to what extent these interpretations coincide with those of other viewers remains unanswered. If one wishes to offer even the beginnings of an answer to that intriguing question, empirical research is unavoidable. Some work in this area has already been done. Experiments pertaining to the interpretation of metaphors are reported for instance in the articles by Verbrugge, Malgady and Johnson, and Connor and Kogan in Honeck and Hoffman (1980). A weakness in these studies is that they provide the metaphors with no, or a highly abridged, context – a circumstance whose impact on interpretation is insufficiently taken into account, as McCabe (1983) demonstrates with a series of counter-experiments. Generally speaking, there is an increasing awareness that metaphors should be studied in context and not in isolation (see e.g., Fraser 1979; Bosch 1985; McCabe 1988; Gruber 1988; Katz 1992; Forceville 1995b).

Another point that has hitherto received insufficient attention in metaphor studies is the matter of individual subjects' interpretations. What holds for metaphors holds for texts in general: there may be significant differences in interpretation across (groups of) individuals (see Morley 1983; Camargo 1987; Ang 1991; Larsen *et al.* 1991). The importance of this issue was realized by Johnson and Malgady. Reporting on some of their own earlier empirical research on metaphor comprehension, they somewhat worriedly make the following observation:

> The problem comes when you attempt to look at the *content* of the
> interpretations provided by individual subjects, and the *variability* of the

goodness judgments provided by subjects. It is frustrating to realize that even though you can find a great deal of regularity in the way in which *populations* of subjects deal with populations of metaphors, we can say much less about how an *individual* subject will interpret an individual metaphor. When you examine the individual responses that subjects give when they are presented with a word to associate to, or a metaphor or painting to interpret, you find that they usually make sense, even though they show considerable diversity in their content.

(Johnson and Malgady 1980: 263)

An experiment testing seventy-five subjects' responses to the metaphor 'People are doors' (originally reported in Johnson 1978) yielded no fewer than twenty-seven different interpretations:

> What we see here are interpretations *suggested* by the stimuli, but it seems as though stimuli can suggest a great many things. What a metaphor suggests to an individual seems to be somewhat dependent upon that individual, and not something we can predict entirely from an a priori knowledge of the stimulus – except, of course, on a probabilistic basis.

(ibid.)

Here we are on familiar ground: as we saw in Chapter 5, individual variation in interpretations is predicted by Sperber and Wilson's relevance theory. On the one hand the principle of relevance explains why, in most cases, the message intended by a communicator is more or less understood as such by the addressee; on the other hand, as we saw, there is often room for weak implicatures to be derived by the addressee, and the weaker the implicatures are, the more responsibility for deriving them rests with the addressee rather than the communicator. Now the two main communicators in *Relevance* were Mary and Peter, and although Sperber and Wilson never quite satisfy our curiosity about the exact status of their relationship, Mary and Peter obviously know each other quite well. Thus, to sum up an aspect that was discussed at greater length in Chapter 5, it is fairly easy for Mary to make a correct assessment of Peter's cognitive environment. In mass-communication, it was argued, the situation is different. Both the experiments reported by Johnson and Malgady and the situation as it obtains in advertising pertain to the circumstance wherein a fairly anonymous communicator (the experimenters, the advertiser) addresses a relatively anonymous audience (the experiments' subjects; the advertisement's target group).

The point raised by Johnson and Malgady is important enough to warrant closer investigation. In the context of the present book this means that it would be illuminating to have some idea about the responses a specific pictorial advertising metaphor evokes in different people. This chapter aims to provide insight into this matter. Specifically, it reports the results of an experiment in which the responses of two groups of people, one in Amsterdam (The Netherlands) and one in Ghent (Belgium) to three IBM billboards were tested, the three being part of the same campaign and containing a verbo-pictorial metaphor. Two central questions were whether the participants understood the pictorial phenomena in the billboards as metaphors and, if so, to what extent they agreed on the metaphors' interpretations. Thirdly it was hoped to gain insight into the question what associations, if any, the billboards evoked in participants besides those associations the participants thought the ad-makers intended to evoke.

It should be emphasized that the experiment had a highly exploratory character. Although the testing conditions were as strictly controlled as possible, the whole design of the experiment entailed that the participants had to be given considerable freedom in volunteering their responses. This inevitably had an impact on the methodological rigour with which the responses could be evaluated. Moreover, some participants were not completely naive as to the researcher's scholarly pursuits, which may, as will be explained, have influenced their responses. Consequently, some of the results need to be presented with caution. Nonetheless, certain conclusions can be drawn with a fair degree of confidence, while the wealth of data also permits a number of reasoned speculations meriting further empirical research.

BACKGROUND: MICK AND POLITI (1989)

Mick and Politi, questioning the idea that all consumers interpret advertisements in the same way, report the findings of an experiment testing the responses of 17 undergraduate students to a Gordon's gin advertisement. This ad was chosen, as Mick and Politi indicate, for the dominance of visual over verbal material, the supposed relevance of the product advertised to the subjects tested, and its sexual innuendo. The participants were interviewed individually and their responses were taped. Preliminary instructions informed them that the experimenters were interested in their 'natural thoughts and feelings in answering some questions about each ad they were about to be shown' (Mick and Politi; 1989: 87).

After the protocols had been transcribed, one of the authors distilled three themes in the responses given, a theme being defined as 'represent[ing] the central, dominating idea expressed by the subject' (ibid.: 88). Subsequently the authors independently classified each subject's protocol according to the themes identified by the first author. A fourth category was available for subjects expressing no identifiable theme. The experimenters' doubts were indeed confirmed: significant variations in interpretations were found among the participants, the differences between male and female responses being particularly marked.[1]

Mick and Politi's experiment is pertinent for two reasons. In the first place, my own interest in people's responses to metaphors in advertisements can be considered as a more specific variant of Mick and Politi's more general interest in how ads as a whole are interpreted, and in the second place their methodology can easily be adapted to fit present purposes.

HYPOTHESES

The present experiment was intended to shed light on the following hypotheses:

1 The subjects (from now on: participants) are capable of identifying and interpreting the verbo-pictorial metaphors in the three advertising billboards, even though they have not been explicitly instructed to look for verbo-pictorial metaphors. Since a substantial number of the participants were not totally naive as to the researcher's interest in metaphor (see the section in this Chapter on Participants and procedures), the findings with regard to this hypothesis should be taken with appropriate caution.
2 Among the participants interpreting the metaphor there will be considerable, but not unanimous, consensus about the nature of the features projected from the secondary subject upon the primary subject. The former can be profitably rephrased in terms of Sperber and Wilson's concept of a message's 'strong implicatures' while the latter would then be 'weak implicatures' (see Chapter 5). The prediction that different weak implicatures will be processed by different people derives from the claim that 'relevance is always relevance to an individual', entailing that people's personal character, preferences, history, interests, as well as their relation to the communicator, to a degree co-determine their interpretation of messages that allow variations in interpretations.

Both the processing of strong and that of weak implicatures of the metaphors is likely to be influenced and constrained by viewers' awareness of the 'genre' to which the word and image texts under consideration belong, namely advertisements. This knowledge affects and steers the associations perceived as appropriate. More specifically, viewers know that advertisements always intend to sell, and hence make a positive claim about, a product or service (see the beginning of Chapter 4). Consequently, when asked to interpret the billboards in terms of their maker's intentions, viewers are expected to acknowledge the advertiser's aim to make a positive claim about the product advertised.

STIMULUS MATERIAL

Three Dutch IBM billboards were selected as stimulus material (see Figures 7.1, 7.2 and 7.3). The billboards are here reproduced in black and white, but they were presented to the test groups in their original colours. In each of them, one object is depicted in the same blue-and-white striped pattern as the IBM logo underneath the picture. The choice of these billboards was motivated by the following considerations. In the first place they all contain a verbo-pictorial metaphor, i.e., a metaphor in which one of the terms is rendered pictorially, whereas the other is rendered verbally.[2] Secondly, the textual component in each is minimal. In two of the billboards it is restricted to the IBM logo below the picture; in the third, in addition to the logo, a piano in the picture features the letters 'STEIN . . . ' suggesting the famous brand name 'Steinway'. In terms of the anchoring function of text (see the discussion on Barthes in Chapter 4), this means that the anchoring is (virtually) restricted to the logo – although the information transmitted by this logo is of course essential, since it contains the name of the product advertised. Put differently, whatever it is that is conveyed by the billboards, this is triggered to an unusual extent by pictorial elements or (non-verbal) contextual factors. Since we saw in Chapter 4 that verbal (con)text plays a considerable role in guiding and restricting interpretations, it is interesting to see how a metaphor with minimal textual anchoring is interpreted. Thirdly, since the three billboards were part of one campaign, responses lent themselves to easy comparison. Fourthly, there was no need to manipulate the three billboards in any important sense; they could be presented in their original form. The importance of this circumstance can be gauged from criticisms by Kreuz and Roberts. In a review article, the authors mention as one of the weaknesses of many recent empirical studies of the comprehension of metaphor and other forms of figurative language that 'for the most part . . . these studies have utilized artificial texts as stimulus materials' (Kreuz and Roberts 1993: 152). With respect to 'metaphor', which Kreuz and Roberts identify as the most frequently occurring variant of figurative language in their corpus of literary texts, the authors describe the stimulus materials used in most experiments as having been 'typically . . . produced by the experimenters themselves rather than selected from a naturalistic sample, and the dependent measure of choice is typically reaction time, rather than qualitative verbal protocols that tap the comprehenders' interpretations' (ibid.: 155). While experimenters' texts have the advantage of allowing fairly tight control of theoretically relevant variables, there is one great drawback: 'The results may have very little to do with how people actually process real texts' (ibid.: 152). Although the stimulus material in the present experiment is of a pictorial-cum-verbal rather than a purely verbal nature, Kreuz and Roberts' observations are no less pertinent. It is one of the strengths of the experiment, I believe, that the stimulus material used comes very close to what Kreuz and Roberts call 'real-world texts' (ibid.).[3]

A final bonus of the absence of text (apart from the internationally known acronym 'IBM' and the brand name 'Steinway') was that it was possible to present the billboards to non-Dutch participants without any translation being necessary.

The selection of these three particular billboards from the campaign rather than others was partly motivated by the fact that two of them had already been reflected upon in Forceville (1992), in the same vein as in Chapter 6 of the present study. Another consideration that played a role in making the selection was that one billboard (Figure 7.1) supposedly contained a fairly conventional metaphor, while another (Figure 7.3) was expected to be more challenging and to evoke a wider range of responses, while the third (Figure 7.2) was presumed to be of medium conventionality.

METHOD

The method followed in my experiment is based on Mick and Politi's (1989).[4] A difference between the experiment presented here and that carried out by Mick and Politi is that individuals were not assessed individually and orally, but collectively and in writing, so that relatively many participants could be processed in a brief time span. A second difference is that while Mick and Politi presented an ad and then asked all four questions about it, then presented a second ad and asked the same four questions, and so on, in the experiment reported here participants were asked to answer question 1 for each of the three billboards; subsequently they were asked to answer question 2 for the same three billboards, etc. The reason was that participants should give their responses to each question without knowing what the next question would be, since otherwise their responses to the second and third billboard might have been affected by what they knew would be the next questions. A price was paid for this: since all three billboards were from the same campaign and designed on the same basic pattern, a learning effect very probably took place *within* the time span of answering the first question. This was not considered problematic.

All participants were given a ten-page questionnaire. The cover page contained instructions explaining to the participants that the aim of the experiment was to gain information about the way advertising billboards were interpreted. They were informed that they would be presented with three billboards four times, and that each time they would be asked a different question about them, each billboard being on display during two minutes each time. At the end of the experiment the participants were requested to fill in an information sheet attached to the questionnaire.

The four questions asked were adapted from those asked in Mick and Politi's experiment, and ran as follows:

Question 1 : 'Describe in your own words billboards A, B, and C.'
Question 2 : 'Ignore what the advertiser may have meant by billboards A, B, and C, and describe point by point the personal feelings and associations each of the billboards' pictures evokes in you. Could you please indicate how important you find each of these feelings and associations by preceding the most important one by the number 1, the second-most important by the number 2, etc.? If you consider several

Figure 7.1 Source: Advertising agency: GGK Amsterdam

Figure 7.2 Source: Advertising agency: GGK Amsterdam

Figure 7.3 Source: Advertising agency: GGK Amsterdam

feelings/associations equally important, you can indicate this by marking each of these with the same number.'
Question 3 : 'What do you think the advertiser has wanted to communicate with each of the billboards A, B, and C? If the message in your view has several aspects, could you then please indicate the relative importance of each aspect by marking the most important aspect with the number 1, the second-most important by the number 2, etc.? If you consider several aspects equally important, you can indicate this by marking each of these with the same number.'[5]
Question 4 : 'What proof or evidence do you find in each of the billboards A, B, and C to support your ideas about what the advertiser has wanted to communicate?'

Each question was printed on a different page which further contained the phrases 'Billboard A', 'Billboard B', 'Billboard C', equally spaced out, leaving room to write down responses under each of them. The pages with questions were separated by a page containing the text 'PLEASE DO NOT TURN THIS PAGE UNTIL THE PROJECT LEADER ASKS YOU TO DO SO'. Participants were allowed to turn back to previous questions and expand on their answers, provided they indicated later additions with an asterisk (*).
    The last page contained a number of questions relating to personal

information concerning the participants. Participants were invited to write down their name (not compulsory), give an approximation of their age, as well as indicate their gender, nationality (in the group in Ghent), and current type of work/research. Furthermore participants were asked (1) whether they had seen one or more of the billboards before; (2) what product or service they thought was advertised in the billboards shown; (3) whether the product or service advertised was relevant to them; and (4) what, if anything, they knew about the experimenter's research project. Finally, they were given an opportunity to write down any additional comments they wished to make.

PARTICIPANTS AND PROCEDURES

The experiment was carried out twice, once in Amsterdam (The Netherlands) and once in Ghent (Belgium). In Amsterdam, the participants were eighteen members of the Faculty of Arts at the Vrije Universiteit, both post-graduates and members of staff. Prior to their participation in the experiment, they had listened to two papers on word and image relations. They had been told that I would give a paper on 'responses to advertisements'. The instructions and questions were in Dutch. Two non-native speakers asked whether they could answer in French and English respectively, which was permitted.

In Ghent the experiment was carried out during the annual conference of the Poetics and Linguistics Association 1992. The experiment took place on the third day of the three-day conference. Participants had by then been exposed to a wide range of papers on topics pertaining to literature, communication, advertising, popular culture, and linguistics. The experiment, scheduled as a 'workshop' in the conference's timetable, was announced under the title 'responses to advertisements'. The workshop, in which twenty-five people participated, was one of three parallel sessions. The instructions were in English. The order in which the three billboards were presented was different from the order adhered to in Amsterdam, the idea being that any learning effects that might occur during the experiment should not be attributable to the particular order in which the billboards were shown.

IDENTIFICATION OF THE METAPHORS: RATING METHOD

The open-ended way of questioning participants precluded a simple way of classifying their answers. Such an open-ended response was necessary in view of the fact that one of the hypotheses was that participants would spontaneously identify the metaphors in the billboards, that is, without explicitly having been asked to do so. In order to reduce the subjectivity in rating the responses with regard to this hypothesis, a second rater besides the author independently decided whether participants had identified the metaphors.[6] The criteria employed to assess metaphor identification and interpretation were the same as those used in Chapter 6: to qualify as having identified and interpreted a metaphor, participants' responses should reveal that they had implicitly answered the following three questions: 1) Which are the two terms of the metaphor? 2) Which is the metaphor's primary subject and which its secondary subject? 3) What feature or features is/are mapped from the secondary on to the primary subject? In the present experiment, this meant the following: for a participant to have identified and interpreted the metaphor, he or she had to show an awareness that in each advertisement IBM was presented by the advertiser in terms of something else. This something else was, each time, the blue-and-white object in the picture, the link between the IBM logo and the object being the identical blue-and-white striped pattern. Moreover, the participants had to show an awareness that IBM was being presented in terms of the blue-and-white object rather than vice versa. In terms of the terminology used by Black (1979a), they had then identified IBM as the primary subject and the blue-and-white object as the secondary subject of the metaphor. In addition, they should mention at least one feature or attribute of the blue-and-white object and show an awareness that the attribute(s) was/were to be applied to IBM.

To make the matter of identification and interpretation more concrete, the criteria for identification were formulated as follows: 'Does the participant explicitly mention both IBM and the blue-and-white object?'; 'Is it explicitly or implicitly acknowledged that IBM is to be understood in terms of the blue-and-white object (rather than vice versa)?' 'Is at least one feature of the blue-and-white object mentioned that is to be attributed to IBM?' If the answer to all these – related – questions was 'yes', it was established by the raters that the participant had interpreted the metaphor. The matter of *how* a particular metaphor was interpreted will be discussed later.

IDENTIFICATION OF THE METAPHORS: RESULTS

Before reporting the results, it must be acknowledged that eleven out of the eighteen participants tested in Amsterdam mentioned on the information sheet they filled in at the end of the experiment that they knew I worked on metaphor. This familiarity ranged from a very vague awareness to a fairly extensive knowledge. It is difficult to measure the influence any previous knowledge may have exerted on responses, but there is no denying that this awareness may have affected the results. Nine of the eighteen Amsterdam participants indicated that they had seen at least one of the billboards, or one from the same campaign, before.

Sixteen out of the twenty-five participants tested in Ghent said that they knew at least something about my research project. Only two of the twenty-five Ghent participants, who had a variety of national backgrounds,[7] stated that they had seen at least one of these Dutch billboards before, while a third was unsure. Not surprisingly, the first two were Dutch.

The two raters immediately agreed that all participants tested in Amsterdam mentioned IBM and the blue-and-white object, acknowledged that IBM was to be understood in terms of the blue-and-white object (and not the other way round), and mentioned at least one feature that was attributed from the blue-and-white object to IBM. It was also investigated *at what stage* they did so. The latter is relevant for the following reason: it was deemed probable that the repeated exposure to the three (related) billboards might in itself constitute a learning process. Since the participants had to answer question 1 for billboard A, B and C, respectively; question 2 for billboard A, B and C, respectively; and the same for questions 3 and 4, they had twelve opportunities to write down their responses. The earlier the participants acknowledged the brand name IBM, the correspondence between IBM and the blue-and-white object, and a feature that was attributed from the blue-and-white object to IBM, the quicker they could be said to have identified the metaphor. The raters assessed that sixteen out of eighteen participants mentioned IBM under question 1A, that is, when they were exposed to the first billboard for the first time. Similarly, 15 out of 18 were scored as having recorded the correspondence between IBM and the blue-and-white object as soon as question 1A.[8] Finally, while each of the eighteen participants mentioned at least one feature of the blue-and-white object that was attributed to IBM, nine spontaneously did so as early as under question 1A.

Twenty-three of the twenty-five participants tested in Ghent mentioned IBM. Of these, eighteen did so under 1A, that is, on first exposure to the first billboard shown during the experiment. Two mentioned IBM under 1B, two under 1C, and one under 4A. The remaining two did not mention IBM at all, thus failing to recognize the primary subject of the metaphor as such. Hence they cannot be said to have identified the metaphor. In the results to be reported henceforth, these two will be left out of consideration. Since, however, their protocols are highly revealing for different purposes, they will be discussed separately (see the section at the end of this chapter on Further reflections on the experiment's results). Twenty-two of the remaining twenty-three participants (the exception being participant G8)[9] also mentioned the correspondence between IBM and the blue-and-white object, although only eight of these did so under question 1A[10] – which provides a marked contrast with the Amsterdam participants. The raters immediately agreed that twenty-one out of twenty-three participants attributed one or more features to IBM, while both raters had doubts about the remaining two. After discussion, one of the remaining two was scored as having identified and interpreted the metaphors and the other (participant G8) as not having done so. This leaves twenty-two protocols in the Ghent experiment. While twenty-two participants were thus scored as having mentioned at least one feature of the blue-and-white object that was attributed to IBM, only two of them spontaneously did so as early as under question 1A. With three exceptions the twenty-two participants interpreted all three metaphors. The raters had doubts whether G9 had interpreted IBM IS OARS, whereas G13 and G20 were unable or unwilling to interpret this billboard.

It can thus be concluded that in Amsterdam all eighteen participants identified and interpreted the three metaphors IBM IS A BLUE-AND-WHITE OBJECT. Twenty-two of the twenty-five participants in the Ghent group were judged to have identified and interpreted the metaphors (although three did not interpret IBM IS OARS). As we have seen the participants in Amsterdam seem to have been quicker to identify and interpret the metaphors than those in Ghent. What is meant by this is the following: somebody who mentions IBM *and* the correspondence between IBM and the blue-and-white object *and* at least one feature to be attributed from the blue-and-white object to IBM – *doing so all under question 1A* can be said to have processed and interpreted the metaphor straightaway. The *later* any of these observations occurs, the more time, or the more exposures to the billboards a participant seems to have needed to understand the metaphor. This needs to be qualified, of course, for participants may well have understood the metaphor straightaway on first being exposed to the first billboard, but not have shown this in their written responses to 1A. To be on the safe side, the ratings had to be consistently cautious. Nonetheless, the Ghent participants seem to have been slower in processing the metaphors than the Amsterdam participants. This could be attributed to several factors. I offer the following speculations for consideration: 1) The Amsterdam participants' greater previous familiarity with the billboards may have positively influenced their responses; 2) The first billboard shown to the Amsterdam participants (IBM IS A BEACON) was easier than the first one shown to the Ghent participants (IBM IS OARS) and may have put Amsterdam participants on the 'right track' at an earlier stage than the Ghent ones; 3) Theoretically, it is also possible that the IBM billboards having been aimed at people with a Dutch cultural background, Dutch cultural 'schemas' were better tapped than non-Dutch ones. Notice that since relatively more Ghent participants indicated a degree of familiarity with my research project (fifteen out of twenty-two – almost seventy per cent) than did Amsterdam participants (eleven out of eighteen – a little over sixty per cent), this factor cannot be held responsible for the difference signalled.

A final word needs to be said on the identification of the metaphors. It is noteworthy that only two participants tested in Amsterdam *explicitly* identified the metaphors as such by actually mentioning the word 'metaphor' or one of its derivations. If certain affiliated terms ('symbolism' and 'analogy') and their derivations are counted as explicit identification as well (following the practice in Steen 1992: 158), then four of the eighteen Amsterdam participants can be said to have explicitly identified the metaphors. Among the Ghent participants, eight out of twenty-two explicitly identified the metaphors, six of these using the word 'metaphor' and two the word 'analogy'. Hence, many participants unproblematically identify and interpret metaphors without being aware that *that* is what they are doing. This corroborates Steen's finding that people are perfectly capable of interpreting metaphors without explicitly identifying them as such (Steen 1994: 62–3).[11]

INTERPRETATION OF THE METAPHORS: SCORING CRITERIA

In this section I will take a closer look at *how* the metaphors were interpreted. To reduce the degree of subjectivity in interpreting participants' responses, a scoring method was envisaged that is similar to Mick and Politi's. In their case, the first author identified a number of 'themes' in the participants' responses, and subsequently both authors pigeon-holed the responses as exemplifying one of these themes. The equivalent of Mick and Politi's themes in my experiment were the features or attributes that participants judged transferable from each metaphor's secondary subject (the blue-and-white object) to its primary subject (IBM). In practice, these interpretations took the form of predicates projected from the blue-and-white object upon IBM. Thus, participants volunteered 'IBM is . . .', or 'IBM has . . .', or 'IBM does . . .', or 'With IBM one can . . .' or something similar. A difference from Mick and Politi's approach is that whereas they identified each participant's response in terms of one (dominant) theme, in the present approach it was possible for participants to score as having mentioned more than one theme. This was allowed so as to enable a discussion of the interpretations in terms of Sperber and Wilson's (1986) strong and weak implicatures, one of the crucial ideas behind that distinction being that not all assumptions in a message can be taken as communicated with equal force, nor with the same degree of strength to different people.

While the identification and the fact of interpretation of the metaphors as such, as discussed in the previous section, could be established with a high degree of reliability, an assessment of the how of interpretation proved more difficult to chart. The main reason for this is that the wide variety of responses volunteered by the participants had to be somehow classified in a limited amount of categories. Inevitably, there was an element of arbitrariness involved on the first rater's part in deciding 1) how many categories were to be distinguished to do justice to the variety of responses without relinquishing the possibility of making any generalizations whatsoever and 2) how these categories were to be labelled.

In view of the exploratory character of the experiment, I will briefly dwell on some aspects of this categorization problem. In the first place, many attributes mentioned by the participants were contiguously related. Take, for instance, IBM IS A TUNING FORK. If one participant mentions IBM's 'quality' as the key feature here, while another ventures that 'with IBM you have matters under control', the question arises whether these responses exemplify one or two categories. One could argue that the responses do not reflect the same attributes, 'having things under control' being more specific than 'quality' – in which case one would need two categories to accommodate the responses. On the other hand it is plausible to say that *because* IBM is high-quality it has things under control (or vice versa), so that the responses are virtually the same – in which case one category would suffice. And, again, if someone mentions with reference to IBM IS A BEACON that IBM is 'robust', should this be scored in a separate category, or be seen as exemplifying 'reliability'? In both these cases it was decided, on the basis of other comments offered by participants, that the two attributes were sufficiently different to deserve a separate category. Similar decisions had to be taken in other cases. Because of this, the boundaries between some categories were rather fuzzy – a fact that was to have consequences for the degree of consensus the two raters could reach about scoring a certain response in a certain category.

The matter was further complicated by the fact that participants used a wide variety of phrases and expressions; it was the raters' job to determine whether these different phrases reflected the same attribute or not. It is to be noted that the request to number and prioritize the attributes deemed relevant seldom resulted in clearly separated attributes. Sometimes, the raters judged, a participant mentioned more than one attribute under one number; while in other cases the same attribute was mentioned in slightly different words under two numbers. Thus, the requested numbering of attributes yielded no ready-made categories.

A third factor should be taken into account. As we saw in Black's example of the metaphor 'marriage is a zero-sum game' (see Chapter 2), each mapping of attributes from the source domain on to the target domain of a metaphor involves a degree of 'translation'. The responses to the metaphors in the experiment vary in the extent to which this translation process has been completed, and this in turn poses problems as to the scoring of responses as similar or dissimilar. The problem can be rephrased as follows: to what extent have the relevant attributes of the source domain been translated for the domain of the target? For example, several participants mentioned with reference to IBM IS A TUNING FORK that IBM made harmony possible. These participants, that is, report responses that are more closely connected to the source domain (TUNING FORK) than to the target domain (IBM). By contrast, there is also a participant (A2) who reports that IBM helps a business firm 'to keep relations with your good clients OK', while another (A19) interprets that 'IBM tunes in to your company's infrastructure'. These latter two focus on the target rather than the source domain. In terms of scoring, responses of this sort pose problems of categorization: while the responses of A2 and A19 suggest a greater degree of translation, they are not necessarily incompatible with responses that mention the rather general feature 'harmony'. This begs the question whether these responses should be scored in the same category or not. Since a decision to do so would risk the accusation of offering an over-interpretation of the responses, these 'target domain-related' responses were kept separate. In practice, this meant that they ended up in the category **other themes**. It should be realized, however, that the responses in this category could in fact well be seen as reflecting 'translated' versions of explicitly identified themes. The problem mentioned here alerts us to the possibility that participants not only reveal a certain variety in the *kinds* of interpretation; their responses also suggest variety in the *extent* to which the metaphorical transfer process has actually been carried out – this second variety unfortunately not being clearly visible in the division into categories. I want to suggest that the issue of the extent of interpretation is no less important than the issue of the variety of interpretation and deserves further empirical testing.

A final obstacle to unambiguous scoring of responses is that even when two participants mention the same attribute, they may significantly differ in the emphasis they give to it. Thus IBM IS OARS suggested to some people that IBM provides a quiet and pleasant atmosphere *at work*, whereas to others this metaphor signified that IBM enabled one to experience quiet and lack of stress *after work*. Similarly, some people saw in IBM IS A TUNING FORK an exhortation 'tune in to IBM!' whereas others interpreted that IBM tuned in to one's company.

The fuzziness of the boundaries between categories meant that quantification of the results proved possible for only some categories. But there is compensation for this on the qualitative side: thanks to the open-ended way of questioning participants, the present experiment is able to show that consensus on a general level often goes hand-in-hand with small but relevant interpretation differences by individual participants – a finding that is in keeping with Sperber and Wilson's emphasis on relevance to an individual. Since qualitative rather than quantitative results are central in this part of the experimental results, a generous number of sample responses from the protocols will be given.

INTERPRETATION OF THE METAPHORS: RESULTS

IBM IS A BEACON

IBM IS A BEACON was the billboard shown first to the Amsterdam participants and second to the Ghent participants. On the basis of the responses I constructed the following categories, in which I myself and the second rater were subsequently to score the participants' responses.

1 **safety** theme;
2 **robustness** theme;
3 **quality** theme;
4 **other** themes (attribute mentioned by 2 or less participants).

The **safety** category yielded immediate agreement between the two raters on fifteen out of the eighteen Amsterdam responses, and on eighteen out of the twenty-two Ghent responses.[12] On the **robustness**, **quality**, and **other** themes, the raters achieved no clear agreement on what responses should be slotted in what categories. Apparently, the category labels I had chosen proved rather subjective, and it therefore makes no sense to quantify the number of participants scoring in each of these categories. What matters most, however, is that many participants *did* mention various other features besides **safety** that they judged transferable from the blue-and-white object to IBM. In order to give an impression of the variety of responses, I will retain my original categories in the sample responses presented below. It is to be realized, however, that this is done for the practical purpose of being able to roughly subdivide responses into smaller categories, and that other subdivisions into categories are possible:[13]

Safety theme

A1   'The IBM is as safe as a beacon at sea.'
A4   'IBM = safety, certainty, trustworthiness, you can rely on it.'
A7   'IBM = rescuer in emergencies . . .'
G3   'IBM serves as a beacon in the rough waters of the business world, helping to avoid dangers, and ensuring that customers arrive at their destination.'
G10   'IBM is there to save you in case you're having a "rough" time; IBM can survive stormy weathers. Trust the company and you will be able to survive them too.'
G15   'The lifebuoy and light represents IBM's ability to guide the client through stormy weather.'
G20   'IBM is a kind of lead star, a beacon in the hectic world of modern technology.'

Quality theme

A10   'You can decide on your course due to IBM: trend-setting.'
A16   'Radar reflector/light – new techniques.'
A19   'IBM towers above all competitors.'

Robustness theme

A15   'Tower of strength in turbulent world, tho' if so I don't understand why lighthouse(?) is *leaning*; tower of strength *survives* buffeting environment (thru' use of logo colour scheme).'
G3   'IBM is firm, steadfast, and does not move with the ever-changing waves, but will always be there.'
G24   'The resistance of the buoy – stays afloat.'

Other themes

A2   'The more chaotic, the more efficiently IBM intervenes.'

A12   'Attractive high-tech design of IBM-products.'

G2   'IBM products can generate excitement, exhilaration for the consumer of these products.'

G9   'Buoys are official artefacts guarding the seas; this one is in IBM colours; therefore IBM has its influence in all kinds of places and is a benevolent influence on all the work.'

IBM IS A TUNING FORK

IBM IS A TUNING FORK was the billboard shown second to the Amsterdam participants and third to those in Ghent. The variety in responses was significantly greater than in the case of IBM IS A BEACON. The attributes mentioned by the participants were labelled by me as manifestations of one of the following themes/categories:

1 **quality** theme;
2 **harmony** theme;
3 **reliability** theme;
4 **necessity** theme;
5 **omnipresence** theme;
6 **art** theme;
7 **guidance** theme;
8 **other** themes.

The **quality** theme resulted in immediate agreement between the two raters on eight out of twelve Amsterdam responses; and on four out of eight Ghent responses. For the other themes there was no clear agreement. Again, for the practical purposes outlined in the previous section, I will retain my original subdivision into themes:

Quality theme[14]

A8   'IBM sets the tune = IBM is the first brand of computers in the world.'

A11   'IBM is a top-class brand, like Steinway.'

A19   'IBM only cooperates on the basis of first-rate quality.'

G2   'IBM products are as cool, sophisticated, and as perfectly tuned as a concert grand piano; they give out a perfect note. They respond with perfect pitch like the grand piano responds to a virtuoso. The consumer of IBM products will perform like a virtuoso at a perfectly tuned concert grand.'

G23   'IBM "calls the tune". Forget the tuning-fork and your sonata and concerto may turn out to be an unpleasant experience. . . . It might mean something like IBM sets the standards.'

Harmony theme

A2   'IBM is necessary just before a false note occurs; your company can be protected against this false note.'

A4   'Ensemble becomes possible.'

A16   'An IBM (however small) is absolutely necessary to enable the big (company or so) to run; all this happens in complete harmony.'

G18   'The analogy is between the tuning fork and IBM sharing presupposed properties as being both able to strike the key, to be of assistance when needed in the right or most simple way.'

Art theme

A5   'IBM is also geared to music.'

A19   'IBM is also sensitive to culture.'

A20   'Automatization is art.'

G9   'The fusion of technology and art.'

G24   'Modern image in terms of "art"; link to music and a culturally accepted "upmarket image"; link to composition and thus the use of a tool (piano/IBM) to create music/information etc.'

Guidance theme

A5   'With IBM you have matters under control.'

A11   'Even the best pianist needs a tuning fork; the same holds in "business" where IBM plays the role of guide.'

Reliability/precision theme

A17   'IBM equipment can be used in the most refined situations; IBM equipment is extraordinarily refined.'

G5   'We, IBM, help you to play in tune. We ensure the precision and the appropriateness of your actions.'

Necessity theme

G7   'The product is a small but essential element; the whole system depends on it.'

G10   'IBM is the necessary complement to all activities.'

Omnipresence theme

G10   'There is not a single domain IBM has not reached and has not proved itself indispensable in.'

G21 'A strange object again. Being unique in shape (like the previous one) may[be] the IBM company wants to show the multitude of uses it can have. Moreover, we have, I think, a significant balance between the classical (piano) and the modern in shape and use object. The old technology is living together with the new one.'

Other themes

A2 'Keep relations with your good clients all right.'
A12 'The seemingly so small, but in fact essential role of sophisticated techniques in all great human achievements.'
A14 'IBM: it is so simple.'
G19 'The IBM equipment has a creative potential – it can set one free to let the mind become inventive.'

IBM IS OARS

Scoring the responses to IBM IS OARS (shown third to the group in Amsterdam, first to the Ghent group), I distinguished the following attributes mentioned by the participants:

1 **progress** theme;
2 **tranquillity** theme;
3 **omnipresence** theme;
4 **other** themes.

On the **progress** theme the two raters achieved immediate agreement on eleven out of twelve Amsterdam responses, and on ten out of twelve Ghent responses. On the **tranquillity** theme, there was immediate agreement on six out of nine Amsterdam responses, and on five out of seven Ghent responses. The **omnipresence** and **other** themes yielded no clear agreement.

Progress theme

A4 'You make progress with [IBM].'
A5 'IBM has driving power.'
A7 'IBM-oars provide good rowing instruments.'
A8 'With IBM one has the (strong, solid, tough, effective) instrument to move forward, go on a discovery (metaphor), live (metaphor of life as a journey).'
G3 'IBM can help to hasten the journey (to ?). The company provides the locomotive power, the navigational competence, and helps those who are left "up the creek without a paddle".'
G4 'I find the association very remote and vague. Really forcing something – IBM is everywhere, even in non-technological

walks of life (??). The oars propel the boat – IBM propels your business (??). Not evident!'

G5   'We (= IBM) make the world move. We provide the energy and the force to go forward.'

Tranquillity theme

A2   'If you make use of IBM, you can finish your day's work in tranquillity; no managerial stress; there will be no chaos.'

A4   'IBM stands for rest-after-work.'

A15   'If you own an IBM, everything is nice and beautiful; it is as if IBM *brings about* the weather.'

A19   'IBM likes to promote a good and pleasant atmosphere in the company.'

G19   'That IBM has something which could provide in one's need for leisure-time; presumably the fact that their equipment saves time, leaves more available leisure-time to be enjoyed, or makes life *a lot easier* in general. (If only that were true!)'

Omnipresence theme

A11   'Whether for private or for business purposes, you can't ignore IBM.'

G12   'IBM, although it is a modern computer company, is being associated with pleasant, leisure and country scenes; so, it is becoming integrated with aspects of life it would not normally be connected with; IBM is part of the fabric of life?'

Other themes

A12   'Integration of well thought-out modern technique in an age-old world; the beauty of the product that matches the great old beauty.'

A19   'IBM is always ready for you; IBM computers can always and everywhere be used straightaway.'

A20   'I like the implicit suggestion that the "user" (of boat/oars + IBM) will have to "work" himself. The choice of the material alone does not guarantee that the goal will be achieved. ... Suggestion that IBM is good by coupling the brand with such a familiar means of transport as a rowing-boat. IBM, too, is familiar, so it will hold out as long as the boat.'

G15   'The striped oars represent IBM's innovativeness; Captatio benevolentiae.'

PERSONAL ASSOCIATIONS OF PARTICIPANTS

These sample responses report results that were based on participants' responses to the question what message they thought the advertiser had intended to convey (question 3). Participants had also been asked to respond to the billboards with the request to indicate personal feelings and associations evoked by the billboards, ignoring the commercial message (question 2). The aim of this question was to gain insight into how billboards trigger responses that are not constrained by the necessity of taking into account the advertiser's intentions (for instance, making a positive claim for a product). After all, as Cook points out,

> Even if the majority of ads have the function of persuading their addressees to buy, this is not their only function. They may also amuse, inform, misinform, worry or warn. It can be argued that these other functions are all in the service of a main function which is usually to sell; alternatively, even selling ads perform multiple functions which are more or less autonomous (whatever manufacturers may believe).
>
> (Cook 1992: 5)

In this section I will take a closer look at participants' reactions to the billboards in response to the question about their personal feelings and associations. No formal rating or quantification method has been employed here. The proposed categories should therefore be seen as provisional, suggestive, and in need of further experimental corroboration. I have distinguished three types of responses to question 2, although again, boundaries between categories are fuzzy ones:

a) general associations evoked by the blue-and-white object or the context in which that object has been placed;
b) private associations that have nothing to do with IBM or advertising at all;
c) comments on the advertiser or the billboard itself.

The associations classified as belonging to type a), *general associations*, reflect a range of culturally determined connotations. Some samples:

IBM IS A BEACON

A2   'Wild sea; danger.'
A14   'Robust, strong, solid; certainty, safety; clarity, order in chaos, light in the darkness; saevis tranquillus in undis.'
G5   'To me, the light in the storm symbolizes safety in a very aggressive and dangerous environment.'
G6   'Imperturbability.'
G19   'Turbulence; ominousness; violence; associations with cold + harsh conditions to be avoided.'

IBM IS A TUNING FORK

A1   'Musicality; elegance.'
A12   'The combination of technique on a high level and art on a high level; for great human achievements technique is required: tuning is necessary to accomplish coherence.'
A14   'Unity, cooperation.'
G2   'Sophistication, wealth, discrimination.'
G11   'This picture does not really have much impact for me; straight lines and oblique lines which I can intellectualize to offer interpretations or perhaps associations but few feelings; neatness/efficiency/cleverness; but this is just an academic exercise in interpretation which does not seem very genuine.'

IBM IS OARS

A7   'Repose, relaxation; mild summer evening.'
G5   'The paddles do not fit into the environment, they very much attract the attention which makes me [wonder] why they have been placed there. They are the ones who make the boat move.'
G8   'Serenity, calmness, quiet.'
G21   'Exploration of new territory.'

As will be clear, the associations recorded here ignore the IBM logo. They are part of what in the IBM IS A BLUE-AND-WHITE OBJECT metaphors functioned as these metaphors' source domains. Since participants need not worry about advertisers' specific intentions while answering question 2, it is not at all surprising that they pay less attention to the blue-and-white object. While perceived from the viewpoint of the advertisers' intentions all pictorial elements apart from the blue-and-white object are contextual elements somehow qualifying that object (which in turn is used to predicate something about IBM), here these contextual elements can be responded to in their own right. From the perspective of personal associations, as we will see under c), the blue-and-white objects are often seen as irritating and distracting.

The associations classified as belonging to type b), *private associations*, provide insight into how billboards may trigger effects that have nothing to do with the selling proposition inherent in them, and moreover reflect how advertisements may suggest specific things to specific individuals. Some samples:

IBM IS A BEACON

A9   'Jan den Hartog – television series/Op Hoop van Zegen.'[15]
A14   'Artificial photography.'

A16   'Shakespeare sonnet.[16] ... Nice perspective – [beacon] only visible when you are half-drowned.'

G1   'Altogether it is an extremely boring picture.'

G2   'Storm, energy, excitement; this has good rather than bad associations. I've always liked living near the sea and am happiest near or on it. Storms at sea always seem exhilarating to me; there are also associations with fine art. People like Turner it seems to me like to paint the sea either in flat calm or as storm tossed.'

G4   'Discomfort – that water looks cold!; fear – I don't like choppy seas!'

G9   'This one takes me back rather too vividly to sailing weekends as a child, especially one stormy morning in Poole Harbour when I stood in the cockpit getting faceful after faceful of rain and spray.'

G11   'I associate this picture with turmoil, but seen as a very aesthetic phenomenon. This prevents me from associating the picture with danger or disaster.'

G20   'I associate this with sailing on the Waddenzee at gale/force 8; a minor association is with Dutch sea-painting, notably the Hague School of painting.'

IBM IS A TUNING FORK

A1   'Jackstraws (the game with the coloured sticks); one never tunes a piano with a tuning fork, hence a bit nonsensical.'

A2   'Wonderful evening in the "Concertgebouw" [= famous concert hall in Amsterdam]; ... Festivity, warm atmosphere; [my?] piano needs tuning.'

A4   'Music, Steinway quality; tuning fork = absurd, made of wood? Wrong form?'

A14   'Is a tuning fork a sweetie (and thus edible)? ... Play the piano when I am home; is a Bosendorfer all right as well?'

A16   'Ugly tuning fork – obviously not a genuine one.'

A17   'What an irritating tuning fork on that black piano; a tuning fork in prison-colours.'

G8   'It looks rather cold – although pianos usually evoke warm feelings. Something to do with the texture of the piano.'

G9   'The tuning fork: taking up music again after several years' gap – the first thing I did was buy a tuning fork.'

G13   'Childhood memories. A lady-teacher during singing lessons at school performing mysterious tricks with a tuning fork (I don't think I knew what it was then), after which we (the pupils) were asked to sing to the accompaniment of the piano.'

G15   'The striped tuning fork suggests a smart-arsed unconventionality; the piano suggests solidity and materialism that has more to do with it as a prestige object than an instrument which is played.'

G17   '*Strong* evocation of childhood, when I played the piano + took lessons; includes remembering a piano-tuner who was blind + whom I envied because of his ability to play so well; memories of my dog, who used to lie on my feet + make it impossible to use the pedals; I can almost hear the note of the tuning fork + wonder whether I still have "perfect pitch"; *many* other related thoughts, esp. wondering whether a musical "ear" + a linguistic are (*provably* [sic]) related.'

G23   'It means relatively little to me – as the picture bears little relationship to actually *playing* the piano. *Tuning* it is an altogether different experience + not necessarily a pleasant job. Not something which puts one into contact with people or which gives (on a short-term basis) any aesthetic pleasure.'

IBM IS OARS

A2   'Picnic on the island; island of Torcello near Venice.'

A4   'Romantic, kitsch, painting/unreal.'

A9   'Summer evening; holiday; gnats; Vrije Universiteit promotion campaign making use of "rowing": "rowing with the oars one has at one's disposal" – in my view a rather unfortunately chosen image.'[17]

A10   'A pity to start rowing and disturb nature's tranquillity.'

A14   'Biking along [rivers] Gein and Waver: rowing I gladly leave to others.'

G2   'It reminds me of holidays I have spent in Wales and in the Norfolk Broads. These associations are good ones – for me it is an image of rest and recreation; also there is something to do with absence. Who has left the boat there with the oars. Lovers?'

G8   'Reminds me of a late evening walking alongside the Thames at Oxford.'

G13   'This picture evokes my childhood. As a boy I spent hours in the rowing-boat of my grandfather, who was a fisherman. It also reminds me of one of the opening sentences of C.P. Snow's "Time of Hope": ". . . it was one of those long afternoons of childhood".'

G17   'The ochre colouring reminds me of old photos, and evokes sensations of mustiness.'

G20   'I have the most awful associations with this picture. I made a similar (very similar) picture in Sweden at the burial (at the lake) of the daughter of a friend of mine. She was murdered in Sweden; no other associations.'

Notice that some of the responses recorded above under b) could, but need not, be interpreted as (mostly negative) comments on IBM, or the billboard itself. Sometimes, however, participants explicitly say something about their personal response to the billboard as a billboard, and by extension to IBM. In several cases they present a subversive or ironical reading of the billboard. Sample responses in category c), *comments on the advertiser/billboard*:

IBM IS A BEACON

A10   'IBM-advertisements are always beautifully and expensively designed: IBM is a prestigious brand; IBM strikes me as a rather arrogant company.'

A11   'IBM is a beacon on the sea. You can rely on it. So you must (be so stupid as to) buy an IBM.'

A20   'Nice idea; [but] the advertisement does not provide the viewer with any insight into the product that IBM stands for.'

G4   'IBM is a beacon in the rough seas of life/ business (note to the unworldly: you should not treat your IBM computer like this).'

G17   'IBM again. A striped marker buoy on a rough sea. It seems the stripes are "flavour of the month" for the IBM marketing people. The lowering grey sky seems to imply that the "light" in a storm is provided by IBM. I dislike this ad. . . . Again I find myself tending to a sarcastic interpretation – IBM are all at sea.'

IBM IS A TUNING FORK

A16   'An IBM (however small) is absolutely necessary to let the (big) company run smoothly; all this happens in complete harmony. (If you have a puny little piano, incidentally, you shouldn't buy an IBM).'

A20   'Nice, too, is the connotation top quality that is evoked by the connection Steinway/IBM.'

G2   'This just reminds me of other adverts especially Benson & Hedges Silk Cut which tend to be highly allusive.'

G20   'IBM sets/is the tune/norm for computer developments. (I am not supposed, I suppose, to add that I think this third billboard preposterous and out of place).'

IBM IS OARS

A14   'On a summer evening I don't want to be reminded of computerization. . . . While rowing, you must constantly look back over your shoulder (tiresome), even with IBM-oars.'

A3   'Apparently this is what life looks like if you opt for IBM, but the connection between advertisement and the product to be sold is very far-fetched here! . . . Weak!!!'

G4   'Puzzlement – what the hell has this got to do with IBM?; annoyance that IBM are toying with the public by introducing totally irrelevant adverts.'

G9   'No serious photographer can any longer get away with this kind of thing as art; it must be an advertisement.'

G10   'IBM is as necessary to present-day situation as these oars are in this boat. . . . Oars can sometimes get lost, can't they?'

G12   'Is the brown colouring meant to suggest an early morning or late evening "feel", or is it meant to suggest that the picture was taken many years ago? Probably the former as the IBM "effect" must be modern.'

G17   'Confused message – I want to interpret it as "IBM has moored the boat + gone off somewhere", which I'm sure was not the intended message!'

Quite a few participants voice anger or irritation about the billboards, or towards IBM. As to the reason for this one can only speculate. It may be that the professional background of the groups participating in the experiments – all academics working in the field of language or literature – has a role to play in this respect. In the first place, the people participating are in all probability not the type of people that were IBM's target group; for this reason, the interest in the product among the participants may have been rather low. As a corollary, the very fact that the participants were all working in university language and literature departments may well have increased their irritability. Since these people are used to analysing fairly complex, and/or aesthetically highly rated (cultural) phenomena, the billboards may have 'offended' some of them, due to either the lack of cognitive depth or the type of visual design of the billboards. Then again, this group, being used to analysing discourses of various kinds, may simply be particularly critical anyway. However this may be, it would be interesting to see how, say, a group of business managers would respond to these billboards, not only in terms of the identification and interpretation of the metaphors, but also in terms of any personal emotions and associations. Individuals sharing a number of background assumptions – having to do, for instance, with their profession – may systematically differ in their interpretations from individuals with other background assumptions.

FURTHER REFLECTIONS ON THE EXPERIMENT'S RESULTS

Apart from the light that the experimental findings shed on the hypotheses proffered earlier in this chapter and on the personal associations billboards may trigger, the protocols invite reflection on yet other aspects of the interpretation of pictorial metaphors, some of which have been touched upon in earlier chapters of this book. These issues are the role of cultural context; the effects of repeated or extended exposure to an advertisement; the influence of language; and Sperber and Wilson's distinction between strong and weak aspects of communication. They will be discussed in the next few sections.

Two interesting cases

It was concluded that, with two exceptions, all participants in the Amsterdam and the Ghent groups at the very least *mentioned* IBM, usually somewhere in their answer to question 1. The two exceptions, both in the Ghent group, are worthwhile examining in more detail. The first (G16), an Australian (age 30–40) apparently had not spotted the IBM logo below the picture. That means that he was by definition unable to identify the (verbo)pictorial metaphors IBM IS OARS/BEACON/TUNING FORK. That did not prevent him from perceiving what was the focus of attention in each billboard, as his answers to question 1 ('describe in your own words billboards A, B and C') reveal:

A) 'A boat, a row boat in an "idyllic" lake or river setting, probably early in the morning. There is a sense of isolation, of nature (the reeds or plants). Focus, however, is on the boat and its contents, which look like oars.'
B) 'A science fiction scene: something out of "War of the Worlds" in the middle of a raging storm at sea. The object being buffeted is very futuristic, there are notions of strength, light (is it a lighthouse?) and autonomy.'
C) 'View of part of a piano. That can be said because part of the keys are visible. There is an object on the piano which reminds me of the oars from the first billboard (the colours are similar). A very unusual kind of focus/framing here. What is the object?'

Similarly, in his answers to question 3, this participant gropes around for an attribute that is of importance:

A) 'The only "message" I see being pushed is the compatibility of nature and technology/craft. The way technology/culture blends into nature. Or again, the compatibility of the human in [and?] nature.'
B) 'The strength, reliability, autonomy of something buffeted by nature. The power of the cultural artefact.'

C) 'Smoothness, polish, finish: all high cultural attributes. A certain kind of poise, taste, distinction is being produced here. We are being "called up" as part of this notion of taste, of distinction.'

It could be ventured then, that, even though he does not realize what product these billboards are advertisements *for*, this participant's knowledge of the 'genre' to which the pictures belong (i.e., advertising) guides him into identifying attributes that might be applicable to the product. Put differently, the expectations that the genre or framework of advertising activates are those of positive claims for a product or service; these remain intact even if the product itself is not identified. It is interesting, incidentally, to see how this participant answered the question (on the information sheet) what he thought was the product advertised. Apparently thinking that each advertised a different product, he came up with: 'A. Cigarettes/Technology. B. Technology (batteries!?). C. Wine, expensive food/drink'.

A highly intriguing series of responses was provided by G14 (age 20–30) who, although she did not give her nationality, almost certainly was Chinese.[18] Here are her answers to question 1:

A) 'It is a very beautiful scene of nature, with river, little boat. It is an evening scene with little trees around. It reminds me of the Chinese phrase: the sun is extraordinarily good, but sorrily it's close to evening.'
B) 'It is a sailing boat, it seems to me there is much wind and storm at this moment while the sailing boat is in water.'
C) 'It has presented part of the piano, but I am wondering what is on the top of the piano. The several keys which are visible are really beautiful.'

Clearly, this participant does not realize the importance of the oars in A), while in B) she mistakes the beacon for a sailing boat. Moreover, in C) she fails to recognize the tuning fork for what it is. Here are her responses to question 3:

A) 'I think the advertiser has wanted to tell people that nature is beautiful and quiet and peaceful. Instead of going to live and stay in big cities, why not return to nature to enjoy the eternal beauty.'
B) 'The advertiser wants to communicate through this that people should dare to challenge the wild nature.'
C) 'It can be an advertisement from one of the piano factories to communicate that you can always buy a beautiful piano with reliable and good quality from our factory and most beautiful music can be produced from it.'

Not surprisingly, this participant did not fill in anything when asked to identify the products advertised – although she guesses, as we have seen, that C) might advertise pianos.

While both G16 and G14, lacking the insight that these are ads for IBM, have difficulties interpreting the billboards presented, G14's are greater. If we assume she is indeed Chinese, this entails, I speculate, that she is less familiar with the Western cultural code in which these billboards are embedded. We do not know what she made of the oars (she does not mention them in any of her answers), but she obviously mistook the beacon for a ship, while she refers to the tuning fork (in her answer to question 4) as 'the little decoration at the top of the piano'. Moreover, she may be confused about the aims and objectives of commercial advertising. Although this interpretation of G14's responses is largely speculative, her answers suggest that pictures are not necessarily more 'international' than words, some of them presupposing considerable cultural background knowledge. It may be added that research into cross-cultural interpretation of pictures might well benefit from using pictorial advertisement metaphors as stimulus material.

'Temporal effects'

An element that was largely lost in the evaluations of participants' responses is the coherence and, sometimes, development in the series of answers given by individual participants. Although strictly speaking beyond the concerns of the present study, a few observations will be made on this aspect.

Clearly, the repeated exposure to the three related billboards for several participants constituted something of a 'learning process'.[19] This is partly suggested by the (albeit sparse) use of the asterisk (*) – to indicate later additions – and partly by such phrases as 'Now I see . . .' For instance, not all people straight away spotted the IBM logo under the picture while the colour correspondence dawned upon some only gradually. Thus, G13 answers question 1A: 'Rowing boat; oars; reeds; IBM; I fail to see any connection between IBM and this idyllic landscape. *The only relation I see is in the colour of the oars and that of the caption IBM'. Moreover, some people did not immediately recognize the tuning fork as such, mistaking it for an arrow, a pen, or a metronome, while later they usually came to see it for what it was. Similarly, various people at first thought the beacon was a lighthouse, although several were puzzled why, in that case, it was leaning. One participant (A12) did not recognize the radar-reflector on top of the beacon, describing it as 'a kind of futuristic white disk', while another (G21) doubtfully referred to the 'light above the [beacon] and kite(?) above it . . .'

A clear example of somebody who, although he admits it grudgingly, increasingly seems to appreciate what is going on is G4. Here follow his responses to IBM IS OARS, in temporal order:

Q1 'Rowing boat containing 2 crossed, striped oars in foreground on tranquil stretch of water (evening, early morning?) IBM logo (hence blue stripes). Boat is moored to stake on bank. Relevance to computers – zilch.'

Q2 'Peace, tranquillity of scene; Holiday associations of rivers; Puzzlement – what the hell has this got to do with IBM?; Annoyance that IBM are toying with the public by introducing totally irrelevant adverts.'

Q3 'I find the association very remote and vague. Really forcing something – IBM is everywhere, even in non-technological walks of life (??). The oars propel the boat – IBM propels your business (??). Not evident!'

Q4 'Very little. It's up to the spectator to cudgel his brains on this one. It's obviously the oars which are the item in focus – hence my second suggestion above might be more probable.'

One participant (A10) stated under 'additional remarks': 'The first ad was clear to me from the very beginning, the second one became clear to me in the course of this experiment, the third [IBM IS OARS] I still don't get: you have to make do with whatever is at hand, even if it's only IBM?' [20] Finally, one participant saw elements of a rudimentary 'narrative' in the series of billboards. Thus, after having been exposed earlier to IBM IS A BEACON, A13 in his description of the IBM IS OARS billboard commented, 'perhaps a narrative link? The tranquillity, the port, the inactive oars point to a happy end. The water is calm, the storm is over'.

Influence of language

It is noteworthy that even though language is virtually absent in the billboards used as stimulus material, it *does* play a role in some of the comments participants offer. Thus, as we saw, several Amsterdam participants with respect to IBM IS OARS mention the expression 'roeien met de riemen die je hebt' with its negative connotations, causing participants to reject its pertinence. Not surprisingly, the (mostly non-Dutch) participants in Ghent did not come up with this expression. Moreover, A8, whose mother tongue is French, commented that the IBM IS OARS billboard would in France not be suitable, since it evokes the expression 'mener quelqu'un en bateau', 'taking somebody in the boat', meaning 'deceiving somebody'. Oddly enough, the same expression, with the same meaning, exists in Dutch ('iemand in de boot nemen'), but *none* of the Dutch participants mentioned this.

Similarly, IBM IS A TUNING FORK evoked in many participants the expression 'being in tune with', or 'being attuned to', the latter having a Dutch equivalent in 'afstemmen op'. Inasmuch as these expressions are in themselves often used in verbal metaphors, they have clearly influenced the interpretations of the pictorial metaphors.

Sperber and Wilson's strong vs. weak implicatures

The main issue on which the experiment was intended to shed light was the question to what extent participants would agree among themselves on the interpretation of the billboards' metaphors. It was hypothesized, let it be recalled, that 'among the participants interpreting the metaphor, there will be considerable, but not unanimous, consensus about the nature of the features projected from the secondary subject upon the primary subject'. As we saw, this expectation was confirmed, albeit that the consensus about IBM IS A BEACON and IBM IS OARS was considerably greater than about IBM IS A TUNING FORK. The latter proved to give rise to a greater variation in interpretation among the participants – which could also be formulated as a claim that this last billboard proved the most suggestive, interesting one.

Let us return for a moment to Sperber and Wilson's concepts of strong and weak communication (Chapter 5), and see how the present findings can be rephrased in these terms. For a start we should ideally be able to decide what to do with Sperber and Wilson's distinction between explicatures and implicatures. An explicature was defined as 'a combination of linguistically encoded and contextually inferred conceptual features. The smaller the relative contribution of the contextual features, the more explicit the explicature will be, and inversely' (Sperber and Wilson 1986: 182), which immediately confronts us with a problem, since the billboards do not only contain *linguistically* encoded conceptual features – namely, 'IBM' – but also *pictorially* encoded (?) conceptual features – most notably the blue-and-white objects. It would seem to me counterintuitive, however, to maintain that for instance IBM IS A BEACON, as embodied in Figure 7.1, and the linguistic utterance 'IBM is a beacon' led to fundamentally different conceptualizations.[21] If this is correct, the identification of the pictorial metaphor itself would count as an explicature, since the propositional attitude of an utterance is an explicature of that utterance (ibid.: 180). But that is not all; I would propose that the identification of various objects and phenomena in the billboards (the beacon, the sea, the storm, etc.) is a matter of 'reference assignment' (see p. 92) and should hence count as explicatures as well.

As was stated in Chapters 4 and 5, the fact that the pictorial metaphor occurs in a billboard advertising a certain brand suggests that 'This is an advertisement' and 'This is an advertisement for brand X' are strong implicatures of the billboards. The interpretations of the metaphors are also implicatures. But what would be strong, and what weak implicatures? Apart from the awareness that advertisers want to make a positive claim about their clients' products, we have no access to intentions against which we could measure participants' responses. Of course the uncertainty is increased by the paucity of verbal anchoring of the billboards – which was one of the reasons in the first place to select them for the experiment.

Moreover, as stated above, the degree of consensus about the features projected from the blue-and-white object upon IBM differed per billboard. Hence it is a difficult issue to establish which are strong and which are weak implicatures of the billboards.

Now we could solve the problem of what are to be considered strong and what weak implicatures by deciding on quantitative grounds that in the case of BEACON, 'IBM provides safety' is more strongly implicated than 'IBM products are beautifully designed', simply because more participants offered the first than the second interpretation, while with reference to TUNING FORK 'IBM stands for quality' is more strongly implicated than 'IBM brings together old and new technology', which was suggested by only one participant. This sounds plausible – as long as we realize that these outcomes might change if the composition of the group of participants were changed. Not only a systematic variation in the national background of the participants might affect the results, but also, for instance, a system-atic variation in the kind of work participants do. Theoretically it might be the case that while the imagination of academics in language and literature departments is stimulated by an art-related metaphor such as that in TUNING FORK, a group of harbour pilots might come up with far more attributes in BEACON than in TUNING FORK. This, of course, would be entirely consistent with Sperber and Wilson's claim that relevance is always relevance to an individual. Keeping these considerations in mind, we can nonetheless conclude that for the groups of participants under scrutiny some 'attributes' were more strongly implicated than others; to what extent their responses can be generalized remains a matter for further research.

Let us for a moment return to an example in Sperber and Wilson concerning weak implicature to which the present cases can be fruitfully compared:

> Mary and Peter are newly arrived at the seaside. She opens the window overlooking the sea and sniffs appreciatively and ostensively. When Peter follows suit, there is no one particular good thing that comes to his attention: the air smells fresh, fresher than it did in town, it reminds him of their previous holidays, he can smell the sea, seaweed, ozone, fish; all sorts of pleasant things come to mind, and while, because her sniff was appreciative, he is reasonably safe in assuming that she must have intended him to notice at least some of them, he is unlikely to be able to pin her intentions down any further.
>
> (Sperber and Wilson 1986: 55)

I would argue that the situation we have with the three IBM billboards under scrutiny is similar to the one sketched in this seaside scene. While in Sperber and Wilson's example verbal information is completely absent, in the IBM billboards it is restricted to a minimum. In both cases we find an illustration of Sperber and Wilson's claim that 'to varying degrees, all non-verbal communication is weak communication . . . : one can never be sure which of a variety of assumptions made manifest by the communicator she herself actually had in mind. The set of assumptions which have been communicated can be defined in general terms, but the individual members of this set cannot be enumerated' (ibid.: 175). If we take Sperber and Wilson to mean, as I think they do, that any enumeration constitutes necessarily a partial and non-exhaustive list, we find that roughly the same applies to the attributes that participants project from secondary subject upon primary subject in the metaphors of the IBM billboards.

In the context of Sperber and Wilson's theory, it is useful to devote a last observation to the requested prioritization of both participants' personal and the presumed intended associations evoked by the billboards. This prioritization did not lead to analysable data. There is one phenomenon, however that deserves mentioning: a substantial number of people in answering questions 2 and 3 deviate once or more from the 'normal' prioritizing order 1, 2, 3 etc.[22] Put differently, after having written down the personal associations requested (question 2) or the presumed intended associations requested (question 3), these participants in some cases decided that the order in which they had hit upon these associations was not equivalent to the order of their importance. This could be seen as a finding that sheds light on the matter of effort versus effect in Sperber and Wilson's theory. Whereas in strong communication the principle of relevance predicts that it is the *first* interpretation that comes to the addressee's mind which is the one intended, it would seem that no such thing can be predicted about weak communication. If we surmise, as seems reasonable, that participants write down their responses in the order in which they come to mind, then the fact that various participants *subsequently* number the relative importance of these responses in an order that deviates from the order in which they came to mind is interesting, since it suggests that in the case of weak implicature it is not necessarily the first interpretation that comes to mind which is understood as the most relevant.

SUMMARY

In this chapter the results were reported of a highly exploratory experiment testing if and how verbo-pictorial metaphors in three related IBM billboards were identified and interpreted by two groups of participants, all of them based in language or literature departments. Although for reasons outlined above the results must be approached with some caution, a number of tentative conclusions can be drawn.

The first hypothesis to be tested was that participants would identify and interpret the verbo-pictorial metaphors in the three advertising billboards, even though they had not explicitly been warned to look for metaphors. The fact that forty of the forty-three (18 + 25) participants identified and interpreted the metaphors warrants the conclusion that this hypothesis was confirmed. Most participants identified the metaphor without explicitly mentioning the term 'metaphor' or an equivalent term, supporting Steen's (1994: 62–3) findings. The circumstance that many participants were not completely unaware of the author's interest in metaphor, however, was potentially a biasing factor, necessitating further research with naive participants.

Second, it was hypothesized that among those participants interpreting the metaphor there would be considerable, but not unanimous, consensus about the nature of the features projected from the secondary subject upon the primary subject – that is, about the interpretation of the metaphor. This was confirmed, although there was more consensus on IBM IS A BEACON (interpretation: 'IBM provides safety') and IBM IS OARS ('IBM helps you make progress' and 'IBM fosters an atmosphere of peace and tranquillity') than for IBM IS A TUNING FORK ('IBM guarantees quality'). The last one seemed to give rise to a greater variation in interpretation among the participants – which could also be formulated as a claim that this last billboard proved the most suggestive, interesting one.[23] Apart from these more or less shared interpretations, participants voiced a wide range of more idiosyncratic ones. The occurrence of idiosyncratic interpretations besides shared ones supports Sperber and Wilson's (1986) distinction into weak and strong implicatures of a message, as well as their insight that relevance cannot be objectively established but must always be specified in terms of relevance-to-a-certain-individual.

In addition, the protocols suggest not only that interpretations showed variation in *kind* from one participant to another, but also in *extent*: the degree to which attributes projected from the source domain upon the target domain have been 'translated' reflects marked differences between participants. It is also probable that certain differences in interpretations are group-specific. In future research, national background of the participants would be a variable meriting investigation, and so would, for instance, participants' professional backgrounds. Theoretically it might be the case that while the imagination of academics in language and literature departments is stimulated by an art-related metaphor such as that in IBM IS A TUNING FORK, a group of harbour pilots might come up with far more attributes in BEACON than in TUNING FORK. Keeping this in mind, we can nonetheless conclude that for the groups of participants under scrutiny, some attributes were more strongly implicated than others. Further empirical research testing the responses of other types of groups is imperative.

Furthermore, the experiment yielded suggestive data about other associations evoked by a billboard besides those associations participants think the ad-makers intended to be evoked. These personal associations and (largely critical) comments on IBM or the billboards' design occur, of course, mainly in response to question 2, where participants were explicitly asked to do so. Interestingly, the critical comments occasionally also occur in the answers to question 3, where the ad-maker's presumed intention was asked after – but if so they are usually hedged in ways that suggest participants' realization that these are not part of the intended message. This can be seen as a corroboration of the view that 'genre' plays an important contextual role in the attribution of meaning.

Finally, some reflections were volunteered on the possible influence of cultural background, the influence of language, and the repeated exposure to the billboards upon the interpretation of the metaphors under consideration, as well as on the dichotomy between strong and weak implicatures with reference to non-verbal stimuli.

8 Closing remarks

INTRODUCTION

In this final chapter I want to sketch briefly how the insights of this book may give rise to further research. Suggestions pertain, first, to widening the scope of investigating pictorial metaphor (a label which in this chapter will cover verbo-pictorial metaphor and simile as well). Second, since pictorial metaphors are virtually never unaccompanied by text – whether in a relaying or in an anchoring function (see Chapter 4) – the approach outlined in the previous chapters also provides starting points for examining the relationships between words and images in more general terms. Third, the insights obtained can function in analyses of advertisements. Finally, the present study offers some suggestions for a more extensive examination of other pictorial tropes.

VARIABLES IN THE COMMUNICATION SITUATION

The case made for (verbo)pictorial metaphors in this book consists of an application of Black's (1962, 1979a) interaction theory of metaphor to a corpus of selected advertisements. More precisely these advertisements are static ones, either printed ads or billboards. Even more specifically, they are Dutch, French, British, and German ads. That is, various choices had to be made to narrow down the corpus material to manageable proportions – choices which were justified in Chapter 4. The decisions that had to be made can all be related to the communication model represented in Figure 4.1, inspired by Jakobson (1960). It will be illuminating to take a second look at that model and consider how more extended research in the area of pictorial metaphor needs to examine what happens if the various slots in the model are filled differently. In the following sections I will briefly consider the original six slots of that model under four headings – word and image text, code/channel, communicator/addressee, and context – and indicate how varying the way each of these slots is filled affects interpretation. It is to be realized, of course, that the four categories can be separated only in theory and not in practice.

Word and image text

The pictorial metaphors under scrutiny in this book all occur in advertisements. One of the vital reasons for selecting this type of word and image text for developing a model of pictorial metaphor was the fact that a clear intention can be established in advertising. Inevitably the question arises whether the types of pictorial metaphor distinguished also manifest themselves in other types of word and image texts. As we have seen in various studies considered in Chapter 4, attempts to locate pictorial tropes (whether tropes in general or metaphor in particular) have been undertaken in other text genres as well. Some specifically focus on visual art (Wollheim 1987, Forceville 1988, Hausman 1989, Whittock 1990), others take into account different kinds of texts (illustrative pictures in a didactic text, cartoons, operation instructions) as well (Johns 1984, Kennedy 1982, 1985). It is worthwhile to investigate in more detail which other word and image texts besides ads can manifest pictorial metaphor. In pursuing this question, the matter of 'intention' remains a factor of critical importance. The degree to which an intention can be unequivocally established has consequences for the study of any metaphors occurring in a word and image text. As postulated before, three necessary conditions for the identification and interpretation of anything that purports to be a metaphor are the answerability of the following questions:

1) Which are the two terms of the metaphor?
2) Which is the primary subject and which is the secondary subject?
3) Which feature(s) of the secondary subject is/are projected upon the primary subject?

I propose that, generally speaking, the easier it is to establish the intention underlying the utterance (in whatever medium) of a metaphor, the easier it is to answer these questions, and hence the less complicated the analysis of the metaphor will be. That is, inasmuch as pictorial metaphors – and indeed pictorial tropes in general – occur in word and image texts, it is to be expected that their investigation will be relatively fruitful in, for instance, cartoons and didactic texts. After all, a metaphor employed in a cartoon needs to bolster the cartoon's point – and if the metaphor is not understood, the joke will miscarry.[1] Similarly, a didactic text has the intention to instruct, and any pictorial tropes used will have to enhance that understanding – on penalty of creating confusion otherwise. The intentions underlying artistic texts, on the other hand, can in many cases not be unambiguously established. Whereas in non-artistic word and image texts there is a high premium on the communication of a certain fairly narrowly circumscribed message, such constraints hold to a lesser extent for artistic word and image texts. The primary aim of a work of art, let us assume, is to provide aesthetic pleasure, rather than the communication of a clear set of assumptions. Art frequently prohibits definitive and exhaustive interpretations, and favours suggestiveness and polyinterpretability (see Schmidt 1982). This considerably increases the difficulty of identifying and interpreting pictorial metaphors in art. As I show in Forceville (1988, 1990), Surrealist paintings and collages sometimes even forbid a satisfactory answer to the second of the three questions judged essential for using the label 'metaphor' ('Which is the primary subject and which is the secondary subject?'), rendering the third question ('Which feature(s) of the secondary subject is/ are projected upon the primary subject?') even more difficult to answer (see the section on Forceville 1988 in Chapter 3).[2]

No sooner, however, has the difficulty of tackling artistic pictorial metaphors been assessed than it should immediately be emphasized that the study of this type of metaphor is nonetheless not to be neglected. The reason for focusing on a corpus of word and image texts characterized by clear intentions was that it provides a better angle for the development of a *theory* of pictorial metaphor. In turn, the insights thus gained should be employed to analyse artistic metaphors, which usually are more open-ended and suggestive than those in ads. In Black's terms they tend to be more resonant (Black 1979a: 26); in Sperber and Wilson's terms they have a wider spectrum of weak implicatures (see the section on 'relevance theory' in Chapter 5). Whittock's (1990) cinematic metaphors convincingly show that the examination of artistic pictorial metaphors is a valid activity – and an absolutely necessary part of the critical evaluation of the films in which they occur.

There is reason to dwell a little longer on Whittock's study. Recall that he proposed to focus on 'marked' metaphors, i.e., metaphors that 'proclaim themselves to be such or those that the film maker seems to be declaring as such' (1990: 50). The very fact that Whittock is able to come up with dozens of persuasive examples of pictorial metaphors might seem to contradict my contention that studying pictorial metaphors in artistic texts is a difficult enterprise. My original claim, therefore, must be narrowed down. In order to do so, we first need to recall Whittock's position concerning intentionality (see the section on Whittock 1990 in Chapter 3). The sentence quoted above suggests that Whittock regards certain cinematic phenomena as being probably intended by the director to be understood as metaphors. While he acknowledges that a film may contain phenomena interpretable as pictorial metaphors that were not consciously worked into the film by their directors, Whittock proposes to focus on marked metaphors rather than on cinematic metaphors that are 'so unobtrusive, so subliminal, that their very existence may become matters of dispute' (ibid.). But of course the *intention* to metaphorize alone is not enough; this intention must be substantiated in the film in such a way that a phenomenon can indeed be located and analysed in terms of metaphor.

Now why, then, are cinematic metaphors a type of artistic metaphors that lend themselves fairly well to identification and analysis? I submit that this is because most feature films have a narrative character. And as soon as an artistic utterance, in whatever medium, embodies a 'story', it becomes more easy and valid to locate a degree of intentionality in it. A story has a point or even a plot and this fact structures and constrains the ways in which it can be interpreted. This holds similarly for the metaphors that occur in that story. While I still maintain my original claim that it is less difficult to identify and interpret non-artistic metaphors than artistic ones, artistic genres cannot be simply all lumped together. I propose the further hypothesis, therefore, that phenomena occurring in artistic manifestations with a narrative character lend themselves better to identification and interpretation in terms of metaphor than phenomena in artistic manifestations with no, or less, narrative character.

Code/channel

The codes used in the advertisements discussed in this book arc on the one hand the code of language and on the other the pictorial code – at least inasmuch as pictorial representations can be said to be codified (see Chapter 4). Two types of ads were distinguished, printed advertisements and billboards, the latter generally featuring less verbal text than the former. The very nature of the phenomena discussed in this book, i.e., pictorial metaphors in their various manifestations, means that the consideration of alternative channels and their potential codes (aural, olfactory, gustatory, tactile) on the whole falls outside the scope of this section. One exception, however, deserves closer attention since it pertains to a natural extension of the corpus material considered in this book. As the previous section suggests, moving images may feature pictorial metaphors as well. It makes sense, therefore, to study pictorial metaphors not just in printed ads and billboards, but also in commercials. However, modern films and commercials not only have textual anchorage or relay in various forms (spoken dialogue or subtitles; written notices of various kinds *within* the film frame), allowing for verbo-pictorial metaphor in addition to pictorial metaphor, but also a layer of non-linguistic sound. The latter admits a type of metaphor not possible in printed advertisements. A recent commercial broadcast in Holland shows a man shaving with a reassuringly old-fashioned razor-blade while the sound-track features the noise of a revving car. The visual layer suggests the domain of shaving, while the soundtrack suggests the domain of cars. Since the commercial turns out to be one for Toyota, the metaphor is TOYOTA IS RAZOR, with as projected feature for example the razor's supposed quality, reliability, design, and/or the smoothness of its movements. Another commercial, for KLM, shows in slow-motion a swan landing, while the background noise features snippets of exchanges in an airport's control tower and of a braking plane, suggesting the metaphor PLANE IS SWAN, with 'elegance', 'beauty', and/or 'naturalness' among the projectable features. Notice, incidentally, that the metaphor in the KLM ad is similar to the TYRES ARE LIFE BUOYS metaphor (Figure 6.9) in that here, too, the primary subject is not visually depicted; it is the domain of the secondary subject that is visually rendered. That is, the product advertised is *not* visualized.

Apart from allowing 'auro-pictorial' metaphor, moving images differ in yet another technical aspect from those discussed in this book. Whilst in static, printed pictures both terms of the metaphor must be *simultaneously* present (MP2s, similes, VPMs) or suggested (MP1s), in films this need not be the case: because of film's unfolding in time, one term can be displayed (or suggested) *after* the other. To give an example, in a TV commercial against hooliganism sponsored by the Dutch government ('Postbus 51') one first sees three young tough guys, unshaven, grim-looking, in leather jackets, jeans, heavy boots – in short, three prototypical 'hooligans' – destroying public property. In the last shot, when they are walking away, something has changed: now all three are wearing diapers. Together with other contextual clues (such as the baby-music played, and the final textual reinforcement that, translated, runs: 'Hooliganism is *so* childish') we can conceptualize the metaphor as HOOLIGANS ARE BABIES with the projected feature 'childish behaviour'.[3] The point is that here the second term of the metaphor, 'babies', is suggested after the first term. Film, like language, unfolds linearly in time, and does therefore not need to present, or suggest, the two terms synchronically in a single shot, as must be the case in static pictures such as those used in ads and billboards.[4]

Communicator/addressee

In Chapter 5 the position was advanced, with the aid of concepts derived from Sperber and Wilson's (1986) relevance theory, that analysing an advertisement must take into account the identities of the communicator and the addressee. The communicator was identified as the advertiser while the addressee was taken to be the group of potential consumers. Since one of the crucial tenets of Sperber and Wilson's theory is that relevance is always relevance to an individual, an analysis of advertisements and the pictorial metaphors they may contain needs to show an awareness at whom the advertisement is aimed. A delimitation of the target audience can involve many different dividing lines. One criterion is whether an advertisement has a local, national or international scope. Since the advertiser needs to provide a stimulus that she considers the best possible one to make an impact on the cognitive environment of the envisaged audience, it can make a difference whether the advertiser is a small beer brewery advertising in the village paper hoping to reach local customers; whether she is promoting a certain brand of beer nationwide; or whether she is promoting that same brand internationally. In each case the advertiser must make an assessment of the cognitive environment of a different group of addressees, including what they can be presumed to know, believe, like and dislike. While this holds generally for all kinds of connotations that may inhere in an ad, for present purposes it is specifically pertinent to the choice of source domain for a pictorial metaphor. After all, the interpretation of a metaphor consists in mapping a selection of features from the source domain onto the target domain – the latter constituting the product or being metonymically related to that product. From the viewpoint of the advertiser, therefore, the metaphor's source domain should embody or suggest a network of facts, opinions, connotations and beliefs that are understood by, as well as appeal to, the envisaged audience. Clearly, what the local, national, and international brewers can take for granted as known by and appealing to their respective addressees is bound to vary.

A glimpse of what may happen if a pictorial metaphor is presented to somebody from a very different culture surfaced in the discussion of a Chinese woman's responses to three IBM billboards (see the end of Chapter 7). It will be obvious that a more systematic study of how pictorial metaphors are interpreted by people from different countries may yield valuable insights into the degrees to which objects and events may evoke culturally similar or different connotations (for a related approach, see Camargo 1987), and into the order in which these connotations strike various (groups of) addressees.

But the addressees' geographical background is only one of the factors that may affect the interpretation of pictorial metaphors. Several advertisements considered in this book make use of metaphors that are aimed at specific subgroups of potential addressees: car-owners rather than non-car owners (Figure 6.16, PARKING METER IS DYING CREATURE); retailers rather than consumers (Figure 6.20, LIQUORICE IS BLACK GOLD); young boys rather than girls (Figures 6.21, BMW MOTORBIKE IS GIRLFRIEND and 6.24, CONDOM IS COAT); upmarket rather than average consumers (Figures 6.1, SHOE IS TIE and 6.4, GROLSCH IS CHAMPAGNE). Studying pictorial metaphors in advertising thus requires taking into account the target audience of an advertisement.

Extended research on pictorial metaphor that wishes to focus on the identity of (groups of) addressees could take the following, more or less complementary forms. On the one hand, experiments such as that reported in Chapter 7 can be carried out with a systematic variation in one factor deemed important in the backgrounds of potential addressees. Cultural background is an obvious candidate for this, but as Mick and Politi's (1989) experiment suggests (see Chapter 7), gender can also be a pertinent variable. Moreover, in discussing my own findings in Chapter 7, I proposed that professional background may also affect interpretation. But theoretically any systematic distinction between two or more groups of people may yield significant variations in interpretation (see for instance Larsen *et al.* 1991). This type of research, then, investigates what features, if any, a certain group of people chooses to map from the source domain on to the target domain (usually, the product), and whether these choices differ systematically from those made by a certain other group. These investigations, of course, are necessarily of an empirical nature.

Another approach is to focus on the production rather than the reception side of pictorial metaphors in advertisements. One could investigate whether advertisements promoting a specific type of product, for instance cars, use different metaphorical source domains depending on the envisaged audience. Thus, a question could be whether, and if so which, different metaphorical source domains are used to try and sell cars to men as opposed to women, to Europeans as opposed to North-Americans, to businessmen as opposed to industrial workers, etc. In turn, it can be ascertained which features from these respective domains are suggested for mapping – and hence also which features are *not* selected, and thus ignored or at least downplayed. Such research can shed light on the kind of stereotypical attitudes that advertising presupposes – or even constitutes.

Alternatively, it is possible to trace how a given concept is used as a source domain in different advertising metaphors, that is, which projectable features it is supposed to embody. Any metaphor hinges on the projection of a selection of features from the source domain of the secondary subject upon the target domain, and therefore the secondary subject needs to exemplify these features quite strongly for the metaphor to be effective. Moreover, since the advertiser needs to employ these secondary subjects in ways that she believes are relevant to the envisaged addressees, she is compelled to activate, and appeal to, existing (self)schemas (see Chapter 5) of these addressees. Consequently, it may be illuminating to consider which features of a phenomenon are 'used' in an advertising metaphor's secondary subject in order to gain an impression of this phenomenon's 'reputation' in a particular society (see for instance Casillo's [1985] study of the feature 'Italianness' in American advertisements, and Williamson's [1988/1978] various 'referent systems', discussed in the Introduction of Chapter 4). Since advertisements always make some positive claim about the product or service promoted, and since in metaphors it is the secondary subjects which are mined for their ability to provide these positive claims (sometimes antonymically), examining secondary subjects is bound to yield insight into the hopes, beliefs, principles, desires, fears and other values a society lives by.[5]

Context

As we saw in Chapter 4, the notion of context is not a fixed category, but can include a wide variety of aspects, depending on the purpose of analysis. Several of these aspects were already discussed under different headings in the preceding sections of this chapter, but there are yet other factors that could be taken into consideration. In the previous sections it was explained how geographical context plays a role in the interpretation of advertisements, and of pictorial metaphors occurring in them specifically. But of course contextual factors can affect interpretation on a far more local level as well. That is, a complete analysis of an advertisement may benefit from taking into account the immediate physical surroundings in which it occurs. For a printed ad, this can mean that the analysis must take cognizance of such factors as the kind of newspaper or magazine in which it appears, and the type of texts that occur in its immediate environment (other commercial advertisements? personal ads? news articles?). Commercials usually appear not in isolation but in a block, which in turn is framed in between two programmes, or alternatively, which interrupts a programme. Again there is a potential interaction between a commercial and other commercials in the same sequence[6] or with the programme in which it is embedded. Even the physical location of a billboard can, usually in a modest way, affect its interpretation, as advertising people are increasingly aware. It can make a difference whether a billboard stands in a park, a railway station, a university building, or in front of a business centre.

Besides location in its various manifestations, time is also a factor that may affect the interpretation of a pictorial metaphor. For instance, an advertiser can depend on the expectation that certain events will be, at a given moment, uppermost in her addressees' minds. Olympic Games, important football matches, Christmas, holidays, continuing good or bad weather, the award of a famous prize, natural disasters, certain political developments and a host of other things can be presumed to be so prominent in the envisaged addressees' cognitive environment at a certain moment (but not a week, a month, or a year later) that an advertisement can trust readers/viewers to supply facts or emotions that are not made explicit in the advertisement itself.

Considered from a long term perspective, time can play yet another role. Over time the connotations of any object, event, or person used as a source domain in a metaphor can change. Reputations do not remain constant. A doping affair can degrade a one-time sports hero to a fraud. The notion of a 'hippy' had different connotations in the 1960s than it has in the 1990s. A typewriter is now – but was not twenty years ago – likely to evoke the notion of being (ridiculously or honestly) old-fashioned. In our era of increased awareness of threats to the environment plastic cutlery will be seen by many no longer as sophisticatedly efficient but as unacceptably wasteful.

A contextual element whose importance I have repeatedly emphasized is that of 'genre attribution'. It was argued, for instance, that the genre attribution 'advertising' strongly implicates 'this is an advertisement for product X', which in turn generates the strong implicature 'something positive will be claimed for product X'. By contrast, in a genre attribution 'art', for instance, neither of these implicatures is pertinent.[7] However, advertisements and billboards may in various ways problematize the matter of genre attribution. For one thing, ads sometimes try to disguise their true nature by attempting to pose as a different type of text. Thus, ads in sponsored magazines may take the form of, allegedly, critical articles (so-called 'advertorials', see Myers 1983); or they may try to 'merge' with surrounding articles by making use of the same typeface, or style, or conventions, as these articles (see also Cook 1992: 31 ff.). Another variant of this is ads' incorporation of complete 'texts' that originally belonged to a different genre. Paintings or news photos, for instance, can be re-used in ads. Matters become even more complicated when there is a deliberate blurring of genres. This issue, I believe, is the central problem underlying the fierce controversies surrounding the international Benetton campaigns of the past few years. Can a word and image text be simultaneously an advertisement for a brand of clothes and a protest against racial prejudices, environmental pollution, social injustice, or war? Or does the relatively minor (in terms of space) addition of the Benetton logo ineluctably and completely transform what otherwise could well have been a news photo into a commercial message? And would changing the genre attribution from 'advertising' to 'sponsoring' change the answers to the aforementioned questions at all?

Finally, the issue of context of course plays a role within the physical boundaries of the advertisement itself. As we saw in Chapter 6, the subdivision into MP1s, MP2s, similes and VPMs hinges to a considerable extent on where 'metaphor' ends and 'context' begins. Further research concentrating on this issue might try to answer such questions as the following: What principles govern the choice of any one of these varieties of metaphor/simile rather than one of the others in advertising? Is it technically possible to transform any of these types into one of the others? Which elements in the context are essential, and which optional, for the interpretation of the metaphor? Are there yet other sub-types of pictorial metaphor besides those identified in Chapter 6? Questions pertaining to metaphor/ context divisions may moreover shed light on issues connected to part/ whole relations (see Chapter 6, note 7).

OTHER PICTORIAL TROPES

The proposal to accept the existence of pictorial metaphor inevitably raises the question whether other tropes have pictorial counterparts as well. As we saw in Chapter 3, Kennedy (1982), Johns (1984), and Durand (1987) all give an affirmative answer, and their many examples suggest that pursuing the study of pictorial tropes is a valid enterprise, in the interests both of a better understanding of tropes and of greater insight into the processes of picture comprehension. None of these authors, however, provides a satisfactory theoretical framework for the examples given. At this stage it is possible to delimit some criteria that such a framework should take into consideration.

A comprehensive framework of pictorial tropes needs to be developed within the boundaries of a more general theory of communication and cognition. We may provisionally hypothesize that Lakoff and Johnson's (1980) discernment that metaphor is first and foremost a matter of thought also holds for other rhetorical figures (see also Gibbs 1993). If symbolism, paronomasia, metonymy, paradox, irony, etc., are a matter of cognition first, and of language second, it should be possible to define their characteristic properties in medium-neutral terms. But even in that case, an elaboration of a framework of pictorial tropes will have to be founded on existing theories, and these have in many cases been developed in the realm of language – although tropes like symbol and allegory are familiar from art-historical studies as well (see for instance Gombrich 1975/1972).

Sperber and Wilson's (1986) relevance theory provides a further starting point for the development of an all-encompassing framework of pictorial tropes. The principle of relevance, after all, involves the mutual awareness of communicator and addressee that the former is trying to make some sort of impact on the cognitive environment of the latter. Inasmuch as rhetorical tropes constitute ways to achieve these effects, relevance theory can provide parameters within which the pictorial tropes can be described, characterized, and illustrated. Various contextual factors, both text-internal and text-external, need to be taken into account. One of the most vital of these is the assessment to which genre the text featuring the said trope belongs.

Within a cognition-based and relevance-oriented approach the description and characterization of the tropes itself can be undertaken. Such a description must take cognizance of, and compare, any authoritative definitions and classifications of tropes that are already available. While some of these (e.g., symbolism, allegory) have been applied to pictorial phenomena, many have been hitherto primarily or exclusively familiar from the verbal realm. In the latter case investigations need to be made to see if, and how, they can fit certain pictorial phenomena. It should be emphasized that finding plausible correspondences between verbal and pictorial phenomena is often by no means a simple, mechanical matter. To some extent the application of labels that have gained currency in the description of certain verbal phenomena to pictorial phenomena is in itself a creative act: the similarity between the verbal phenomenon and the pictorial phenomenon is often not pre-existent, but needs to be created.

The degree of creativity involved in transposing or translating verbal tropes to the pictorial realm is constrained in at least two obvious ways. First, any transpositions must respect intuitions about what is essential in any verbal trope. Thus, whatever candidates may be suggested for pictorial hyperbole, an element of exaggeration is crucial. Similarly, a pictorial paradox, if it exists, needs to embody a phenomenon that features an apparent contradiction. Second, internal relations in the framework of the verbal tropes, in terms of similarity and dissimilarity, should be maintained as much as possible in the envisaged pictorial framework. Anything labelled 'pictorial meiosis,' for instance, should contrast with 'pictorial hyperbole'. Likewise, it needs to be investigated whether the verbal distinction between paradox and oxymoron has a parallel in the visual realm. And, to give a third example, both the shared characteristics of pictorial metaphor, symbolism, and allegory, and their differences should be charted.

In order to facilitate the development of a framework of pictorial tropes, a range of 'tests' needs to be designed similar to those I have proposed to differentiate between the various types of metaphor in Chapter 6. These tests could take the form of questions such as the following: what contextual levels are (in)dispensable for ensuring the envisaged interpretation of a specific pictorial trope? If a specific pictorial trope concerns two terms, by what means do we establish their order? Does the trope involve a necessary or optional physical distortion of an object depicted? Is the picture in which the said trope occurs bound to one pictorial medium or is it translatable into another one (e.g., from a drawing into a photo)? Does changing the style in which an object is depicted affect the classification of the trope? Would it be possible to execute the trope in three dimensions?

The description and characterization of pictorial tropes furthermore needs to accommodate the following complicating factors:

1) pictures seldom occur without any verbal accompaniment, so that usually word/image relations will have to be taken into account as well. If a trope, analogous to the verbo-pictorial metaphors identified in the case studies in Chapter 6, involves two terms belonging to different media, the question can be asked whether the trope could have been rendered with a switch of medium of the terms;

2) the boundaries between various tropes cannot always be drawn with absolute confidence. Thus some tropes may shade into one another. It is thinkable for instance that one might hesitate, in classifying a certain pictorial phenomenon, between the categories 'pictorial metaphor' and 'pictorial pun' (see Forceville 1994a; for a discussion of pictorial puns, see also Abed 1994);

3) tropes do not necessarily occur in isolation: various tropes can manifest themselves in combination with other tropes. As we saw in Chapter 6, many metaphors involve metonymy as well. Other combinations are conceivable. In advertising, a product could for instance be depicted both as a person (personification) and in giant-sized proportions (hyperbole). This potential co-occurrence, however, is not exclusively a complicating factor. Establishing which tropes can and which cannot co-occur may help define them.[8]

SUMMARY

Extending the already rich topic of metaphor from the verbal to the (semi)pictorial multiplies the opportunities for research, both from a theoretical perspective and with a view to applications. All the theoretical issues in studies of metaphor that have been raised about verbal specimens must be discussed with reference to its pictorial variants, too, in order to increase the understanding of the similarities and differences between verbal and pictorial metaphor. Moreover, the systematic transposition of Black's model of verbal metaphor to pictorial phenomena enables students of cognitive metaphor to verify any claims derived from delimiting metaphor in language by checking them against pictorial specimens. In turn, Black's theory should be employed to examine whether metaphors are expressible via yet other modes of perception: the auditory, the gustatory, the olfactory, the tactile – or any permutations of these as well as combinations with the verbal and the visual mode.

The study of pictorial metaphor, and of other pictorial tropes, furthermore, is a useful instrument to help develop a theory of images and word and image texts, and of how these communicate. The modern world makes an increasing use of pictorial modes of conveying information, but theories of how this is achieved are still in their preliminary stages. The model of pictorial metaphor offers an angle on the analysis of the rhetorical strategies employed in word and image texts in more general terms. While in this book the corpus of texts has been restricted to (static) advertisements, the insights can be extended to subcategories of other types of texts, be they artistic, didactic or informative in nature. Inasmuch as these latter are governed by identifiable intentions, the link between linguistic metaphor and narrative as discussed in Ricoeur (1977) and Johnson (1993) should be translatable to the realm of pictures and word and image texts.

Finally, the existence of metaphor, no matter in what medium, is a constant reminder of the crucial fact that the world as we know it is always a world perceived through the filter of our preconceptions, values, and goals. Representations of the world, whether verbal or pictorial in nature, are inevitably distortions of the infinitely rich and infinitely chaotic phenomenon we call reality. On the one hand such distortions are simplifying structures without which we would fail to survive either individually or as a species; on the other hand they tend to make us forgetful of rival conceptualizations that could be, and are, based on that selfsame 'reality'. Investigating the largely unexplored area of pictorial metaphor, from theoretical and experimental angles, provides us with a powerful tool to examine both sides of this issue.

Notes

ACKNOWLEDGEMENTS

1 Substantial parts of Forceville (1991, 1994a and 1994c) have found their way into Chapter 6. An earlier version of Chapter 5 appears in Forceville (1994b), while a shorter version of Chapter 7 has been published as Forceville (1995a).

1 INTRODUCTION

No notes

2 MAX BLACK'S INTERACTION THEORY OF METAPHOR

1 Note Mooij's claim that Bühler (1934) and, even more, Stählin (1914) propose views on metaphor that in many ways anticipate Black's interaction theory (Mooij 1976: 78–80).

2 Possibly Black's confusion is caused by the particular example he uses here: Stevens's 'society is a sea'. The circumstance that the primary subject under consideration, 'society', happens to be a network of (social) relationships anyway may have misled Black into thinking that it would be superfluous to stipulate that a primary subject is no less 'a system of things' than a secondary subject.

3 Lakoff and Johnson discuss this aspect of metaphor in terms of 'highlighting' and 'hiding' (1980: 10 ff.).

4 For a compelling analysis of the network of metaphors underlying the US policy makers' decision to defend Kuwait in the Gulf war, see Lakoff (1992).

5 In situations where a metaphor is used to aid learning or the making of new discoveries, structural mappings are often crucial (see for accounts Gentner 1989; Gentner and Jeziorski 1993).

6 Incidentally, it is defensible to argue that an attribute such as 'carnivorous' is not a trivial one in 'man is a wolf'. Since human beings are both herbivorous and carnivorous, while wolves are only the latter, there is a tension between 'man' and 'wolf' on this score as well. In the metaphorical transfer from wolf to man the carnivorousness could be interpreted as 'bloodthirstiness'.

7 Kittay uses this metaphor for metaphor as well (Kittay 1987: 269).

8 This notion is also captured by the name of Verbrugge's (1980) variant of Black's interaction theory, i.e., the 'transformation view' of metaphor.

9 Following the practice initiated by Lakoff and Johnson (1980), I will in this book capitalize metaphors when their CONCEPTUAL status is at stake. *Italicized, lower case print* indicates the metaphorized parts in the linguistic manifestation a metaphor can take.

10 In contemporary writing on metaphor, the term 'domain' is generally used for

what Black labelled 'implicative complex'. More specifically, the implicative complex of the secondary subject is called the 'source domain', whereas the implicative complex of the primary subject is the 'target domain'. In view of their greater currency, these latter terms will henceforth be used.

11 And even in so-called ordinary language a statement's truth or falsity can only be assessed within a certain conceptual framework that is not objectively given. Lakoff and Johnson specify a number of aspects that are central to this presupposed conceptual framework, such as categorization, the imposing of entity structure and orientation towards phenomena that do not inherently possess either. See for a detailed discussion of these claims Lakoff and Johnson (1980), specifically Chapter 24.

12 Kjärgaard (1986: 126) makes the same point.

13 MacCormac (1985) is one of the theorists who tries to salvage the notion of literal truth/falsity for metaphor by arguing that metaphors are partially true and partially false.

14 Unless, of course, 'X' and 'smiled' are not part of the same frame. In this case what we have is one metaphor that is embedded in another one. The principle remains the same.

15 Alternative expressions used in this book are 'transferred from the secondary to the primary subject' and 'mapped from the secondary on to the primary subject'.

16 For more discussion of the asymmetry and irreversibility of the two terms of a metaphor, see Chapter 3 and Forceville (1995b).

3 TOWARDS A THEORY OF PICTORIAL METAPHOR: RELEVANT STUDIES

1 This paper is concerned with what metaphors mean, and its thesis is that metaphors mean what the words, in their most literal interpretation, mean, and nothing more. Since this thesis flies in the face of contemporary views with which I am familiar, much of what I have to say is critical.

(Davidson 1979: 29–30)

2 In the second half of his Lecture, Wollheim claims that it is not necessarily the *human* body that is metaphorized in many paintings. He argues that there are certain paintings featuring 'architecture or . . . buildingscapes' that 'metaphorize the same thing as the great canvases of Bellini and Titian. They possess corporeality to a high degree' (1987: 338), and discusses them at length.

3 Wollheim (1993), which expands on the insights of Wollheim (1987), came to my attention too late for extended discussion here. In spite of some theoretical refinements, however, the article does not refute the criticisms voiced in this section. Judged from the perspective of developing a theory of pictorial metaphor, one of the main problems with Wollheim's account remains his claim that 'though I have no arguments for this last piece of my account of pictorial metaphor . . . I believe that there is just one thing that all (at any rate) *great* metaphorical paintings metaphorize: and that is the human body' (1993: 119).

4 This idea was also proposed by Ricoeur (1977: Study 7).

5 The reason for this misunderstanding, incidentally, is that Hausman focuses too much on the *linguistic* level of the metaphors, whereas, as Lakoff and Turner's analysis shows, the five 'terms' Hausman identifies can actually be shown to be manifestations of only three terms (or rather domains) on the *cognitive* level (see p. 33 for more discussion on the difference between the two).

6 Kittay's (1987: 66 and 289 ff.) analysis of the same Shakespeare passage seems to corroborate my reading. Incidentally, in Forceville (1990) I discuss a drawing by Max Ernst, entitled 'Chimaera', which could be interpreted as a *pictorial*

metaphor with six terms. These, however, are circularly related, and I propose we understand them – if we do so at all – by postulating one term at a time as the primary subject and one term as the secondary subject. For a discussion of metaphors with two terms where the order of the terms is difficult or even impossible to assess, see Forceville (1995b).

7 I note in passing that Hausman here confuses Black's remarks on the metaphor 'Man is a wolf' (Black's example in his main text) with those he makes with reference to the difference between 'Man's face is like a wolf mask' and 'Man's face is a wolf mask' (which happens only to be the example in this particular note).

8 This would furthermore be consistent with his own earlier reminder that he has 'no quarrel with the use of metaphors (if they are good ones) in talking about metaphor. But it may be as well to use several, lest we are misled by the adventitious charms of our favorites' (Black 1962: 39).

9 The interpretation of the metaphor can only be a provisional one as long as its context of utterance is not given. This issue will be discussed at length in Chapters 4 and 5.

10 Notice that this is a possible elaboration, even though the notion of 'home-' has no place in the source domain PRISON.

11 Indurkhya (1992) explicitly comments on the confusion this sentence causes. 'This [sentence] clearly implies a symmetry in the interaction between the source and the target. However, at other places in [Black's] discussion there is a clearly implied asymmetry' (1992: 4). For a sympathetic but critical review of Black's interaction theory see Indurkhya (1992: 68–73). Indurkhya also briefly discusses Hausman's variety of Black's interactionism, implicitly rejecting the latter's ideas about the symmetry of the two metaphorical terms (Indurkhya 1992: 75–6).

12 As such, there is no reason why 'tenor' and 'treatment' could not have been reversed – although in that case the trope under discussion would no longer have been an anticlimax, but rather its opposite; instead of the solemn atmosphere evoked by the Greek temple being deflated by Alfred E. Neumann's presence, the presentation of this young man would then gain solemnity by the presence of the temple. That such a reading is not plausible, I would suggest, is because of the wider context of the picture in question. Since it appears in the satirical magazine *Mad*, we *expect* anticlimaxes rather than their opposites (meioses). Hence, I would venture, it is our expectation of anticlimaxes occurring in *Mad* that determines our reconstruction of temple as 'tenor' and Alfred E. Neumann as 'treatment'. The 'genre' to which a picture or word and image text belongs thus constitutes an important contextual factor.

13 Kennedy's own sustained interest in research with congenitally blind people led him to investigate the interpretation of 'pictorial runes' (Kennedy 1982: 600) – graphic devices used for instance in comic strips to indicate pain, smell, motion, speed, etc. Kennedy claims that pictorial runes, while having no equivalent in language, are clearly metaphoric in character. See also Kennedy (1985; 1990) and Kennedy and Gabias (1985).

14 Johns moreover is mistaken in thinking that Black (1962) discusses the concept of metaphor in the *broad* sense.

15 Durand begins his article as follows: 'This study was done in the sixties, when I worked at the French advertising agency, Publicis, and studied with Roland Barthes at the Ecole Pratique des Hautes Etudes' (1987: 295).

16 Specifically, the labels 'frame' and 'focus' are used where 'primary subject' and 'secondary subject' would have been preferable. Moreover, the use of the mathematical ' = ' instead of 'is' in the verbalizations of the metaphors discussed seems in retrospect misleading, since it encourages the idea that the two terms of

a metaphor are reversible, whereas both in the article itself and in this chapter it is repeatedly emphasized that this is not the case.

17 Indeed, it was perhaps somewhat naive to expect that *any* sort of model could be based on an artistic movement that tried to subvert existing modes of seeing and thinking.

18 The list formulates necessary, not sufficient criteria.

4 ADVERTISING: WORD AND IMAGE AND LEVELS OF CONTEXT

1 It must be conceded, however, that Cook does not seem to draw this conclusion gladly, since generally speaking he attempts to close rather than widen the gap between advertising and literature. See also Cook (1992: 152).

2 Not quite, of course: the size of the reproduction is smaller and, unless indicated otherwise, the advertisements were originally in colour. Moreover, the immediate context in which they originally occurred has disappeared.

3 Although Cook primarily focuses on the linguistic message, his awareness of the difficult question of what anchors what surfaces when, in his comparison between the five billboards, he mentions that 'variation of the opening phrase of the written text *dictates* [*or is dictated by*] changes in the pictorial text' (1988: 154, emphasis mine). For more discussion of word and image relations in an advertisement, see Pateman (1983: 192 ff.). Examples and analyses of interconnections in other types of word and image texts can be found in Kress and van Leeuwen (1992).

4 Johnson's (1987) fascinating exploration of how the workings of the human body influence human conceptualizing and language suggests where we may look for anthropological universals.

5 For interesting examples of cross-cultural misunderstandings see Druce (1990: 36, note 18) and Kennedy (1985: 56–7). For an example of subcultural differences in the interpretation of a television programme, see Morley (1983).

5 COMMUNICATOR AND ADDRESSEE IN THE ADVERTISING MESSAGE: RELEVANCE THEORY PERSPECTIVES

1 For critical commentaries by scholars from a wide range of disciplines, see the 'Open Peer Review' section following Sperber and Wilson (1987). Two critical reviews are Levinson (1989) and Seuren (1988), the latter replied to in Wilson and Sperber (1988). An accessible elaboration of Sperber and Wilson's views can be found in Blakemore (1992).

2 Another summary of *Relevance* by the authors themselves is to be found in Wilson and Sperber (1989). A brief overview of its central tenets is provided by Smith and Wilson (1992). The responsibility for any mistaken interpretations of Sperber and Wilson's theory as presented in this section remains of course entirely mine.

3 Assumptions can also take the form of impressions (Sperber and Wilson 1986: 59). Wilson and Sperber (1989b: 111 ff.) go into more detail about the communication of impressions and attitudes. See also Blakemore (1994), replying to Culpeper (1994) on this subject.

4 In line with Sperber and Wilson's practice, the communicator of a message will here be taken, unless specified otherwise, to be female, while the addressee is male. This solution elegantly pairs positive discrimination to unambiguous referring conventions.

5 Naturally, in an oral exchange between two people that are simultaneously present, the participants continually switch roles, being in turn communicator and addressee.

6 Sperber and Wilson have been criticized for making both stimulus and context variable factors, for instance by Seuren (1988: 140–1). Consequently, Seuren claims, the notion of relevance becomes circular. Sperber and Wilson counter the criticism by pointing out that the matching of stimulus and context always involves the active evaluation of an individual, that is of 'a mechanism capable of accessing a variety of contexts' (Wilson and Sperber 1988: 154). The authors, I take it, want to emphasize here that assessing relevance is not a matter of mathematical calculation, but a process undertaken by a specific individual capable of weighing probabilities, matching bits of information, etc. The importance of 'relevance-to-an-individual' is elaborated on in the next section.

7 Various commentators have criticized Sperber and Wilson for being rather speculative about the assessment of the effort involved in processing a stimulus. See for instance Bach and Harnish (1987: 711); Clark (1987: 715); Russell (1987: 731); Levinson (1989: 459).

8 There is, in fact, a far more profound affinity between Johnson's (and Lakoff's) work and Sperber and Wilson's than this brief reference can suggest (see particularly the section 'Meaningfulness and linguistic meaning' in Johnson 1987: 176 ff). For this reason it is all the more surprising that Johnson (1987, 1993) is apparently unaware of Sperber and Wilson's work (although in the former of these he refers to Grice's work) – and vice versa: Sperber and Wilson 1986 contains no references to either Lakoff or Johnson. Since both Lakoff and Johnson's and Sperber and Wilson's work have influenced many scholars, and continue to do so, cross-fertilization is highly desirable.

9 Pilkington explores the implications of 'poetic effects' for poetry and concludes that 'a poem is successful and has value to the extent that it communicates poetic effects' (1991: 60).

10 'A logical form is *propositional* if it is semantically complete and therefore capable of being true or false, and *non-propositional* otherwise' (Sperber and Wilson 1986: 72). 'Logical form', in turn, is the sum total of the 'logical properties of a conceptual representation' (ibid.).

11 Cooper even sees the achievement of intimacy as metaphor's primary characteristic: 'It is reasonable to modulate from seeing intimacy as merely one among several sustaining functions of metaphor to seeing it as *the* general sustaining function. . . . The cultivation of intimacy, I suggest, is the best candidate for that "need and power of the spirit and heart" which, according to Hegel, metaphor manifests' (1986: 168). This, however, is far too strong a claim: surely the pre-eminent role of metaphor as a pedagogical or heuristic device cannot be subsumed under the theme of the enhancement of intimacy.

12 This is a good moment for a reminder that relevance is always relevance to an individual. A necrophiliac, for instance, might not at all agree that 'graveyards are sad and boring places'; on the contrary, he might find them highly exciting locations. Consequently, he might come up with a different metaphorical projection. The communicator of the metaphor, if she wished to convey that museums are sad and boring places to this particular person, obviously made the wrong assessment of the cognitive context of her addressee! And even then the necrophiliac, if he is aware of the relative rarity of his predilections, might realize that the speaker did not intend to suggest museums' exciting, but rather their boring atmosphere. I owe the example to Lachlan Mackenzie.

13 The pertinence of Sperber and Wilson's work for the study of advertisements was signalled already by Pateman (1983). Pateman's article was based on an early, fairly short version of relevance theory (Wilson and Sperber 1979). The present account builds on later, and more extended versions, and can thus be more precise and detailed. Tanaka's (1994) application of relevance theory to advertising will be discussed in the next section.

14 Ricoeur, incidentally, proceeds by saying that 'this abolition of the ostensive character of reference is no doubt what makes possible the phenomenon we call "literature", which may abolish all reference to a given reality'. Interesting though it might be to speculate to what extent the referential function is similarly weakened for advertising, I will not pursue this matter further here. . . .

15 Sperber and Wilson suggest that in broadcast communication, 'a stimulus can even be addressed to whoever finds it relevant. The communicator is then communicating her presumption of relevance to whoever is willing to entertain it' (1986: 158). This, of course, holds for all forms of mass-communication: it is for instance equally applicable to the example I gave about the presumed relevance to various readers of the present text (see p. 89).

16 Of course there are varieties of pictorial communication that belong in the category 'strong communication', such as the stylized, and heavily coded, pictures usually called 'pictograms'. I owe this observation to Adrian Pilkington.

17 The aiming for intimacy in advertising is acknowledged by Cook as well (1992: 172).

6 PICTORIAL METAPHOR IN ADVERTISEMENTS AND BILLBOARDS: CASE STUDIES

1 All figures are originally in colour, unless specified otherwise. Translations of texts from non-English advertisements and billboards are all mine.

2 It is to be borne in mind that this emphasis on relevance to an individual also has consequences for my own analyses of the advertisements in this chapter: although I will try to be as unbiased as possible, I can never lay claim to having provided the one and only, or even the 'best' interpretation of the metaphors under discussion.

3 For instance that Grolsch is a brand of beer, that beer is often sold in bottles, that beer usually contains alcohol, etc.

4 As a matter of fact, the Grolsch bottle in the cooler also appeared in one of the Grolsch TV and cinema commercials. Awareness of this kind of 'intertextuality' – very common in advertising – of course also facilitates interpretation. Bex elaborates on this type of intertextuality by emphasizing that 'each specific contribution to a generic type [here: advertising] contributes a particular token which both modifies what has gone before and offers possibilities for future adaptation' (Bex 1993: 729).

5 The two last words, 'proost' and 'gezondheid' are in fact not German but Dutch, although the former is close enough to its German equivalent to be recognizable to a German audience. Both are common toasts in Holland. Moreover it is to be noticed that 'altes Haus' (old house) is also used as an informal form of address among men, while the heading may also pun on the expression 'Einfälle wie ein altes Haus haben', which roughly means, 'to hit upon the most curious ideas'. I thank Marieke Krajenbrink for pointing this out to me.

6 When this billboard was shown to Word and Image students at Trinity College, Dublin (April 1994), two of them suggested that the heading also punningly referred to the expression 'Stuff a cold and starve a fever'.

7 It is furthermore to be noticed that the two alternative verbalizations proffered have to do with part-whole relationships, which Lakoff sees as crucial to basic-level categorization. He approvingly refers to Tversky and Hemenway (1984), who observe that

the basic level is distinguished from other levels on the basis of the type of attributes people associate with a category at that level, in particular, attributes concerned with *parts*. Our knowledge at the basic level is mainly organized around part-whole divisions. The reason is that the way an object is divided into parts determines many things. First, parts are usually correlated with functions, and hence our knowledge about functions is usually associated with knowledge about parts. Second, parts determine shape, and hence the way that an object will be perceived and imaged. Third, we usually interact with things via their parts, and hence part-whole divisions play a major role in determining what motor programs we can use to interact with an object.

(Paraphrased by Lakoff 1987: 47)

8 As an afterthought, however, I wish to observe that the situation can be quite complicated. If we were to verbalize the metaphor NIB IS KEY in Figure 6.14 as NIB IS BIT (OF KEY), it would be an MP1. What could be said to be in favour of such a verbalization is that there *is* a separate word to name that part of a key (namely 'bit'); what would count against it is that 'bit', unlike 'key', is not a concept with 'great cultural significance', nor is it 'perceived holistically, as a single gestalt'. Conversely, a case could be made for verbalizing the metaphor in Figure 6.8 as NIB IS ALARM CLOCK rather than NIB IS HAMMER, the result being a shift from MP1 to MP2. Confirmation (or disconfirmation) of my proposal to distinguish between the two categories requires empirical testing.

9 An advertisement in the same series juxtaposes the Eiffel tower and a giant sized bottle of Dommelsch beer.

10 Ortony uses the term 'predicates' for what are here called 'features'. As suggested in Chapter 2 in the outline of Black's theory, a feature 'x-ness' can be rephrased as a predicate 'is x'.

11 Later on in his article Ortony also discusses the possibility that in a simile (or a metaphor), the B-term suggests predicates that are non-predicates of the A-term. These predicate introduction similes or metaphors Ortony sees as 'one of the cornerstones of insight' (1979: 200). This remark captures the notion of 'creating similarity' of Black's interaction theory.

12 The difference outlined here between a simile and a non-literal comparison is not an absolute one, as Ortony himself acknowledges (1979: 193), inasmuch as the distinction between salient and non-salient predicates cannot be made absolutely. For one thing, it is to be added, the decision about the (non)salience of predicates in a metaphor involves the assessment of relevance, and hence requires taking into account the context and situation in which the metaphor is used. In the zero-context in which Ortony presents his examples, of course, default values concerning the terms under discussion obtain.

13 Corroboration for the proposal can be found in Kaplan (1992), which came too late to the author's notice to be discussed at length in the present study. Kaplan distinguishes between juxtaposition and identity type of visual metaphors, a dichotomy that is equated with (verbal) simile and metaphor respectively (1992: 203).

14 Of course in some cases the text is inscribed on the primary subject itself and thus helps to identify it: the TICKET metaphors (Figures 6.6, 6.7, and 6.13) all have the text 'Air France' inscribed on the ticket; and the bottle in Figure 6.4 contains the brand name 'Grolsch'.

15 The Dutch word 'verkering' means both 'dating' and 'the person one is dating'.

16 It is to be noticed that in the Dutch original, the pronoun used to refer to the BMW motorbike is 'hij' ('he'). This might seem to conflict with a reading of the motorbike as a rival girlfriend. It is to be pointed out however, that what is at stake here is grammatical gender, not biological sex.

17 The fact that the features mapped from source on to target domain change their value from 'negative' to 'positive' (e.g., 'not-long-lasting relationship' becomes

'long-lasting relationship') because of its sustained regularity does not at all affect the principle (cf. Figure 6.12).

18 A more recent Dutch billboard ad for a brand of mopeds, Puch, ran as follows: 'When you are young you've only got one thing on your mind. [Follows Puch Logo, and underneath, in small print:] All right, let's say two'. Here again, the erotic overtones can hardly be missed.

19 In Forceville (1995b) I examine this latent transfer from primary to secondary subject in the light of Black's notion of 'interaction', and propose the label 'subsidiary transfer' of features for it, as distinct from the dominant transfer that, as in any metaphor, runs from secondary to primary subject.

20 It is to be noted that 'regenjasje', the diminutive form of the Dutch word for rain coat, has 'condom' as a secondary meaning.

21 The link between coitus interruptus and preventing pregnancy is acknowledged for instance in the erotic dictionary of Heestermans *et al.* (1980/1977).

22 Presumably there is the clearly commercial idea behind this that even if people do not wish to take the time or make the effort to read the body-copy, the picture + heading/pay-off provides them with enough information to be relevant.

23 Perhaps Figure 6.3, where the word 'semences' ('seeds') generalizes the depicted 'sweet corn', should count as an exception.

24 For some interesting examples of the role of cultural context in promotion and advertising, see Druce (1990: 36–7). The article contains a number of perceptive analyses of word-image relationships in adverts, book covers and others.

7 INDIVIDUALS' RESPONSES TO THREE IBM BILLBOARDS: AN EXPLORATORY EXPERIMENT

1 For more detailed discussion, see the article itself. A second hypothesis, derived from MacCannell (1987), was tested, namely that sexual desire was associated with brand desire.

2 To be sure, the classification of the IBM metaphors as *verbo*-pictorial can be challenged: both because of the fact that the 'verbal' component is a logo and because there is a colour correspondence between the logo and an element in the picture, the verbal component has clearly pictorial aspects as well. As so often in the complex relations between word and image that characterize advertising, traditional distinctions tend to get blurred. For present purposes, however, it is not important whether the specimens under consideration are labelled pictorial metaphors or verbo-pictorial ones.

3 Contextual factors that were beyond my control include the precise physical context in which the billboards would have been originally encountered and, more importantly, the testing circumstances (a 'laboratory situation' versus a passing glance – if that). Furthermore the size of the billboards was in the experiment reduced to a slide format.

4 For another experiment based on Mick and Politi's (1989) design, see Elliott *et al.* (1993).

5 The requests to prioritize in questions 2 and 3 were not made in Mick and Politi's experiment. They were incorporated in the hope that the responses would be interpretable in terms of Sperber and Wilson's 'strong' versus 'weak' implicatures'.

6 I would like to thank Etienne Forceville for carrying out this task.

7 Of the twenty-five participants, eight were British, three Belgian, three Dutch, two Greek, two Australian; the other seven were, respectively, Canadian, Spanish, Chinese(?), French, Danish, South-African, and Belgian-Dutch-Moroccan.

8   Here the two raters reached immediate consensus on thirteen out of eighteen responses; the others were resolved through discussion.

9   The responses of participants tested in Amsterdam have been coded as 'A + number'; those of participants tested in Ghent as 'G + number'.

10   The raters achieved immediate consensus on seventeen out of twenty-three on this score; the remaining responses were resolved through discussion. For those who did not mention the correspondence under question 1A, the scores were as follows: six under 1B; two under 1C; five under 3A; 1 under 3B; one not at all.

11   The fact that in Amsterdam eleven out of the eighteen participants indicated awareness that my project was concerned with metaphor, while only four explicitly identified metaphors (the Ghent numbers being sixteen and eight out of twenty-two respectively) can be adduced as circumstantial evidence that the degree of possible bias caused by participants' previous knowledge about my interest in metaphor should not be overrated.

12   'Immediate agreement among the raters on fifteen out of eighteen' here means the following: In Amsterdam the **safety** theme was scored as being exemplified *by both raters* in the responses of fifteen of the eighteen participants. In the responses of three participants the **safety** theme was identified by only *one* rater.

13   The total number of responses identified exceeds the number of participants. This is due to the fact that many participants mentioned more than one attribute. In order not to complicate matters further, no attention has here been paid to the relative importance claimed (if at all) by participants for attributes (i.e. the prioritization as requested in questions 2 and 3; see the section earlier in this chapter on Method; but cf. the section later on Sperber and Wilson's strong vs. weak implicatures). Here and later, sample responses do not necessarily reflect *all* the text written in response to a particular subquestion. The responses of participants tested in Amsterdam have been translated by me (except for A15's, who responded in English), while those of participants tested in Ghent were already given in English; some punctuation and spelling mistakes have been silently corrected; comments in square brackets are mine; numbers indicating prioritization have been removed and, where originally present, replaced by a semicolon.

14   It is to be noted here that several participants, even though they already had acknowledged the colour correspondence between IBM and the tuning fork, focus on the (Steinway) piano rather than the tuning fork, thus effectively interpreting the metaphor IBM IS A (STEINWAY) PIANO rather than IBM IS A TUNING FORK.

15   The Dutch writer Jan de Hartog often chose seafaring settings for his books. *Op Hoop van Zegen* is a famous play by the Dutchman Herman Heijermans, situated in the fisherman's world.

16   This participant, when asked for clarification, stated that one of Shakespeare's sonnets (no. 116) suggests a beacon:

> [Love] is an ever-fixed mark,
> That looks on tempests and is never shaken;
> It is the star to every wandering bark,
> Whose worth's unknown, although his height be taken.

17   The Dutch expression 'roeien met de riemen die je hebt' literally translates as 'to row with the oars that one has at one's disposal' but means 'to make do with whatever is available'. Several other participants tested in Amsterdam were reminded of this expression, and voiced their incomprehension, since they realized that IBM would surely not have wanted to convey such a negative sentiment.

18 Circumstantial evidence for this is that there was (only) one Oriental-looking woman among the 25 participants, she being the only one who had not given her nationality. Moreover, as her answer to question 1A reveals, she is familiar with the Chinese language.

19 It may be observed, incidentally, that the 'real life' presentation of the billboards allowed a similar 'learning effect'. Several specimens of the series were simultaneously on display out on the streets for a week or so. People were thus bound to come across them repeatedly over time.

20 For more discussion concerning this last interpretation, see the next section.

21 There is, of course, one crucial difference between the two: the former contains an amount of informative context that is absent in the latter.

22 Across the two groups twenty out of the forty participants whose responses were used did this at least once (where they had the chance to do this six times, i.e., under questions 2A, 2B, 2C, 3A, 3B, 3C).

23 The difference spotted here between IBM IS OARS and IBM IS A BEACON on the one hand and IBM IS A TUNING FORK on the other is only valid, of course, to the extent that my categories are seen as reflecting the variety in participants' responses.

8 CLOSING REMARKS

1 Corroboration of this idea can be found in an illuminating article by Danto (Danto 1993). The first example he discusses is a cartoon in which king Louis Philippe is metaphorically represented as a pear. Danto furthermore astutely comments on the irreversibility of terms in a pictorial metaphor (see Chapter 3) and on the cultural context (see Chapter 4) in which a pictorial metaphor is embedded.

2 Moreover, the importance of an identifiable intention is not only necessary for analysing pictorial metaphors, but can be extended to other aspects of the analysis of pictures. In an article attempting to formulate criteria for the application of the concept 'depicting', Max Black (1972) reaches the same conclusion. After having rejected various criteria as necessary and sufficient to characterize 'depiction', he observes:

> There is something of the first importance lacking from our account, namely all consideration of the purposes of the activities in the course of which, what we, in our culture, recognize as 'pictures' are produced. And no account of the concept of depicting, or of the various related concepts bundled together under that label, could be adequate without some examination of such purposes.
>
> (Black 1972: 128)

3 And the interpretation can be expanded with implicatures of various weakness or strength. As John Woods (University of Lethbridge) suggested to me, babies are incontinent, they cannot control themselves, they produce shit, which other people will have to clean up, the hooligans look ridiculous in the diapers . . .

4 Although technically this would be feasible in billboards as well: since advertising agencies nowadays sometimes present a series of related, 'developing' billboards not simultaneously, but over a certain period of time, it would in principle be possible to present the two terms of a metaphor *after* each other.

5 For a discussion of how metaphorizing and other ways of making sense of the world are inextricably connected to ethics, see Johnson (1993).

6 For instance when, as currently happens in a lot of Dutch commercials, a 30 or 45 second commercial has a 5 second 'sequel' a few commercials later, presumably to reinforce the message.

7 Although forms of art with a didactic element feature something that is perhaps comparable to this notion. As Gombrich (1982/1972: 155) reminds us, 'even in the sphere of art the dimensions of communication are observable, although in more complex interaction'. Thus artistic forms that aim not just at aesthetic pleasure, but also want to educate the viewer, may embody a strong implicature that bears a close resemblance to that claimed for advertising, namely 'something positive will be claimed for product X'.

8 To be sure, the features mentioned under 2) and 3) hold for purely verbal texts as well.

Bibliography

Abed, F. (1994) 'Visual puns as interactive illustrations: their effects on recognition memory', *Metaphor and Symbolic Activity* 9,1: 45–60.

Abelson, R.P. (1976) 'Script processing in attitude formation and decision making', in J.S. Carroll and J.W. Payne (eds) *Cognition and Social Behavior*, Hillsdale, NJ: Lawrence Erlbaum, 33–45.

Adler, J.E. (1987) 'Comparisons with Grice', *Behavioral and Brain Sciences* 10,4: 710–11.

Ang, I. (1991) *Desperately Seeking the Audience*, London: Routledge.

Arnheim, R. (1958) *Film as Art*, London: Faber and Faber.

Bach, K. and Harnish, R.M. (1987) 'Relevant questions', *Behavioral and Brain Sciences* 10,4: 711–12.

Barthes, R. (1986/1961) 'The photographic message', in *The Responsibility of Forms* (trans. R. Howard), Oxford: Blackwell, 3–20.

—— (1986/1964) 'Rhetoric of the image', in *The Responsibility of Forms* (trans. R. Howard), Oxford: Blackwell, 21–40.

Beijk, J. and Van Raaij, W.F. (1989) *Schemata: Informatieverwerking, Beïnvloedings-processen en Reclame* [Schemas: Information Processing, Persuasion Strategies and Advertising], Amsterdam: VEA.

Berlin, B., Breedlove, D.E., and Raven, P.H. (1974) *Principles of Tzeltal Plant Classification*, New York: Academic Press.

Bex, T. (1993) 'The genre of advertising', *Revue Belge de Philologie et d'Histoire* 71,3: 719–32.

Black, M. (1962) 'Metaphor', in *Models and Metaphors*, Ithaca, NY: Cornell University Press, 25–47.

—— (1972) 'How do pictures represent?', in M. Mandelbaum (ed.) *Art, Perception, and Reality*, Baltimore/London: Johns Hopkins University Press, 95–130.

—— (1979a) 'More about metaphor', in A. Ortony (ed.) *Metaphor and Thought*, Cambridge: Cambridge University Press, 19–43.

—— (1979b) 'How metaphors work: a reply to Donald Davidson', in S. Sacks (ed.) *On Metaphor*, Chicago: University of Chicago Press, 181–92.

Blakemore, D. (1992) *Understanding Utterances: An Introduction to Pragmatics*, Oxford: Blackwell.

—— (1994) 'Relevance, poetic effects and social goals: a reply to Culpeper', *Language and Literature* 3,1: 49–59.

Bosch, P. (1985) 'Context dependence and metaphor', in W. Paprotté and R. Dirven (eds) *The Ubiquity of Metaphor: Metaphor in Language and Thought*, Amsterdam: John Benjamins, 141–76.

Boyd, R. (1979) 'Metaphor and theory change: what is "metaphor" a metaphor for?', in A. Ortony (ed.) *Metaphor and Thought*, Cambridge: Cambridge University Press, 356–408.

224   *Bibliography*

Brooke-Rose, C. (1958) *A Grammar of Metaphor*, London: Secker and Warburg.
Bühler, K. (1934) *Sprachtheorie: Die Darstellungsfunktion der Sprache*, Jena: Gustav Fisher.
Camargo, E.G. (1987) 'The measurement of meaning: Sherlock Holmes in pursuit of the Marlboro man', in J. Umiker-Sebeok (ed.) *Marketing and Semiotics: New Directions in the Study of Signs for Sale*, Berlin: Mouton de Gruyter, 463–83.
Casillo, R. (1985) 'Dirty gondola: the image of Italy in American advertisements', *Word & Image* 1,4: 330–50.
Clark, H.H. (1987) 'Relevance to what?', *Behavioral and Brain Sciences* 10,4: 714–15.
Cohen, T. (1979) 'Metaphor and the cultivation of intimacy', in S. Sacks (ed.) *On Metaphor*, Chicago: University of Chicago Press, 1–10.
Connor, K. and Kogan, N. (1980) 'Topic-vehicle relations in metaphor: the issue of asymmetry', in R.P. Honeck and R.R. Hoffman (eds) *Cognition and Figurative Language*, Hillsdale, NJ: Lawrence Erlbaum, 283–308.
Cook, G. (1988) 'Stylistics with a dash of advertising', *Language and Style* 21,2: 151–61.
—— (1990) 'Goals and plans in advertising and literary discourse', *Parlance* 2,2: 48–71.
—— (1992) *The Discourse of Advertising*, London: Routledge.
Cooper, D. (1986) *Metaphor*, Oxford: Blackwell.
Culpeper, J. (1994) 'Why relevance theory does not explain "the relevance of reformulations"', *Language and Literature* 3,1: 43–8.
Danto, A.C. (1993) 'Metaphor and cognition', in F.R. Ankersmit and J.J.A. Mooij (eds) *Metaphor and Knowledge* (*Knowledge and Language*, vol. III), Dordrecht: Kluwer, 21–35.
Davidson, D. (1979) 'What metaphors mean', in S. Sacks (ed.) *On Metaphor*, Chicago: University of Chicago Press, 29–46.
Druce, R. (1990) 'Colorless green signifieds sleep furiously: reconciling the image and the word', in T. D'haen (ed.) *Verbal/Visual Crossings 1880–1980*, Amsterdam: Rodopi/Antwerpen: Restant, 15–44.
Durand, J. (1987) 'Rhetorical figures in the advertising image', in J. Umiker-Sebeok (ed.) *Marketing and Semiotics: New Directions in the Study of Signs for Sale*, Berlin: Mouton de Gruyter, 295–318.
Elliott, R., Eccles, S., and Hodgson, M. (1993) 'Re-coding gender representations: women, cleaning products, and advertising's "New Man"', *International Journal of Research in Marketing* 10, 311–24.
Forceville, C. (1987) 'Metafoor en maatschappij' [Metaphor and society], *Massacommunicatie* 15,3: 268–76.
—— (1988) 'The case for pictorial metaphor: René Magritte and other Surrealists', in A. Erjavec (ed.) *Vestnik IMS* 9,1, Inštitut za Marksistióne Študije, Ljubljana, 150–60.
—— (1990) 'Pictorial metaphor: the surrealist interest', Unpublished ms. Faculty of Arts, Vrije Universiteit Amsterdam.
—— (1991) 'Verbo-pictorial metaphor in advertisements', *Parlance* 3,1: 7–19.
—— (1992) 'IMB IS EEN STEMVORK en andere picturale reclamemetaforen in de IBM campagne' [IBM IS A TUNING FORK and other pictorial advertising metaphors in the IBM campaign], *Reclamare* 3, September 1992, 19–23, 25–7.
—— (1994a) 'Pictorial metaphor in advertisements', *Metaphor and Symbolic Activity* 9,1: 1–29.
—— (1994b) 'Pictorial metaphor in billboards: relevance theory perspectives', in J. Müller (ed.) *Towards a Pragmatics of the Audiovisual* vol. I, Münster: NODUS, 93–113.

—— (1994c) 'Towards a delineation of pictorial simile', in E.W.B. Hess-Lüttich and J.E. Müller (eds) *Kodikas/Code* 17,1–4: 187–202.

—— (1995a) 'IBM is a tuning fork – degrees of freedom in the interpretation of pictorial metaphors', *Poetics* 23,3: 189–218. (Reprinted with kind permission from Elsevier Science B.V., Amsterdam, The Netherlands.)

—— (1995b) '(A)symmetry in metaphor: the importance of extended context', *Poetics Today* 16,4: 677–708.

Fowler, H.W. (1926) *A Dictionary of Modern English Usage*, Oxford: Oxford University Press.

Franklin, M.B. (1988) '"Museum of the mind": an inquiry into the titling of artworks', *Metaphor and Symbolic Activity* 3,3: 157–74.

Fraser, B. (1979) 'The interpretation of novel metaphors', in A. Ortony (ed.) *Metaphor and Thought*, Cambridge: Cambridge University Press, 172–85.

Gentner, D. (1989) 'The mechanisms of analogical reasoning', in S. Vosniadou and A. Ortony (eds) *Similarity and Analogical Reasoning*, Cambridge: Cambridge University Press, 199–241.

Gentner, D. and Gentner, D.R. (1982) 'Flowing waters or teeming crowds: mental models of electricity', in D. Gentner and A.L. Stevens (eds) *Mental Models*, Hillsdale, NJ: Lawrence Erlbaum, 99–129.

Gentner, D. and Jeziorski, M. (1993) 'The shift from metaphor to analogy in Western science', in A. Ortony (ed.) *Metaphor and Thought* (second, revised and expanded edition), Cambridge: Cambridge University Press, 447–80.

Gick, M.L. and Holyoak, K.J. (1980) 'Analogical problem solving', *Cognitive Psychology* 12, 306–55.

Gibbs, R.W., jr. (1993) 'Process and products in making sense of tropes', in A. Ortony (ed.) *Metaphor and Thought* (second, revised and expanded edition), Cambridge: Cambridge University Press, 252–76.

Glucksberg, S. and Keysar, B. (1993) 'How metaphors work', in A. Ortony (ed.), *Metaphor and Thought* (second, revised and expanded edition), Cambridge: Cambridge University Press, 401–24.

Gombrich, E.H. (1975/1972) 'Introduction: aims and limits of iconology', in *Symbolic Images: Studies in the Art of the Renaissance*, London: Phaidon, 1–25.

—— (1982/1972) 'The visual image: its place in communication', in *The Image and the Eye*, Oxford: Phaidon, 137–61.

Goodman, N. (1979) 'Metaphor as moonlighting', in S. Sacks (ed.) *On Metaphor*, Chicago: University of Chicago Press, 175–80.

Grice, H.P. (1975) 'Logic and conversation', in P. Cole and J.L. Morgan (eds) *Syntax and Semantics 3: Speech Acts*, New York: Academic Press, 41–58.

Gruber, H.E. (1988) 'Coping with multiplicity and ambiguity of meaning in works of art', *Metaphor and Symbolic Activity* 3,3: 183–9.

Harries, K. (1979) 'Metaphor and transcendence', in S. Sacks (ed.) *On Metaphor*, Chicago: University of Chicago Press, 71–88.

Hausman, C.R. (1989) *Metaphor and Art*, Cambridge: Cambridge University Press.

Heestermans H., Van Sterkenburg, P., and Van der Voort van der Kleij, J. (eds) (1980/1977) *Erotisch Woordenboek*, Utrecht: Spectrum.

Hoffman, R.R. (1977) 'Conceptual base hypotheses and the problem of anomalous sentences'. Paper presented at the annual meetings of the Midwestern Psychological Association, Chicago, Illinois, May 1977.

Hofstadter, D. (1985) *Metamagical Themas*, New York: Basic Books.

Indurkhya, B. (1991) 'Modes of metaphor', *Metaphor and Symbolic Activity* 6,1: 1–27.

—— (1992) *Metaphor and Cognition: An Interactionist Approach*, Dordrecht: Kluwer.

Jakobson, R. (1960) 'Closing statement: linguistics and poetics', in T.A. Sebeok (ed.) *Style in Language*, Cambridge, Mass.: MIT, 350–77.

Johns, B. (1984) 'Visual metaphor: lost and found,' *Semiotica* 52, 3/4: 291–333.

Johnson, M. (1987) *The Body in the Mind: The Bodily Basis of Meaning, Imagination and Reason*, Chicago: University of Chicago Press.

—— (1992) 'Philosophical implications of cognitive semantics', *Cognitive Linguistics* 3/4: 345–66.

—— (1993) *Moral Imagination: Implications of Cognitive Science for Ethics*, Chicago: University of Chicago Press.

Johnson, M.G. (1975) 'Some psychological implications of language flexibility', *Behaviorism* 3: 87–95.

—— (1978) 'Similarities in the comprehension of metaphors and paintings'. Paper presented at the annual meetings of the American Psychological Association, Toronto, Canada, August 1978.

—— and Malgady, R.G. (1980) 'Toward a perceptual theory of metaphoric comprehension', in R.P. Honeck and R.R. Hoffman (eds) *Cognition and Figurative Language*, Hillsdale, NJ: Lawrence Erlbaum, 259–82.

—— Malgady, R.G., and Anderson, S. (1974) 'Some cognitive aspects of metaphor interpretation'. Paper presented at the meeting of the Psychonomic Society, Boston, Mass., November 1974.

Kaplan, S.J. (1992) 'A conceptual analysis of form and content in visual metaphors', *Communication* 13: 197–209.

Katz, A.N. (1992) 'Psychological studies in metaphor processing: extensions to the placement of terms in semantic space', *Poetics Today* 13,4: 607–32.

Kennedy, J.M. (1982) 'Metaphor in pictures', *Perception* 11: 589–605.

—— (1985) 'Syllepse und Katachrese in Bildern', *Zeitschrift für Semiotik* 7,1/2: 47–62.

—— (1990) 'Metaphor – its intellectual basis', *Metaphor and Symbolic Activity* 5,2: 115–23.

—— and Gabias, P. (1985) 'Metaphoric devices in drawings of motion mean the same to the blind and the sighted', *Perception* 14: 189–95.

Kittay, E.F. (1987) *Metaphor: Its Cognitive Force and Linguistic Structure*, Oxford: Clarendon Press.

Kjärgaard, M.S. (1986) *Metaphor and Parable: A Systematic Analysis of the Specific Structure and Cognitive Function of the Synoptic Similes and Parables Qua Metaphors*, Leiden: E.J. Brill.

Kogan, N. and Chadrow, M. (1986) 'Children's comprehension of metaphor in the pictorial and verbal modality', *International Journal of Behavioral Development* 9: 285–95.

Kogan, N., Chadrow, M., and Harbour, H. (1989) 'Developmental trends in metaphoric asymmetry', *Metaphor and Symbolic Activity* 4,2: 71–91.

Kogan, N., Connor, K., Gross, A., and Fava, D. (1980) *Understanding Visual Metaphor: Developmental and Individual Differences*, Monographs of the society for research in child development, Serial no. 183, 45,1.

Kress, G. and Van Leeuwen, T. (1992) 'Structures of visual representation', *Journal of Literary Semantics* 21,2: 91–117.

Kreuz, R.J. and Roberts, R.M. (1993) 'The empirical study of figurative language in literature', *Poetics* 22, 151–69.

Lakoff, G. (1986) 'The meanings of literal', *Metaphor and Symbolical Activity* 1,4: 291–6.

—— (1987) *Women, Fire and Dangerous Things: What Categories Reveal about the Mind*, Chicago: University of Chicago Press.

—— (1992) 'Metaphor and war: the metaphor system used to justify war in the gulf', in M. Pütz (ed.) *Thirty Years of Linguistic Evolution*, Amsterdam: Benjamins, 463–81.

—— (1993) 'The contemporary theory of metaphor', in A. Ortony (ed.) *Metaphor and Thought* (second, revised and expanded edition), Cambridge: Cambridge University Press, 202–51.

—— and Johnson, M. (1980) *Metaphors We Live By*, Chicago: University of Chicago Press.

—— and Turner, M. (1989) *More Than Cool Reason: A Field Guide to Poetic Metaphor*, Chicago: University of Chicago Press.

Larsen, S.F., László, J., and Seilman, U. (1991) 'Across time and place: cultural-historical knowledge and personal experience in appreciation of literature', in E. Ibsch, D. Schram, and G.J. Steen (eds) *Empirical Studies of Literature*, Amsterdam/Atlanta GA: Rodopi, 97–103.

Leech, G.N. (1966) *English in Advertising: A Linguistic Study of Advertising in Great Britain*, London: Longman.

—— (1974) *Semantics*, Harmondsworth: Penguin.

Levin, S. (1979) 'Standard approaches to metaphor and a proposal for literary metaphor', in A. Ortony (ed.) *Metaphor and Thought*, Cambridge: Cambridge University Press, 124–35.

Levinson, S.C. (1989) Review of Sperber and Wilson 1986, *Journal of Linguistics* 25: 455–72.

McCabe, A. (1983) 'Conceptual similarity and the quality of metaphor in isolated sentences versus extended contexts', *Journal of Psycholinguistic Research* 12,1: 41–68.

—— (1988) 'Effect of different contexts on memory for metaphor', *Metaphor and Symbolic Activity* 3,2: 105–32.

MacCannell, D. (1987) '"Sex sells": comment on gender images and myth in advertising', in J. Umiker-Sebeok (ed.) *Marketing and Semiotics: New Directions in the Study of Signs for Sale*, Berlin: Mouton de Gruyter, 521–31.

MacCormac, E.R. (1985) *A Cognitive Theory of Metaphor*, Cambridge, Mass.: MIT.

Malgady, R.G. and Johnson, M.G. (1980) 'Measurement of figurative language: semantic feature models of comprehension and appreciation', in R.P. Honeck and R.R. Hoffman (eds) *Cognition and Figurative Language*, Hillsdale, NJ: Lawrence Erlbaum, 239–58.

Mick, D.G. and Politi, L.G. (1989) 'Consumers' interpretations of advertising imagery: a visit to the hell of connotation', in E. Hirschman (ed.) *Interpretive Consumer Research*, Provo, UT: Association for Consumer Research, 85–96.

Miller, G.A. (1979) 'Images and models, similes and metaphors', in A. Ortony (ed.) *Metaphor and Thought*, Cambridge: Cambridge University Press, 202–50.

Mooij, J.J.A. (1976) *A Study of Metaphor: On the Nature of Metaphorical Expressions, with Special Reference to their Reference*, Amsterdam: North-Holland.

Morgan, J.L. and Green, G.M. (1987) 'On the search for relevance', *Behavioral and Brain Sciences* 10,4: 726–7.

Morley, D. (1983) 'Cultural transformations: the politics of resistance', in H. Davis and P. Walton (eds) *Language, Image, Media*, Oxford: Blackwell, 104–19.

Myers, K. (1983) 'Understanding advertisers', in H. Davis and P. Walton (eds) *Language, Image, Media*, Oxford: Blackwell, 205–23.

Nöth, W. (1987) 'Advertising: the frame message', in J. Umiker-Sebeok (ed.) *Marketing and Semiotics: New Directions in the Study of Signs for Sale*, Berlin: Mouton de Gruyter, 279–94.

Novitz, D. (1985) 'Metaphor, Derrida, and Davidson', *The Journal of Aesthetics and Art Criticism* 45,2: 101–14.

Olson, D.R. (1970) 'Language and thought: aspects of a cognitive theory of semantics', *Psychological Review* 77,4: 257–73.

'Open peer commentary' [to Sperber and Wilson's relevance theory] (1987) *Behavioral and Brain Sciences* 10, 4: 710–36.

Ortony, A. (1979) 'The role of similarity in similes and metaphors', in A. Ortony (ed.) *Metaphor and Thought*, Cambridge: Cambridge University Press, 186–201.

Pateman, T. (1980) 'How to do things with images: an essay on the pragmatics of advertising', in T. Pateman *Language, Truth and Politics*. East Sussex: Jean Stroud, 215–37.

—— (1983) 'How is understanding an advertisement possible?' in H. Davis and P. Walton (eds) *Language, Image, Media*, Oxford: Blackwell, 187–204.

—— (1986) 'Relevance, contextual effects and least effort' (Review of Sperber and Wilson 1986), *Poetics Today* 7,4: 745–54.

Pilkington, A. (1991) 'Poetic effects: a relevance theory perspective', in R.D. Sell (ed.) *Literary Pragmatics*, London: Routledge, 44–61.

Quinn, N. (1982) 'Metaphors for marriage in our culture', *Proceedings of the 4th Annual Conference of the Cognitive Science Society*, Ann Arbor, Michigan, 4–6 Aug. 1982, 16–17.

—— (1987) 'Convergent evidence for a cultural model of American marriage', in D. Holland and N. Quinn (eds) *Cultural Models in Language and Thought*, Cambridge: Cambridge University Press, 173–92.

Rector, M. (1986) 'Emblems in Brazilian culture', in P. Bouissac, M. Herzfeld, and R. Posner (eds) *Iconicity: Essays on the Nature of Culture*, Tübingen: Stauffenburg, 447–62.

Richards, I.A. (1965/1936) *The Philosophy of Rhetoric*, New York: Oxford University Press.

Ricoeur, P. (1977) *The Rule of Metaphor: Multi-disciplinary Studies of the Creation of Meaning in Language* (trans. R. Czerny *et al.*), Toronto: University of Toronto Press.

—— (1981) 'The hermeneutical function of distanciation', in *Hermeneutics and the Human Sciences: Essays on Language, Action and Interpretation*, Cambridge: Cambridge University Press, 131–44.

Rossiter, J.R. and Percy L. (1987) *Advertising and Promotion Management*, New York: McGraw-Hill.

Russell, S.J. (1987) 'Rationality as an explanation of language?', *Behavioral and Brain Sciences* 10,4: 730–1.

Schmidt, S.J. (1982) *Foundation for the Empirical Study of Literature: The Components of a Basic Theory* (trans. and rev. R. de Beaugrande), Hamburg: Buske.

Schön, D.A. (1979) 'Generative metaphor: a perspective on problem-setting in social policy', in A. Ortony (ed.) *Metaphor and Thought*, Cambridge: Cambridge University Press, 254–83.

Searle, J.R. (1979) 'Metaphor', in A. Ortony (ed.) *Metaphor and Thought*, Cambridge: Cambridge University Press, 83–111.

Seuren, P.A.M. (1988) 'The self-styling of relevance theory', *Journal of Semantics* 5, 123–43.

Shibles, W.A. (1971) *Metaphor: An Annotated Bibliography and History*, Whitewater, Wisconsin: The Language Press.

Smith, N. and Wilson, D. (1992) 'Introduction', *Lingua* 87 (special issue on Relevance Theory), 1–10.

Sperber, D. and Wilson, D. (1986) *Relevance: Communication and Cognition*, Oxford: Blackwell.

—— (1987) 'Précis of *Relevance: Communication and Cognition*', *Behavioral and Brain Sciences* 10,4: 697–710. Authors' response: 736–51.

Stählin, W. (1914) 'Zur Psychologie und Statistik der Metaphern: eine methodologische Untersuchung', *Archiv für die Gesammte Psychologie* 31, 297–425.

Steen, G.J. (1992) *Metaphor in Literary Reception: A Theoretical and Empirical Study of Understanding Metaphor in Literary Discourse*, doctoral dissertation, Vrije Universiteit Amsterdam.

—— (1994) *Understanding Metaphor in Literature: An Empirical Approach*, London: Longman.

Tanaka, K. (1994) *Advertising Language: A Pragmatic Approach to Advertisements in Britain and Japan*, London: Routledge.

Tversky, A. (1977) 'Features of similarity', *Psychological Review* 84,4: 327–52.

Tversky, B. and Hemenway, K. (1984) 'Objects, parts, and categories', *Journal of Experimental Psychology: General* 113,2: 169–93.

van Noppen, J.-P. and Hols, E. (eds) (1990) *Metaphor II: A Classified Bibliography of Publications from 1985–1990*, Amsterdam: Benjamins.

van Noppens, J.-P., de Knop, S, and Jongen, R. (eds) (1985) *Metaphor: A Bibliography of Post-1970 Publications*, Amsterdam: Benjamins.

Verbrugge, R.R. (1980) 'Transformations in knowing: a realist view of metaphor', in R.P. Honeck and R.R. Hoffmann (eds) *Cognition and Figurative Language*, Hillsdale, NJ: Lawrence Erlbaum, 87–125.

—— (1984) 'The role of metaphor in our perception of language', in S.J. White and V. Teller (eds) *Discourses in Reading and Linguistics* (annals of the New York Academy of Sciences, vol. 433): 167–83.

—— (1986) 'Research on metaphoric developments: themes and variations', *Human Development* 29,4: 241–4.

—— and McCarrell, N.S. (1977) 'Metaphoric comprehension: studies in reminding and resembling', *Cognitive Psychology* 9, 494–533.

Vestergaard, T. and Schrøder, K. (1985) *The Language of Advertising*, Oxford: Blackwell.

Vroon, P. and Draaisma, D. (1985) *De Mens als Metafoor* [Man as metaphor], Baarn: Ambo.

Wheelwright, P. (1962) *Metaphor and Reality*, Bloomington: Indiana University Press.

Whittock, T. (1990) *Metaphor and Film*, Cambridge: Cambridge University Press.

Williamson, J. (1988/1978) *Decoding Advertisements: Ideology and Meaning in Advertising*, London: Marion Boyars.

Wilson, D. and Sperber, D. (1979) 'L'interpretation des énoncés', *Communications* 30: 80–94.

—— (1988) 'The self-appointment of Seuren as censor – a reply to Pieter Seuren', *Journal of Semantics* 5: 145–62.

—— (1989a) 'An outline of relevance theory', *Working Papers in Linguistics* 1, University College London, Dept. of Phonetics and Linguistics: Linguistics Section, 1–28.

—— (1989b) 'On verbal irony', *Working Papers in Linguistics* 1, University College London, Dept. of Phonetics and Linguistics: Linguistics Section, 96–117.

Wollheim, R. (1987) 'Painting, metaphor, and the body: Titian, Bellini, De Kooning, etc.', Lecture VI in *Painting As an Art*, Princeton NJ: Princeton University Press, 305–57.

—— (1993) 'Metaphor and painting', in F.R. Ankersmit and J.J.A. Mooij (eds) *Metaphor and Knowledge* (*Knowledge and Language*, vol. III), Dordrecht: Kluwer 113–25.

SOURCES OF ADVERTISEMENTS AND BILLBOARDS

Reclame Jaarboek 1976 (1977) Amsterdam: Art Directors Club Nederland (Figure 6.11).

Jahrbuch 1978 (1978) Düsseldorf: Art Director's Club Deutschland (Figure 6.26).

Jahrbuch der Werbung, Marketing-Kommunikation in Deutschland, Österreich und der Schweiz 18 (1980). Düsseldorf/Wien: Econ (Figure 6.10).

Reclame Jaarboek 1980 (1981) Amsterdam: Art Directors Club Nederland (Figure 6.12).

10 Ans de Publicité (Stratégies no. 294, 30 October 1981) Paris: Stratégies (Figure 6.5).

Reclame Jaarboek 1981 (1982) Amsterdam: Art Directors Club Nederland (Figure 6.23).

Reclame Jaarboek 1982 (1983) Amsterdam: Art Directors Club Nederland (Figure 6.24).

Reclame Jaarboek 1983 (1984) Amsterdam: Art Directors Club Nederland (Figure 6.20).

Reclame Jaarboek 1984 (1985) Amsterdam: Art Directors Club Nederland (Figure 6.21).

Dossier Agences 1985 (1985) Paris: Stratégies (Figures 6.1, 6.3).

Dossier Campagnes 1986 (1986) Paris: Publications Professionelles Françaises (Figures 6.6, 6.7 and 6.13).

Gesamtverband Werbeagenturen 1987 (1987) Moisburg: Siegmund (Figure 6.17).

British Design and Art Direction 1988 (1988) London: Polygon Editions SARL (Figures 6.9 and 6.16).

Reclame Jaarboek 1990 (1991) Amsterdam: Art Directors Club Nederland (Figures 6.8 and 6.14).

Volkskrant 6 April 1991 (Figure 6.22).

En Toen Ging er een Lampje Branden: Het Beste uit 25 Jaar Nederlandse Reclame en Grafische Vormgeving (1991) Amsterdam: Art Directors Club Nederland (Figure 6.27).

Vrij Nederland 14 December 1991 (Figure 6.18).

Reclame Jaarboek 1991 (1992) Amsterdam: Art Directors Club Nederland (Figures 7.1, 7.2 and 7.3).

Kunst en Wetenschap 1:2, Summer 1992 (Figure 6.19).

Index

This index provides a selective guide to names and topics referred to in the book. The addition 'n' means the reference occurs in a note.